That Man of Granite with the Heart of a Child

That Man of Granite with the Heart of a Child

Biography of J. C. Ryle

Eric Russell

Christian Focus

ISBN 1 85792 631 5

Published in 2001 by Christian Focus Publications, Geanies
House, Fearn, Ross-shire, IV20 1TW, Great Britain.

Cover design by Owen Daily

Contents

Abbreviations

JCRSP. P. Toon, ed, *J. C. Ryle, A Self-Portrait.*

ETG. J. C. Ryle, *Expository Thoughts on the Gospels* (1856 -1873)

TCLLC. J. C. Ryle, *The Christian Leaders of the Last Century* (1869)

KU. J. C. Ryle, *Knots Untied* (1874)

H. J. C. Ryle, *Holiness* (1877).

OP. J. C. Ryle, *Old Paths* (1877).

PCh. J. C. Ryle, *Principles for Churchmen* (1884)

TUR. J. C. Ryle, *The Upper Room* (1888).

LOT. J. C. Ryle, *Light from Old Times* (1890).

AHEPCE G.R. Balleine, *A History of the Evangelical Party in the Church of England* (1908)

AMHER. M. H. Fitzgerald, *A Memoir of Herbert Edward Ryle* (1928)

JCREB. P. Toon, *John Charles Ryle, Evangelical Bishop* (1976)

HTF. John Kent, *Holding the Fort, Studies in Victorian Revivalism* (1978)

Genealogical Tree

Thomas Ryle   **m**   **Martha Wilton**
1720-1799   **d.1787**

    |

    John   *m*   *Mary Nixon*
    Elizabeth   *m*   *Rowland Gould*
    d.1787   *d.1788*

    |

    Elizabeth Shaw   *d.1842*
    Rowland Gould   *d.1847*

John Ryle   **m**   **Mary Nixon**
1745-1808   **d.1810** |

    John
    Joshua
    Thomas
    Elizabeth   *m*   *John Smith Daintry*
    Mary   *m*   *Charles Wood*
    Sarah   *m*   *Samuel Wood*
    Frances   *m*   *Rev. T. Smyth*
    Jane Harriott   *m*   *Sir Francis Sacheveral Darwin*

John Ryle   **m**   **Susannah Hurt**
1781-1862   **d.1846|**

    Mary Anne   *um*
    Susan   *m*   *Rev. C. Daniel*
    Emma   *m*   *Capt. Travers*
    John Charles   *m*
    Caroline Elizabeth   *m*   *Rev. W. Coulthorpe; James Keners*
    Frederick William   *um*   *d.1846*

John Charles   **m**   **Matilda Charlotte Louisa Plumptre**
1816-1900   **d.1847**

    Georgina Matilda

                m   **Jessie Elizabeth Walker**
                          d.1860

    Jessie Isabella   *um*
    Reginald John   *m*   *Catherine Scott*
    Herbert Edward   *m*   *Nea Hewish Adams*
    Arthur Johnson   *um*

                     m   **Henrietta Anelia Clowes**
                            d.1889

Foreword

Soon after my conversion I read Norman Grubb's life of his father-in-law, *C. T. Studd, Cricketer and Pioneer*. It told how an English batsman became a missionary who, after serving in China and India, spent his last twenty years taking the gospel to the Congo. This present biography might well have been called *J. C. Ryle, Cricketer and Pioneer*, for it tells how the cricket captain of Eton and Oxford became a clergyman and, after making his name as an evangelical spokesman and strategist, spent his last two decades as Liverpool's first bishop. Ryle gave up cricket after his ordination, but held that being a cricket captain had done him good: 'I believe it gave me a power of commanding, managing, organizing, and directing....using every man in the part for which he is best suited, bearing, forbearing, and keeping men around me in a good temper.' Also, cricket is a highly strategic game, and a captain must ever determine tactics on a basis of strategy. Thus, Ryle took much wisdom about strategy and man-management to Liverpool, and by general consent did a fine job in giving the diocese shape and substance.

John Charles Ryle – 'the frank and manly Mr Ryle' as Archbishop Magee called him in 1868; 'that man of granite with the heart of a child' as his successor described him – was an evangelical to his fingertips. (Has evangelical religion any distinctive principles? I answer, It has. Are they worth contending for? I answer, they are.') Rightly, Ryle read the Thirty-nine Articles and the Prayer Book as broad-based evangelical documents, and he always sought full evangelicalism for the Church of England itself, measuring all its ways by whether they tended towards or away from this goal. As a bishop he was 'commanding, managing, organizing and directing,' and often perforce acted as if he was an Anglican first and an evangelical second, but that was never so. In 1870 he had a Church Congress listening to his vision for reform – 'Repeal the Act of Uniformity: Shorten the Services: Use the laity: Treat the Dissenters kindly!' – and howling approval as he said things would have been better had John Wesley been made Archbishop of Canterbury. He was always an ecumenical evangelical, seeking the fellowship of Anglicans with each other and with their Free Church neighbours on a basis and within a frame of gospel truth. The flip side of this was that he rejected Roman Catholicism as a form of apostasy. God's truth, he held, must set the limits of fellowship at church level.

Anglican evangelicals of Ryle's type are rare birds today; opinions will differ as to whether that is our gain or our loss. Meantime, it is very good to have Ryle's story told afresh by someone who understands it so well. Like Charles Simeon, his great predecessor two generations earlier, Ryle was an Anglican to remember, and many will be grateful to Eric Russell for making remembrance of him possible in these days.

Dr James I Packer,
Regent College,
Vancouver, British Columbia.

Chapter One

I wanted for nothing

'Few men in the nineteenth century did so much for God, for righteousness, among the English-speaking race and in the world as our late Bishop.'[1] The man of whom this was said, John Charles Ryle, was born at Park House, Macclesfield on 10 May 1816, the fourth of six children and the elder son.[2] His father, John Ryle, was the prosperous owner of a silk mill in the town. The Ryle family used to have strong links with the Methodists in the town, but in recent times John and his wife had decided to attend the Church of England and John Charles was baptised in Christ Church, Macclesfield on 28 September. At Park House on the edge of the town the family grew up wanting for nothing and were provided with every luxury and comfort money could buy.

Childhood and early education

From his early days John seems to have been a shy and reserved child who enjoyed his own company best of all. In the spacious grounds of Park House he could go fishing in the lake, sail his model boats or go off on an adventure with bow and arrow through the coppice. He loved reading and some of his happiest hours were spent reading a volume with pictures in his father's library. He later claimed he was a good reader by the time he was four years of age.[3]

Keen that his son should have a good basic education, his father arranged with Isaac Eaton, the Clerk of the Parish Church, to teach the boy reading, writing and arithmetic. In addition to these daily lessons he was also taught the rudiments of Latin by Miss Holland, his governess. She was a strict disciplinarian, and he recalled that she 'boxed my ears unmercifully, though I dare say I deserved it'.[4]

Ryle was often preoccupied with his business affairs and had little time for his growing family, except at weekends and during

11

the holidays. The most enjoyable times were spent at Bridlington on the east coast, where the whole family liked the bracing air and the sea bathing. Every morning before breakfast they would walk the whole length of the pier and back to give them an appetite. Ryle owned a yacht named Seaflower and as a special treat he would take his little boy sailing with him. John was always tied to the mast to avoid any accidents.

On Saturday evenings there was a regular routine in the Ryle household when all the children were washed and scrubbed in turn in a large wooden bath tub before the fire. John remembered this all too well when 'we endured the most painful thing in the week, having our heads combed with a small tooth comb. This was torture indeed'.[5] The family was not particularly religious but on Sunday mornings dutifully attended Christ Church, the tall slender tower of which was visible from the house through the trees. On his first visit to the church, John was puzzled by the sight of the preacher looking down from the high pulpit and thought it was the king. At one service his mother gave him a pontefract sweet to keep him quiet during the service, but he dropped it under the pew, and after searching for it without success, he embarrassed his family by calling out, 'I cannot find it anywhere'.[6]

John reported of the first eight years of his life that 'we had few cares, no sickness, no anxieties and wanted for nothing. We might have been better done for and we might have been worse.' 'They were happy and pretty harmless years,' although, he added, 'destitute of any real religion.'[7] All in all, he had a far better and happier childhood than the hundreds of less fortunate Victorian children working in the mills in Macclesfield, including his father's own mill.

It was customary in Victorian times for wealthy parents to send their boys away to preparatory school at about eight years old, so John was packed off to the Rev John Jackson's Academy at Bowden, near Altringham. John always felt that he had been sent off to his prep school 'too early...by at least two years'.[8] This was nothing like a prep school today. The majority of clergy received very small stipends and many supplemented their income by taking in private pupils at the vicarage.[9] There were sixteen boys in residence in this small private school, mainly from leading middle-class families on the border of Lancashire and Cheshire.

John's early school days were not his happiest, but he worked hard and devoted himself to his books. The school had a good academic record, but unfortunately, Mr Jackson, a parish clergyman, had to give priority to his parochial duties and sometimes the boys missed lessons and were left to their own devices. They got up to all kind of pranks in their dormitories. Blanket tossing was a favourite amusement and there was some bullying by the bigger boys. With Mr Jackson's connivance any boy who found it difficult getting up in a morning was tossed by the other boys. On one occasion, young Ryle, who always required a lot of sleep, was tossed up to the ceiling and fell out of the blanket and was sick for a time. The affair was hushed up and his parents were never told of the incident. When Mr Jackson was offered a preferment by the Bishop of Chester and he moved to the benefice of Over, a tiny village near Winsford in Cheshire, the whole school moved with him. After three and a half years Ryle left his prep school 'tolerably well grounded in Latin and Greek and having learned a vast amount of moral evil and got no moral good'.[10] It would appear that the religious and moral tone of most of the public and private schools in the nineteenth century was pretty low, even though many were run by clergy and ministers.

Family background

The Ryle family had a long association with the land and were well established in Cheshire by the early sixteenth century.[11] John Ryle's grandfather (also John Ryle) had a life of magnificent achievement. He became a prosperous landowner, a successful silk manufacturer. a respected banker, a conscientious alderman, a generous benefactor, a faithful Christian and a dedicated Methodist. When he died on June 16th, 1808, he had achieved in his 62 years far more than most men, and was buried in the family vault on the east side of Christ Church graveyard. More than half a century later Ryle wrote a note in his memoirs about his grandparents:

My grandfather, John Ryle died before I was born; he made an immense fortune in the silk trade. I only know he was a very good man and an earnest Christian, an intimate friend of the famous John Wesley, who frequently came to stay at his house, and who mentions him in his journals. My grandmother also died before I was born. I have heard that she also was a very shrewd, sensible Christian woman.[12]

John, the eldest son, was in his mid-twenties when his father died, and he inherited a fortune of half a million pounds. He was now the master of Park House and its estate, part owner of a flourishing silk mill and a profitable banking business. He married Susanna, daughter of the wealthy manufacturer Charles Hurt and first cousin of Sir Richard Arkwright, industrialist, inventor, and builder of Cromford spinning mill in Derbyshire, regarded as 'one of the wonders of the world'. Susanna brought a dowry of £30,000.

This second John Ryle took an active interest in local affairs. He was appointed a magistrate and often sat on the bench. He was a governor of the Grammar School, a major in the Loyal Macclesfield Troop, treasurer of the Volunteer Fire Brigade and became High Sheriff of Cheshire. He had an interest in politics and was known to be in favour of parliamentary reforms and religious equality. He gave generously to various philanthropic and charitable causes, including the Macclesfield Dispensary for the Sick, of which he was a founder member.[13] Over the years Ryle added considerably to his fortune. He purchased Upton Hall for £21,000, bought the Erwood estate and is also reputed to have rebuilt the famous Cat and Fiddle Inn, high on the Buxton road. The family bank continued to be successful, opening a branch in Norfolk street, Manchester. John 'was exceedingly popular in and around Macclesfield and was almost king of the place.'[14] The family income was at least £15,000 a year, and the property he owned worth more than half a million pounds.[15]

Eton
Although John the second had received a fine education at the local grammar school, he was ambitious for his elder son and determined that he should go to one of the great public schools.

Several cousins were educated at Eton, and Professor Smyth of Cambridge, a family friend, strongly recommended that the youngster should be sent there. Ryle firmly believed that tutelage at a renowned public school followed by residence at either Oxford or Cambridge afforded a boy contacts which might be useful in later life. So young John was enrolled at Eton College in February 1828, under the distinguished headmaster, Dr John Keate, whom his new pupil described as 'a good disciplinarian, a good scholar, and kept good order.'[16] He was not quite twelve years of age and was at Eton for almost seven years.

There were two classes of boys at Eton, the Collegers and the Oppidans. The latter group were always the larger group, being the sons of the rich and titled, who lodged outside the College in town houses. Ryle went to Eton as a Colleger and was fortunate to be placed in Dr Hawtrey's house, considered by the boys to be 'the largest and best house in the School.'[17] The regime at Eton was harsh, especially for those boys who resided in College, but the boys in Hawtrey House lived in reasonably comfortable surroundings, 'well-fed, well-cared for and wanted for nothing.'[18] Dr Hawtrey was a dedicated scholar and unlike most of the other tutors he readily encouraged any boy who showed signs of ability. Ryle appreciated the help and inspiration he received from his housemaster and sixty years on he still retained a warm affection for his former tutor: 'He helped me immensely in my preparation for Oxford,' he wrote. 'Under his guidance I read privately nearly all the books in which I was finally examined at Oxford.'[19]

It took Ryle some months to settle in at Eton, and during that time he wrote several letters home pleading with his father to let him return home. He found it difficult to fit in with six hundred other boys and as 'a northerner', felt excluded. Fagging was one of the established rituals at Eton in those days. Young Ryle hated the daily chores, but as he progressed up the College, he slowly came to recognise some value in the system. He felt that if not abused it inculcated discipline and reminded spoilt boys that they cannot always have their own way in life. When he reached his final term, he seems to have accepted the system without any qualms, 'I had eight fags of my own in my tutor's house, four of them to wait on me in the morning at breakfast, and four in the evening at tea. But the work they did was a mere trifle, taking only a few minutes, and it did them no harm.'[20]

Daily attendance at Chapel was compulsory, yet in spite of this, Ryle's recollection of his spiritual education at Eton was that 'religion was at a low ebb and most boys knew more about the heathen gods and goddesses than about Jesus Christ.'[21] This was fairly typical of public school religion at this time, with the exception of Rugby School, when Thomas Arnold was headmaster. Ryle recalls that the Sunday sermons the boys had to listen to were 'a perfect farce and a disgrace to the Church of England',[22] and the religious instruction he received in preparation for his Confirmation by Dr John Kaye, the Bishop of Lincoln, was 'ludicrously deficient.'[23] One sermon the boys never forgot, however, was given by a visiting preacher, bald on top, who from the pulpit, announced his text, 'My sins are more than the hairs of my head' (Psalm 40:12).

One of the most lasting impressions made on Ryle at Eton was in the Sixth form when he was encouraged by Dr Hawtrey to read for the Newcastle Scholarship, a divinity award established by the Duke of Newcastle in 1829, and considered by Etonians to be the blue ribband of accolades. Candidates were required to make a detailed study of the Thirty-Nine Articles of Religion and sit an examination. Boys who achieved the three highest marks were awarded grants of fifty pounds each. As a youngster Ryle had never treated religion seriously but now he became a diligent student and in the examination he was placed fourth in the list. 'I surprised everyone by the position which I took' and though disappointed at not winning the scholarship he was satisfied that he had not wasted his time.[24] For the required reading gave him an understanding of Christian doctrine he had never before appreciated and he looked back on this period of study as one of the most significant in his life. 'It is a simple fact,' he wrote in his book *Knots Untied* that 'the beginning of any clear doctrinal views I ever attained myself was reading the Articles for the Newcastle Scholarship and attending a lecture at Christ Church, Oxford, on the Articles by a college tutor. I shall always thank God for what

I learned then. Before that time I really knew nothing system-
atically of Christianity. I knew not what came first or what last. I
had a religion without order in my head. What I found good myself,
I commend to others.'[25]

In his last year or two at Eton, Ryle's reputation began to grow,
and he made a name for himself not only in the examination room,
where he proved that he was a pupil of above average ability and
gained some of the School's most coveted awards, but also on the
river and sports field. One summer he spent most of his leisure
hours rowing in preference to playing cricket, but concluded that
'the boating set are less refined and more given to coarse habits
than the cricketing set'.[26] Cricket was his first love. In the fifth
year he gained a place in the College XI and the following year he
was appointed captain of cricket. Cricket is a time-consuming
game and Ryle confessed that his passion for the game often took
him away from his books in the summer term. He was persuaded
however that it was time well spent:

> It gave me a power of commanding, managing, organising and
> directing, seeing through men's capabilities and using every man in
> the post to which he was best suited, bearing and forebearing, keeping
> men around me in good temper, which I have found of infinite use
> on lots of occasions in life, though in very different matters.[27]

In his fourth year Ryle was joined by his younger brother Frederick,
though the two brothers were never close. It was in his last couple
of years that John made some lasting friendships, particularly with
Charles, John and Algernon Coote, the sons of Sir Charles Coote,
William Courthorpe, who later married his sister Caroline, and
George W. Lyttleton, who married his cousin Caroline Hurt and
became a prominent Member of Parliament.

When at the close of his school life he came to leave Eton, he
did so with 'unfeigned regret'.[28] The last two years had been the
happiest of his life. He was top of his class when he entered the
Fifth and consistently retained a high position in the Sixth. He
admits he was 'ambitious and fond of influence' and quite suddenly
he became 'one of the most prominent boys in the school'.[29]

Through prep school and public school he had received a thorough grounding in classics, yet he reveals that during the whole seven years he was at Eton he never learned any arithmetic, algebra or mathematics.[30] Undoubtedly he was a first class scholar, competed well in the Newcastle Scholarship, took a leading part in the Eton Society, a debating group run entirely by the boys themselves, succeeded in bring Oppidians and Collegers into a closer relationship, and became an accomplished oarsman and captain of the cricket XI. His father had been wise to insist that John should stay on at Eton and settle down. Years later he endorsed his father's judgment by stating 'a public school is about the best discipline a boy can be put through', and sent two of his own sons to Eton and the other to Repton.[31]

John Ryle, MP

At the time when Ryle was beginning to bask in his successes at Eton, his father was seriously thinking of entering Parliament. Macclesfield had been a 'rotten borough' until the passing of the Reform Act in 1832. This new Act removed the pocket boroughs, permitted Macclesfield to send two Members to Westminster and gave the vote to every householder rated at £10 or more. John Ryle was encouraged by his friends to stand.

There were three candidates for Macclesfield in the December 1832 election: John Ryle (Reformer), John Brocklehurst (Reformer), and Thomas Grimsditch (Tory). Bitter feelings were aroused at the hustings with demands for more radical reforms. In his election address, given outside his mill on Park Green to a huge crowd estimated at fifteen thousand people, Ryle declared that he was an independent candidate, in favour of greater reforms, and if elected would pursue a reforming policy. He was fully in favour of the new Reform Bill and would encourage universal suffrage. He also insisted that though loyal to the doctrine and discipline of the Church of England he was opposed to the practices of clergy holding livings in plurality and absentee clergy who did not reside in their parishes. He also favoured removing the civic disabilities suffered by Dissenters, such as the registration of births in the baptismal registers of the parish church, the legality of marriages only in the Established Church and the sole right of the clergy to conduct funeral services in the churchyard. By supporting these reforms Ryle clearly hoped to win the support of both Anglicans and Nonconformists in the election. And he succeeded – both John Ryle and John Brocklehurst were elected.[32]

This first local election to the new Parliament passed off peacefully, but at the next election in January 1835 there were serious disturbances outside the Town Hall. Almost everyone who sported Ryle's colours of blue and yellow were set upon by groups of ruffians, resulting in injuries to his supporters. Two years earlier a mob of mill workers had attacked the residence of John Brocklehurst, and windows were broken. In this instance, the attack was not against Ryle personally, but a crowd of drunken revellers turned over the market stalls in the town square and began looting the produce, which led to assaults on local people. The special constables were unable to restore order, and the Mayor was disposed to stop the election.[33] However, extra constables were drafted in and order was restored. During the disturbance, the platform on which Ryle was standing was pushed over and he fell to the ground injuring his back.

In the end Ryle again headed the poll with a slightly increased majority. He was a popular Member of Parliament, but he did not remain long enough in the House to make his mark. Because of business commitments and failing health he decided not to stand at the election in 1837. By this time his son was considering a parliamentary career.

Chapter Two

Launched as a Christian

In mid-October 1834, the eighteen-year-old Ryle, proud son of the Member of Parliament for Macclesfield, went up to Oxford to study at Christ Church. He was allocated a large room on Tom Quad and assigned a scout who attended to his daily needs.

A typical day for Ryle began with prayers, read from a Latin version of the Prayer book compiled at the Reformation for use in college chapels. There was a divinity lecture before breakfast, and during the morning he attended tutorials in Latin and Greek. The students fared well at Christ Church which had a reputation for serving excellent food in the Great Hall. After dinner students usually spent the evening at wine parties, though Ryle seems not to have been interested in these occasions, preferring to spend his time reading. Several friends and acquaintances whom he had known at Eton also went up to Oxford, but as he began to settle in he came to dislike 'the tone of society amongst the undergraduates at Oxford, the more so from its complete unlikeness to what he had been used to at Eton'.[1] He objected in particular to the 'fawning upon wealth and title' and 'a want of sociability and sympathy amongst undergraduates', which he had not observed to the same degree among his contemporaries at Eton.[2]

Academic success

Christ Church had a fine academic record, though at the time its achievements were behind those of Balliol and Oriel. Thomas Gaisford, the dean, was no mean scholar, who during his long tenure of office did all he could to improve standards. Unfortunately some members of the Senior Common Room in receipt of huge stipends cared little for the progress of their students. In his first year Ryle was assigned Augustus Short as his tutor, who offered him little direction or stimulation in his reading. To Ryle's relief he left to become Bishop of Adelaide in Australia.

He described him as 'perfectly useless, and I never learned anything from him'.[3] Ryle's dedication to learning was rewarded at the end of the first year when he was given a Fell Exhibition, a bequest made by Dr John Fell, a former Dean of Christ Church in the seventeenth century, to encourage bright undergraduates of Christ Church.

It was Ryle's good fortune to have George Henry Liddell as his tutor in both his second and third years. Liddell was probably the finest Greek Scholar at Oxford, and from him Ryle learned the importance of studying literature in the original language, especially the Greek text of the New Testament. Liddell had a class of thirteen students whom he described as 'a good set who will keep all my wits at work.'[4] Liddell was a wise and considerate tutor who was always ready to encourage and guide a keen student. He recommended Ryle to try for the Craven Scholarship, a prestigious award much sought after by gifted scholars at Oxford. Ryle was successful and afterwards he was unstinting in his praise of the tutor who had encouraged him to aim high, saying, 'Liddell was a very good tutor and I heartily wish I had been under him during the whole time at Oxford'.[5]

Examinations were a gruelling experience for those few students who hoped to attain first class honours, and included an oral examination before three examiners, conducted in public before dons and fellow students. Ryle was undaunted when his turn came and he was congratulated on his brilliant answers in philosophy and divinity. It was debated whether to put him, along with Henry Highton, who became an eminent scientist and Headmaster of Cheltenham College, and Arthur Penrhyn Stanley, later Dean of Westminster, in a class by themselves in the school of 'Greats', but eventually it was decided they should share the honours with eight other distinguished graduates, and he was awarded 'a very brilliant first class' in classics.[6]

Ryle's love of cricket never waned and he spent many afternoons on the cricket field. He played in the University First Eleven, and in his second and third years was appointed captain of cricket. He worked to revive the annual University match with Cambridge through some of his Eton friends who had gone there.

Due to his efforts the two University teams met at Lords in June
1836. Ryle was made joint-captain and had a marvellous match,
taking four wickets in the first innings and six in the second.[7]

The spiritual environment

The University was an enclave of Anglicanism and when young
Ryle arrived in 1834 several of the colleges were buzzing with
Tractarian teaching. John Henry Newman was preaching to large
congregations in the recently restored University Church of St
Mary's, but despite his reputation Ryle found him 'dull and
lifeless'[8] From the high pulpit John Keble, the author of *The
Christian Year*, had preached, at Newman's invitation, the assize
sermon on 'National Apostasy' in 1833, which Newman believed
marked the beginning of the Oxford Movement. Certainly from
that time on there were signs of a fresh interest in spiritual things,
not noticed since the days of the Evangelical Revival in the
eighteenth century. At Christ Church, Dr Edward Bouverie Pusey
was attracting a great deal of attention as one of the leaders of the
Oxford Movement, encouraging his congregation of
undergraduates to seek God and worship him through a regular
sacramental and holy life. Ryle must have heard him preach in
chapel on several occasions, but he appears to have been unmoved
either by his undoubted scholarship or the sanctity of his life.
Undergraduates were expected to attend the University sermons,
but very few did so. Ryle recalled that only Edward Denison, a
moderate High Churchman, and W. K. Hamilton, an evangelical,
who under the influence of Pusey became a Tractarian and
succeeded Denison as Bishop of Salisbury, did him any good.
Ryle appears not to have shown any interest in the catholic revival,
though it was most strongly represented in Oxford. Neither does
he appear to have been influenced by any evangelical preachers.
Oxford had been the birthplace of Methodism a century earlier
through John and Charles Wesley, and evangelical stalwarts like
George Whitefield, William Grimshaw and William Romaine had
been students in her colleges. Though A. E. Litton, a fellow of
Oriel and W. W. Champneys, a fellow of Brasenose and curate at
St Ebb's, both had an evangelical ministry among the students,

evangelicalism never flourished at Oxford as it did in Cambridge.[9]

Ryle was not particularly religious when he went up to University, and at home the family were only 'nominal Christians'. After his marriage his father loosened his links with the Wesleyans in the town and the family began attending Christ Church on Sunday mornings but spent the rest of the day like any other day.[10] In 1831 the 23,000 people of Macclesfield were served by two Anglican churches and several Nonconformist chapels. Ryle recalled that the Parish Church and Christ Church at the time 'vied with each other for sleepiness and dullness; and the two incumbents were 'wretched high and dry sticks of the old school and their preaching was not calculated to do good to anybody.'[11]

How then did Ryle's conversion come about? The events are remarkable and clearly reveal the hand of God. He had been challenged when he began reading theology for the Newcastle Scholarship. He never forgot the stinging rebuke he received from his friend Algernon Coote, after uttering an oath, and being told 'to think, repent and pray'.[12] His sister Susan and his cousin Harry Arkwright both professed conversion under the ministry of the Rev John Burnet, the evangelical minister of St George's, Sutton, a new church on the edge of the borough, which Ryle says, 'introduced a new kind of religion into the Church of England in that part of Cheshire.'[13] Originally an Independent chapel built on land donated by John Ryle, the building had been handed over to the Bishop following an altercation between members. In 1828 he appointed the Rev William Wade, an evangelical, as minister. In 1834 the Bishop consecrated the church and instituted the Rev John Burnet as Wade's successor.

A serious chest infection confined Ryle to his bed in Oxford at a critical time just before his final examinations, when he was anxious to obtain a good degree. 'That was the time', he confessed, 'when I distinctly remember I began to read my Bible and began to pray'.[14] It was the first time in fourteen years he had opened his Bible or prayed. In retrospect, Ryle recognised that through all these people and events God was working in his life by his Spirit.

The climax to all these spiritual experiences came in the early summer of 1837. Ryle went into a church in Oxford one Sunday after the service had begun, and heard the second lesson, which was from St Paul's Epistle to the Ephesians, chapter 2. As he listened to the reading he became aware of the Word of God addressing his soul. When the reader came to verse 8, each phrase spoke to him with spiritual power, 'For by grace – are ye saved – through faith – and not of yourselves – it is the gift of God'.[15] This testimony is confirmed by W. H. Griffith Thomas, a curate at St Aldate's in the last decade of the century. 'That verse', he comments, 'was like an arrow strung to the bow of the Divine Archer and its flight was winged in mercy to the heart of the chosen mortal'.[16] He left the church a new man, trusting in Christ for salvation. The Rev J. W. Diggle, who served under Ryle in Liverpool before being consecrated Bishop of Carlisle, used to impress upon his ordinands that 'Bishop Ryle owed his conversion to the reading of a lesson in church.'[17] He was converted not by a tract, nor a sermon, but by the Word of God.

Becoming a Christian was a real and meaningful event in his life and for the next sixty or more years his faith in his God and Saviour never wavered. 'By the beginning of 1838', he claimed, 'I think I was fairly launched as a Christian, and started on a road which I think I have never entirely left from that time to this'.[18]

Ryle becomes a Christian

The first few months of his Christian life were a particularly difficult time. He lost some of his former friends, but gained new Christian friends, among them the Rev John Thornycroft and his sisters, his cousin Harry Arkwright, the Leycester sisters of Toft Hall, Malvern, Georgina Best of Falston in Yorkshire, and William Marsh and his daughter Catherine of Leamington, who all gave him support, advice and encouragement. One of the first books he was given to read was by William Wilberforce, with the intriguing title, *A Practical View of the prevailing religious system of professed Christians in the high and middle classes in this country contrasted with real Christianity.*

Ryle left University with a First in Classics, a Blue for cricket, a strong personal faith in Christ and the prospects of one day entering Parliament. Friends tried to persuade him to stay on at

Oxford, assuring him of being elected to a Studentship or a Fellowship in one of the colleges, but he was determined to move on.[19] 'I left Oxford with a brilliant reputation for the honours which I have taken but with very little love for the University and very glad to get away from it'.[20] In one of his published papers there is another insight into his decision. 'No earthly condition,' he writes, 'appears so deadening to a man's soul as the position of a resident Fellow in a college, and the society of a common room at Oxford or Cambridge.'[21] If he had known how suddenly and dramatically the whole course of his life was to change he might well have opted for a Fellowship.

His family and friends gave him a mixed reception. They were delighted at his academic success but displeased that he had become an evangelical Christian and suddenly given up such enjoyable pastimes as the theatre, dancing, cards and billiards. Ryle had been passionately fond of dancing and playing billiards and it was a real sacrifice for him to give up these 'worldly activities'. He admitted that in his family 'evangelical religion in one way and another began to be talked of and too often ridiculed and abused.'[22] Though this caused him pain and sorrow the experience taught him that 'it is useful to have our religious principles readily assailed. What is won dearly is priced highly and clung to firmly'.[23]

What should the next step be?

While Ryle was at Oxford his father had purchased Henbury Hall, about three miles out of Macclesfield, for £54,000. The Ryles were delighted to leave behind the expanding and smoky mills of the town and move to the Cheshire plain.[24] Young Ryle was greatly impressed by his new home, which was surrounded by arable land, rich meadow and woodlands. 'There was much that was extremely beautiful about it', he wrote, 'both in the grounds and the distant views from it, and I soon became exceedingly attached to it'.[25] Yet he felt unsettled, and within a year of returning home decided to go to London to study law, thinking it would be prudent to be better qualified if he should take up a parliamentary career. [So he joined the office of Mr Christie, a conveyancer of Lincolns

Inn, and lodged in Pall Mall.] He did well in his studies, but unfortunately had to give them up after six months because of the recurrence of a chest infection aggravated by the foul air of Victorian London. While there he regularly attended on Sundays the Rev Baptist W. Noel's Chapel in Bedford Row and became a communicant member.[26] Noel was a fervent evangelical, and had been a loyal member of the Church of England until 1848 when he resigned his living and became a Baptist. He could not accept the doctrine of 'baptismal regeneration' as held by some High Church clergy, and felt the last straw was when the Bishop of Exeter refused to institute the Rev G. C. Gorham, an evangelical who also denied the doctrine, into a benefice in his diocese, on the grounds of his 'unsound doctrine'.[27] Ryle's unqualified acceptance of evangelical religion bitterly disappointed his father, and this led to an estrangement so grievous that he could not confide in his son over business matters. Young Ryle now felt that he was only 'a tolerated person' in his own family.[28]

After his return from London Ryle's father took him into the bank, but gave him no responsibilities. With a hint of discontent he wrote of his experience: 'I was never a member of the firm and knew nothing of its inward affairs. My only business was to sign notes, and learn as much as I could generally of banking business. Happily I never got any further'.[29] Daintry and Ryle's bank, as it was called by the locals, was 'a bank of loan' and issued its own notes to creditors and these became familiar currency in the town. A five pound note headed Macclesfield and Cheshire bank, issued on 25 February 1841 and signed J. C. Ryle, hangs on the vestry wall in Macclesfield Parish Church.[30] At least one hundred and nineteen bank notes were signed by Ryle on that day. Years later when writing a tract on Prayer he recalled working in the bank, 'The bank note without a signature at the bottom is nothing but a worthless piece of paper. A few strokes of a pen confers on it all its value. The prayer of a poor child of Adam is a feeble thing but once endorsed by the hand of the Lord Jesus it availeth much.'

Settled again in Macclesfield, young Ryle followed his father's example and gave himself wholeheartedly to public service. He was appointed a magistrate and regularly sat at the weekly sessions.

He took up a commission in the Cheshire Yeomanry which was often a mainstay of public order in 'the Hungry Forties'. Each year Captain Ryle and his fellow officers went with their troops to Liverpool for ten days training on Crosby Sands, where once they were inspected by the famous General Sir Charles Napier.[31]

It was an uncertain period and Ryle still had ambitions of entering Parliament one day, and he soon became a popular speaker at political meetings in and around the town. A local journalist attending on such meeting said he spoke with 'much ability....and at great length'.[32] His ability and talents were recognised and there was a strong possibility that he might be nominated as the next Tory candidate; but he turned the offer down. His heart was not entirely in Tory principles and he preferred his father's stance as a Reformer. When it became known that Ryle had become a Christian he was also frequently invited to address religious gatherings in the district. These were low key affairs since Ryle knew that his father would resent any publicity relating to his son's religious activities. At home he was permitted to have prayers in the housekeeper's room for the housekeeper and her maid, but the men servants were not allowed to attend. Occasionally he was able to visit a sick or dying person to offer prayer and comfort. While he lived in his father's house his Christian witness had to be limited.

Ryle was now an eligible young man in his early twenties and heir to a large fortune. He received many invitations to visit the great houses for dinner parties and dances, but he did not enjoy socializing and declined as many invitations as he could. Those he accepted he found boring. His parents encouraged him to mix with the gentry and would have been delighted if he had married into one of the county families. His father even offered to give him a house and an annual income of £800 when he found the right lady. But he was not interested in marriage at the time and confessed, 'I was very ignorant about women's character in those days', though admitting, 'I have reason to think now there was more than one person who would have said "yes" if I had asked them.'[33] Evangelicals considered dancing and card-playing unseemly activities and Ryle gave up all such when he was converted. Cricket however was a wholesome pastime. He continued to play for two or three seasons after leaving University, and 'took part in all sorts of gentlemen's matches in Derbyshire, Staffordshire, Nottinghamshire and Leicestershire'.[34]

As Ryle looked back over this period of his life he recognised that God had been fitting him for future service:

> I was training much and learning much in passing through a school of experience which afterwards was very useful to me. I often think now that my chief fault in those days was that I was too much wrapped up in my own daily spiritual conflict and my own daily difficulties. I did not sufficiently aim at works of active usefulness to the souls of others. At the same time it is but fair to say that it would be hard to point out what work there was that I could have done. Teaching, preaching, visitations, evangelization and such like work were out of the question. As long as I lived under my father's roof they would have been strongly objected to, and would have given great offence. It seems to me as if God intended that period of my life to be one of patient learning and not for active doing.[35]

He had no inkling of the catastrophe that was to hit his family and change his whole life.

Sudden humiliation

For several months John Ryle senior had known that the company's finances were not secure, and wrote anxiously to Mr W. H. Ravenscroft, the branch manager of the bank in Manchester, 'If you knew a tenth of the bad effects of your management as I see it here, you would say you never heard of a more melancholy and heartbreaking case... I am at my wit's end.'[36] Ravenscroft lacked business acumen, too readily satisfied borrowers without proper security and ran up huge debts. In retrospect, however, Ryle put the blame for the failure of the family bank fairly and squarely on his father's shoulders. 'The plain truth is,' he confided, 'my father was never fit to be a banker. He was too easy going, too good-natured and too careless about details.'[37] He failed to insure his assets against a rainy day and when the storm broke he lost everything. At the end of June 1841, The Macclesfield and Cheshire Bank ceased payment and the partners were bankrupt.

All that the senior Ryle had inherited from his father, including property which had probably doubled in value, was taken from him by the creditors. He lost an income of £15,000 per annum and property valued at between five and six hundred thousand pounds. The summer of 1841 was a miserable time for all the Ryle family, and indelibly etched upon their minds for ever.

When news broke that after forty-one years Daintry and Ryle's bank had crashed there was pandemonium in the town, and crowds queued outside the bank in Jordangate hoping to retrieve their savings. Several people were injured in the crush and one man had his thigh broken.

Weeks before the collapse of the bank young Ryle had suspected that something was wrong, but his father never discussed his problems with him. He had also been feeling that the emphasis on materialism and the disregard of the Sabbath by the family was a complete departure from his grandfather's godly ways and would inevitably lead to disaster. More than thirty years later the sense of shock and shame was as fresh in his memory as on the day when his father confessed that he was ruined. 'We got up one summer morning with all the world before us as usual and went to bed that same night completely and entirely ruined'.[38]

The legal proceedings and the disposal of all Ryle's private property placed the family under a heavy strain. Mrs Ryle was persuaded to go and stay with her brother Edward Hurt in London. Happily at this time, Susan and Caroline were both married to clergymen. Emma went to stay with Colonel Thornhill and his daughter in the New Forest. Frederick was in Europe reading for a degree and John and his sister Mary Anne stayed on to support their father. It was an unpleasant business winding up the estate. 'This occupied about six weeks', he recalled, 'I think about the most trying and miserable six weeks I ever spent in my life'.[39]

The Macclesfield Squadron had almost two and a half thousand pounds deposited in the bank and only prompt Treasury action saved the Yeomanry funds. The creditors claimed everything else, except that Mrs Ryle had the legal right to the £30,000 settled on her at the time of her marriage. The silk mill on Park Green was sold to William Frost and Sons, who continued the business. Until recent times a unique two-faced grandfather clock, bearing the name Daintry and Ryle and the date 1818, stood in the manager's office. The Henbury estate was put up for auction in December, together with 'the life interest of a gentleman aged fifty-eight in the sum of thirty thousand pounds and a policy of assurance five thousand pounds'.[40] Sympathetic relatives purchased the policies and the estate was privately sold to Major Thomas Marsland of Moseley Hall, Cheadle. Members of the family were allowed to keep their personal possessions but everything else had to be sold.

Once heir to a vast fortune, young Ryle left Henbury Hall in August 1841 humiliated and broken, having resigned his commission in the Yeomanry and with only £200 to his name. 'I luckily had two horses,' he recalled, 'which I sold and my yeomanry uniform, saddlery, accoutrements and so on which Colonel Egerton kindly bought for one hundred pounds as a matter of charity.'[41]

Years later he wrote about the home he loved:

> I do not think that there has ever been a single day in my life for thirty years that I have not remembered the great humiliation of having to leave Henbury. During that thirty-two years I have lived in many houses and been in many positions. I have always tried to make the best of them and to be cheerful in every circumstance, but nothing has made me forget my sudden violent expulsion from Cheshire in 1841...Ever since I left Cheshire I have never felt at home, but a sojourner and a dweller in a lodging.[42]

That was the last time he saw Henbury. At the invitation of Colonel Thornhill he went to join his sister in the New Forest. He discloses honestly in his memoirs that after that dreadful summer he experienced days of deep depression which at times almost drove him to taking his own life. 'The blackest chapter of my life,' he admits.[43]

> The plain fact was there was no one of the family whom it touched more than it did me. My father and mother were no longer young and in the downhill of life; my brothers and sisters, of course, never expected to live at Henbury and naturally never thought of it as their

house after a certain time. I, on the contrary, as the eldest son, twenty-five, with all the world before me, lost everything, and saw the whole future of my life turned upside down and thrown into confusion.[44]

In calmer moments he was conscious of the hand of God at work in his change of fortune. As a young Christian he might have been overcome by the trials of these summer months, but he was wonderfully sustained in his Christian faith. 'To feel trouble freely and yet submit to it patiently is what is required of a Christian' was a lesson he learned in that depressing period. Upheld by his trust in the Lord he had 'a firm and deep conviction that all would be well, though he could not see nor feel it at the time:'[45]

> I have not the least doubt it was all for the best. If my father's affairs had prospered and I had never been ruined, my life, of course, would have been a very different one. I should have probably gone into Parliament very soon and it is impossible to say what the effect of this might have been upon my soul. I should have formed different connections, and moved in an entirely different circle. I should never have been a clergyman, never have preached, written a tract or book. Perhaps I might have made shipwreck in spiritual things. So I do not mean to say at all, that I wish it to have been different to what it was. All I mean to say is that I was deeply wounded by my reverses, suffered deeply under them, and I do not think I have recovered in body and mind from the effect of them.[46]

Ryle's father remained at Henbury to complete the final formalities. 'My grandfather,' Ryle observed, 'was the only Ryle who ever attained great wealth, and my father was the first Ryle who left Cheshire after losing every penny of it.'[47] Later John Ryle joined his wife and together they settled in enforced retirement in Anglsey, a small watering place overlooking the Solent. Susanna died in 1846 and John in 1861. When the affairs were wound up, an interim dividend of four shillings in the pound was paid to each of the creditors, but he was determined to make good all his debts if at all possible, Ryle feeling a personal concern for the hundreds of small investors who had lost their savings in his bank. Over the years John, too, made his contribution to a reduction of the debt by his frugal living and through the sale of his religious tracts and books. When his father died a final payment was made out of the will, making a total payment of thirteen shillings and eight pence half-penny in the pound to all who had lost savings in the bank.[48]

Ever mindful of the adversity which so abruptly changed the circumstances of his life, Ryle in one of his sermons, commented, 'Banks may break and money make itself wings and flee away. But the man who has come to Christ by faith will still possess something which can never be taken away from him'.[49]

Chapter Three

It pleased God

Ryle left Henbury having no idea what he was going to do. His hopes of a parliamentary career had been dashed by his father's bankruptcy. His parents could not offer any practical suggestions and just hoped that something would turn up. Friends enquired whether he might be interested in a secretarial post? William Ewart Gladstone, a young up and coming Member of Parliament, was looking for a competent private secretary. But Ryle was adamant in his response, saying he 'felt no confidence in him and would not have it for a moment'.[1] Civil engineering or the law were possibilities for him, but they 'offered no means of support for several years' and he must have a career that gave him an immediate income.[2] A Fellowship at an Oxford college would provide him with an income of £200 per annum, but he loathed the thought of being a private tutor.

The next step clarified

Eventually it became clear that only one course was open to him, for which he was already qualified – that was to take Holy Orders. 'I could see nothing before me but to become a clergyman, because that brought me in some income at once'.[3] The historic role of the two Universities was to prepare men for the Church, and many young men went up to Oxford or Cambridge to read theology and philosophy intending to take Holy Orders after finishing their degree.

Evangelicals have always made much of the importance of prayer in seeking God's guidance at crucial points in their lives, yet Ryle does not claim that it was an answer to prayer that encouraged him to go forward for ordination. Neither did he believe that God intended all converted young men to become clergymen. He seems to have relied entirely on 'sanctified common sense' in making up his mind, being convinced that circumstances led him that way. In the final analysis, he says, 'I became a clergyman because I felt shut up to it, and saw no other course open to me'.[4] He might also have been influenced in this decision by some of his relatives and friends who had become clergymen.[5]

The circumstances leading up to his ordination were remarkable. Quite unexpectedly he received an invitation from the Rev William Gibson, the evangelical vicar of Fawley, to be his curate. Possibly Colonel Thornhill, a family friend who had moved from Cheshire to take up the post of Steward of the New Forest, suggested Ryle's name to the vicar. Gibson was one of that dying breed of absentee clergy in the Church of England, those who enjoyed the benefits of a benefice but were away from the parish for months on end. The Established Church in the first half of the nineteenth century was plagued by non-resident clergy who neglected their parishes in this way, and the bishops were powerless to act until later reforms were brought in.

All that was required of an Oxbridge graduate seeking ordination was to obtain a title, find a bishop to ordain him, attend a short retreat, and give his assent before the bishop and congregation to believe and teach the Scriptures, to be a Christian example and to give obedience to the bishop. Ryle approached the Bishop of Chester, John Bird Sumner, who in turn recommended him to his brother, the Bishop of Winchester. Within a matter of a few months he was ordained in Farnham Castle, the ancient seat of the Bishop of Winchester. Charles Richard Sumner was an Evangelical who welcomed evangelical clergy to his diocese. Ordinations in the diocese were conducted twice a year and it was customary on the evening before the ordination service for Bishop Sumner to give his formal charge to the ordinands in a quiet and dignified manner, exhorting them 'to preach Christ' in all their ministry.[6] To each deacon after his ordination the bishop gave a text of scripture as a motto for his ministry.

Exbury
From this time on Ryle vowed to devote all his gifts and energies to the service of his Lord and Saviour, Jesus Christ. Friends supported the new ordinand by their prayers. He was made deacon

on St Thomas' Day, 21st December, 1841, and may have preached his first sermon as a clergyman on Christmas Day that year.[7] On his arrival in the parish the rector immediately placed him in charge of the Chapel of Ease in Exbury with about four hundred parishioners to care for. He received a stipend of £100 per annum and a house, which was reputed to be haunted, in the neighbouring village of Langley, about a mile away.[8] Ryle was relatively well off compared with the majority of his parishioners who worked on the land for ten shillings per week, when work was available. Out of his stipend he paid sixteen pounds a year rent for the use of furniture the previous curate had left in the house, bought the necessities of life and paid his maidservant and a youth who did odd jobs and looked after a dog, a cat and a pig.[9]

Ryle quickly got into the routine of pastoral work. He carefully prepared two sermons for the Sunday services, regularly conducted cottage meetings twice a week, 'in small crowded cottages, reeking with peat smoke... and was in every house in the parish at least once a month.' His visits were never merely social calls, but always had a spiritual purpose, more so, since his parishioners were 'totally unaccustomed to being...spoken to about their souls'.[10] At each cottage he left a religious tract, which he purchased from the Religious Tract Society in Southampton. He stitched brown paper to the covers so that they would last longer and exchanged them between cottagers on his next visit. Evangelicals set new standards of pastoral care by their house-to-house visiting, sharing the good news of the gospel, praying with the sick and comforting the dying. In Exbury the people appreciated Ryle's caring ministry and his 'church was soon filled on Sunday'.[11]

Country life was different here from Henbury. 'Drunkenness and sin of every kind abounded' and there were fights between local youths after drinking.[12] He also found the 'large rural parish...between Southampton Water and the Solent' a very unhealthy place, and 'never knew a time when ague, scarlet fever and typhus was not to be found in the district.'[13] There was no resident doctor or nurse in the parish and it was left to neighbours to look after the sick. Richard Baxter, the Puritan divine, had recommended that ministers should tend the sick in the absence of a physician, and in addition to prayer, Ryle used a variety of means in his ministry among the sick in the parish. He gave large quanties of beef tea to patients who suffered from scarlet fever, and for typhus, he confessed, 'I had no faith in anything but port wine'.[14] He thus became adept at amateur doctoring, and in a paper he gave some years later to the British Medical Association in Liverpool, he revealed a remarkable knowledge of dispensing medicines. He believed that God had given to the medical profession the knowledge and gift of skills to share in his own healing work, saying, 'Next to the office of him who ministers to men's souls, none is really more useful and honourable than that of him who ministers to the soul's frail tabernacle, the body'.[15]

For most of the time that Ryle was a curate at Exbury his rector was in Malta, and he was left to look after the parishioners at Fawley as well as his own people. If clergy wished to have a curate they generally paid for him out of their own stipend and consequently some clergy felt they had a right to be away from the parish for months on end. After two years in the parish he began to suffer bouts of ill-health, evidently brought on by overwork and the poor environment. His own remedies were not able to cure his constant headaches, indigestion and heart murmurs and he felt he must seek specialist advice. Though he was 'as poor as a rat', he went to see Dr Henry Jepson, a renowned medical practioner in Leamington Spa, who put him on a course of 'blue pills, sulphuric acid, dandelion, Leamington water and frequent cold shower baths.'[16] The prescribed treatment lasted a month, and most generously Dr Jepson would take a fee only for alternate visits. The treatment worked, but Ryle felt that he had to consider moving to another parish.

It was some consolation for him to know that his parishioners were genuinely sorry he was leaving. When the time came in November 1843, he printed *A Minister's Parting Words to the Inhabitants of Exbury* and distributed it throughout the parish. In the tract he confessed his shortcomings and prayed that the Lord would send 'a better Minister than ever I have been'. There followed a word of exhortation to sinners to repent and trust in the Saviour. Believers he urged to glory in nothing but the Cross of Christ and to depend on nothing but the blood of Christ and the work of Christ; to be diligent in prayer and Bible-reading, to be steadfast at Church, not neglecting the Sacraments nor despising the Prayer-book'. Ryle left Exbury with a strong conviction that his ministry had not been in vain and many in the parish now had a real faith in Christ.

Winchester

Bishop Sumner was aware of the sterling work accomplished by Ryle at Exbury and, as he was looking for the right man to fill a vacancy at St Thomas', Winchester, he offered Ryle the benefice. Ryle readily accepted this challenge. St Thomas' was a small, run-down parish of 3,000 parishioners with a stipend of £100 per annum and a house. The stipend was no greater than he had received at Exbury, but a quarter of the livings in the Established Church were worth less. Ryle was delighted with his preferment, which removed him from a very unhealthy parish and placed him in a picturesque town, rich in architecture and historical interests, as well as giving him sole charge of his own parish. Ryle arrived in the parish 'in a very cold, pinching winter' in 1843, and found the church was an old, tumbledown building, holding about 600 people, with old fashioned pews.[17] The previous incumbent had been an Evangelical, but getting on in years and not an active pastor. Before moving to the parish Ryle called to see him, and was surprised to find a clergyman 'in slippers and dressing-gown in the middle of the day. I made up my mind that I should find little had been done in the parish.'[18] His fears were confirmed when he became rector.

He began his ministry in Winchester determined to justify the confidence the bishop had shown in him. He was 27 years of age, energetic, and free from the distractions of a wife and family. Soon he made a name for himself in the town. The tall, youthful rector preached on Sundays with 'a great deal of fire and energy, after a manner that was quite new in Winchester', and made a very great sensation.[19] Within a very short time he had filled the church 'to suffocation and turned the parish upside down'.[20] He also started a mid-week Bible study group in the Infant School which was well attended. Some who attended the Sunday services were from other churches 'occupied by unsatisfactory incumbents', and apparently were attracted by reports of what was now going on at St Thomas'.[21]

Looking back over his ministry in Winchester, however, Ryle felt that he was 'youthful and inexperienced' and was particularly critical of his preaching style.[22] Although his pulpit oratory did draw large congregations, he said:

> My preaching at Winchester on Sundays consisted entirely of written sermons, of a style I should not care to preach now, because they were far too florid, and far less simple and direct than I afterwards found valuable. Nevertheless, they were thoroughly evangelical and being well-composed and read with a great deal of earnestness and fire. I have no doubt they sounded very fine and effective, but I should not wish to preach them now.[23]

Later in his ministry he retained the same biblical content and preached with the same evangelical fervour, but reduced the full written sermon to a few brief notes and preached in a more lucid, pithy and forceful style.

He had not been long in his parish before discovering that being a young, unmarried rector had its drawbacks. He suspected that some of the young women in his congregation were more interested in the minister than his message. He was not naturally gregarious and felt embarrassed in the company of women he did not know. In any case, he felt that marriage was out of the question until he had a stipend of a least £500 a year with a house.[24]

Although Bishop Sumner favoured Evangelicals, the diocese remained predominantly Broad and High Church. Several influential Tractarians in the vicinity of Winchester included John Keble as vicar of Hurley, George Moberley as headmaster of Winchester College, and Samuel Wilberforce, third son of the evangelical philanthropist, who had recently been appointed to the parish of Alvestoke, which included Anglsey where the Ryle family lived. Wilberforce, by his persuasive preaching and frequent visiting, exercised a powerful influence on the family, with the exception of Mr Ryle who disdained High Church practices. When

John travelled over from Winchester to visit his family Wilberforce would invite him to preach, and never raised any objection to his evangelical message, talking with him 'as if we were all agreed in the main'.[25] In spite of Wilberforce's 'great kindness'[26] and occasionally attending St Thomas' when he was in town, Ryle felt his influence on his brother and two sisters was 'extremely pernicious'[27] and they 'suffered greatly from it'.[28] It was Wilberforce who gave brother Frederick his first title when he was ordained, and his sister Emma appears to have been dominated by Wilberforce's brother-in-law, H. E. Manning, a frequent visitor to Alvestoke who later became a Roman Catholic. After four years in the parish Wilberforce was appointed Dean of Westminster, and within a year was consecrated Bishop of Oxford.

An unexpected call

In Victorian times it was not uncommon for a clergyman to remain in his parish for twenty, thirty or even more years, and Ryle expected to spend many years at St Thomas' in the ministry to which he believed God had called him. The parishioners were responding to his evangelical ministry, and he was enjoying his work and not looking for preferment. So it was a complete surprise when after only five months in Winchester he received a letter from Lord Lyndhurst, the Lord Chancellor, inviting him to consider the vacant parish of Helmingham in Suffolk. Crown livings and other important benefices were sometimes offered as a gesture for political services. Was Ryle approached in deference to his father's political successes, or because of his former connections with Eton and Christ Church? We do not know. It is possible that his name was put forward by Mrs Tollemache of Helmingham Hall, who had befriended Ryle soon after he was converted.[29]

Ryle was not particularly drawn to Suffolk, a part of the country he did not know, and he was not enthusiastic about leaving a town church with a full congregation for a country parish of 300 inhabitants. On the other hand, if he remained in Winchester he would always be a poor clergyman and to some extent still dependent on his father's generosity. The Lord Chancellor's offer of a parish with a stipend of £500 a year was very attractive. For the first time in his life he would be independent financially, and might even consider getting married and raising a family. He accepted the offer, tendered his resignation to the bishop, and left Winchester for Helmingham. Not only at the time but even years later he had misgivings about this decision. 'Of all the steps I ever took in my life to this day I feel doubts whether the move was right or not. I sometimes think it was want of faith to go, and I ought to have stayed.'[30] He was instituted into his new parish by Edward Stanley, the Bishop of Norwich.

Helmingham in west Suffolk, where Ryle was rector for seventeen years, is about ten miles north-east of Ipswich and four miles south of Debenham. Today it is little changed from what it was in 1844, when Ryle went to the parish. Nearly all the parishioners were employed by John Tollemache at Helmingham Hall or on the estate. The tiny village of scattered cottages had no village green, no shop, no public-house, no beer house, and until 1853 had no school except a small dame school run by Mrs Tollemache. Helmingham Hall had been the seat of the Tollemache family since 1487 and was set in a parkland renowned for its oaks and shapely elms. It was Tollemache's custom when not resident elsewhere to have the Hall filled with Victorian high society. On these occasions Ryle acted as chaplain, conducted family prayers morning and evening and preached before the distinguished guests on Sundays. Some of the guests were very worldly, but those whom Mrs Tollemache personally invited were 'very thoroughly Christian'.[31] Ryle was delighted at these opportunities of meeting and conversing with eminent evangelicals such as John Bird Sumner, the Archbishop of Canterbury and H. Montegue Villiers, who was to become Bishop of Durham, Admiral Harcourt and Captain Hope. He respected these evangelical stalwarts and took to heart their wise counsels. Gladly, he testified, 'I thank God that I met them and think their acquaintance did me good.'[32]

The Tollemache family
John Tollemache was a fine figure of a man, standing over six foot in height, with broad, muscular shoulders, bold features and a strong chin. He was a man of immense strength, very fond of

sport and a lover of the sea. Twice he beat the champion runner of England over one hundred yards, though he modestly admitted that he was the younger man. A keen cricketer, he challenged local village teams each summer to play against a side drawn from his own family. Twice married, he had twenty-four sons and one daughter, though only twelve sons survived. He was renowned as one of the leading agriculturalists in the country and among the first landowners to give each of his male estate workers a small-holding attached to each cottage. He was determined to make Helmingham a model estate and over the years he spent thousands of pounds building and renovating the semi-detached cottages for his workers. He built the cottages in pairs, 'because' he said, 'a chimney between the two warmed both and in sickness each had neighbours to call on for help'.[33] He was a Member of Parliament from 1841 to 1872 and four years later was created a baron in recognition of his philanthropic endeavours.

He was a devout churchman, and every Sunday morning when he was in residence at Helmingham he and his family drove in carriages down the long drive to church, attended by a retinue of servants attired in black and white livery. The gentlemen in the party carried tall hats and each of the ladies a Prayer-book, a clean white handkerchief and a small posy of flowers. They were welcomed by the rector at the lychgate and led into church, while the estate workers remained standing until the family and their guests were seated in the Tollemache pews at the front of the nave. Tollemache was an Evangelical, a loyal Churchman, a supporter of the Protestant Reformation Society and the Exeter Hall meetings, a strong critic of ritualism and a strict Sabbatarian. He insisted on a strict observance of the Sabbath and allowed only cold meat to be served at dinner. All the servants had some time off on Sundays, but they were expected to attend church when their work was finished. The daily routine at the Hall began and ended with family prayers generally conducted by Tollemache himself. At the appointed hour, one of the liveried servants would take a large family Prayer-book resting on a silver salver into the dining room, and announce, 'Prayers are on the table, sir.'[34]

The lovely old church of St Mary's stands on the edge of

parkland and woodland surrounding the Hall and dates from the late thirteenth century. The Squire had arranged for the church to be completely renovated and restored prior to Ryle's arrival. Inside every available wall between the stain glass windows bears some memorial to the Tollemache family, and there are some very fine marble monuments. It was fashionable at the time for evangelical clergy to have selected texts painted on the interior walls and beams of their churches, and during his long incumbency at Helmingham, Ryle carefully chose twenty-four texts of scripture to be painted on the walls, with important words in red. Beside a tomb in the chancel is the text 'Them that sleep in Jesus will God bring with him'. Over the east window, 'Jesus said, I am the way, the truth and the life, no man cometh unto the Father, but by Me'. Over the chancel arch, 'Being justified by faith, we have peace with God, through our Lord Jesus Christ.' By the pulpit, 'Woe is me if I preach not the gospel', and over the main door, 'Remember how thou hast received and heard and hold fast and repent.'[35]

Unlike the church, the rectory was in a wretched state of repair when Ryle arrived and the Tollemaches insisted on the new rector residing at the Hall until the repairs were completed. Ryle did not relish this prospect, and much to his annoyance it was over a year before he could move into his new home. Even when he did so he 'found the place in a miserable condition and it cost him a lot of money, which he could ill afford, to put it in decent order'.[36] When eventually he settled in he found no difficulty in employing a suitable elderly woman from the village as cook, a young housemaid, and an odd-job man to attend to his horse and gig.

Life at Helmingham
Ryle found the work at Helmingham less hectic than at Exbury and less demanding than Winchester. All his parishioners lived within a mile or so of the church, which made visiting more convenient. He believed with Chalmers, the Scottish divine, that 'a house-going parson makes a church-going people'. His predecessor had been thirty-two years in the parish but in the latter years had neglected his pastoral work, so the parishioners were delighted to have a younger and more active parson. In the winter

months he would trudge through the sleet and snow of East Anglia to meet with a handful of believers to sing a few hymns together and share in prayer and Bible study. Such cottage meetings were popular activities in evangelical parishes, but High Churchmen derided them as 'Methodistical'.[37]

For the first time in his ministry Ryle found that in his small parish he had time for serious reading and study. With an adequate stipend he was no longer dependent on gifts from his father and friends and at last could afford to buy books, even if most of them were from second-hand bookshops. He was particularly interested in the tomes of the Reformation and Puritan writers. These treasured volumes he picked up in Ipswich and London and occasionally from the libraries of retired clergy in the diocese. The break-up of such libraries troubled him and drew forth the observation; 'The end to which good men's libraries finally come is a melancholy subject. Few things are so much loved by some, and despised and neglected by others as books, and especially theological books.'[38] He loved books and derived learning and pleasure from reading them. 'I read everything I can get hold of which professes to throw light on my Master's business and the work of Christ among men.'[39] He was an avid reader of the works of the Reformers. When an undergraduate at Oxford he had often passed the spot where Hugh Latimer, Nicholas Ridley and Thomas Cranmer had died in the flames for their faith, and in Suffolk he lived not many miles from where Rowland Taylor, the Protestant reformer, was martyred. Though he knew that the Reformers were despised in his day, their names vilified and their works ignored, yet they were undoubtedly men who firmly held 'the faith once delivered to the saints'. They were learned theologians, challenging preachers and devout men of God. His study of the Reformers established him in the great principles of Protestant doctrine from which he never departed.

The Puritans

It was in Suffolk also that Ryle discovered the Puritans. 'From the day I was transplanted into the eastern counties, and became a Suffolk incumbent I have made it my business to study the lives

of eminent Suffolk divines,' he admitted.[40] This part of England
had been receptive to the biblical doctrine of 'Justification Sola
Fide' in the sixteenth century. 'In the days of Queen Mary and
Elizabeth the inhabitants of Norfolk and Suffolk were famous for
their deep attachment to the doctrines of the Reformation and in
the days of the Stuarts and the Commonwealth they were no less
famous for their steadfast adherence to Puritan principles.'[41] During
his long ministry in East Anglia his appetite was whetted for
Puritan theology. Some of the best and holiest Puritan divines
were at one time resident in the area. There was the saintly William
Gurnall, Rector of Lavenham, the largest church in West Suffolk.
Thomas Young, a distinguished member of the Westminster
Assembly, and Milton's tutor, was Vicar of Stowmarket, and
William Bridge was 'town-preacher' at Great Yarmouth for seventeen years. Ryle drank deeply of the wells of Puritan theology. He
came to regard men like John Owen, Stephen Charnock and
Richard Sibbs as masters of experimental theology and believed
there were no writers to compare with them on the great biblical
themes of sin, redemption and holiness of life.[42]

He admired the Puritans for their expository preaching.[43] They
were giants in the pulpit and their sermons were a power in the
land. They believed preaching was God's highest calling and their
response in proclaiming the gospel faithfully and diligently was
'a primary duty'.[44] Preaching was God's appointed means of
bringing to himself those he had elected to save, and so the preacher
must humbly proclaim the whole gospel of Christ in his ministry.
To win souls they must preach to heart as well as mind and in turn
believers must be active doers of the Word. He admired the
Puritans too for their industrious pastoral ministry.[45] Faithfully
they went in and out among the people exhorting with carefulness,
reproving with zeal, comforting with cheerfulness, instructing with
erudition and ever watchful over their flock with God's oversight.
Their diligence in ministry was an example he assiduously
followed. In addition he admired the Puritans for their sound
doctrine.[46] Tenaciously they held to the supremacy and sufficiency
of Scripture. They loved to make much of Christ since he is the
only Saviour from the guilt, the power and the consequences of

sin. He endorsed the important place the Puritans gave to the person and work of the Holy Spirit [47] He approved wholeheartedly the Puritan acclamation of the believer's sovereign election, assurance of his present standing in grace and the certainty of his future state in glory He admired the Puritans for applying doctrine to everyday Christian living.[48] They resisted the temptation to treat theology as a dry, theoretical subject, but insisted that the truth must always be put into practice. So the Puritans made much of what they called 'the application' of the Word of God to holy living in daily life. Richard Baxter he considered an example to follow:

> While others were entangling themselves in politics, and burying their dead amidst the potsherds of earth, Baxter was living a crucified life, and daily preaching the Gospel. I suspect he was the best and wisest pastor that an English parish ever had, and a model that many a modern rector or vicar would do well to follow.[49]

Though Ryle admired the Puritans, he was not blind to their faults. Some were quaint and eccentric in their ways, exaggerated in their language and almost all over long in their sermons. These were largely faults of their age. For Ryle, however, their great fault was to allow themselves to be ejected from the Church of England in 1662 by the Act of Uniformity. He felt it was a tragedy that two thousand godly ministers were turned out of the Established Church and forced to become Nonconformists. He wished that more had followed the example of William Gurnall and others who had conformed and continued a useful and blessed ministry in their parishes. The Puritans, he acknowledged, 'with all their faults, weaknesses and defects, alone kept the lamp of pure evangelical religion burning in the times of the Stuarts; they alone prevented Laud's Popish inclinations carrying England back into the arms of Rome. It was they who fought the battle of religious freedom, of which we are reaping such fruits. It was they who crushed the wretched spirit of inquisitorial persecution which misguided High Churchmen tried to introduce into this land. Let us give them the honour they deserve'.[50]

Chapter Four

Simplicity in preaching

Ryle loved preaching and was in his element in the pulpit. He was a commanding figure with a strong voice and a clear delivery. In Winchester his forthright preaching had attracted a congregation which filled his church to overflowing on Sundays and, although Helmingham was only a small rural parish, almost all his parishioners attended church to hear the Rector preach. The second half of the century was the golden age of the popular preacher and men such as Joseph Parker at the City Temple, R. W. Dale at Carr Lane Chapel, Birmingham, F. W. Robertson at Trinity Church, Brighton, and C. H. Spurgeon at the Metropolitan Tabernacle, were household names and attracted large congregations. Nevertheless, with the spread of ritualism in the Established Church, the growing emphasis on the priest rather than the preacher and the altar rather than the pulpit, the question was inevitably raised from time to time in the Church press, 'Is the Pulpit Losing its Power?'[1]

In evangelical churches the sermon often assumed a significance out of all proportion to the rest of the worship (although the preaching was not always of the highest standard). Ryle was not one of the great preachers of the day, but the rural community at Helmingham liked the way he addressed them with sincerity, simplicity and conviction. A visitor to the church in the 1850s remarked on the size of the Sunday morning congregation and the eloquence of the preacher in an impressive setting. 'We found the reverend gentleman preaching in a beautiful Gothic church. He was surrounded by some of the finest statuary the county has to boast of – busts, effigies and tablets, groups of mailed knights, mute representatives of a race of men long since passed away, have their place. But this is not all, for the goodly number of devout worshippers are gathered to listen to the manly voice, and the fervent eloquence of the modern pastor'.[2] The same reporter estimated that 'although the population is not more than 280, the congregation numbered something like 160'.[3]

The 1851 religious census confirmed that more people attended church in the country districts than in the towns, and probably attendances at Helmingham during Ryle's incumbency were above the average for country congregations. In the pulpit Ryle was first and foremost an evangelist and expository preacher, who preached from an open Bible basing his message on a text or passage of scripture. The text he chose for his first sermon at Helmingham was from Luke 7:40: 'I have somewhat to say unto thee.'

The sermon was a comprehensive message of greeting to all parishioners, an invitation to repent of their sins and turn to Christ and finally an exhortation to all believers to live godly lives. The congregation was left in no doubt that the new rector had come to the parish to proclaim the gospel of redemption and reconciliation. He had not been inducted and instituted by the bishop merely to say the statutory services nor simply to enjoy a good stipend in a quiet country living, but to stand before the people as 'an ambassador of Christ, a bearer of the flag of truce bringing the glad tidings of the terms of peace'.[4] He was a pastor with a concern for men's souls. For the benefit of those parishioners who did not attend church that Sunday morning he printed the full text of his sermon and set out in his gig to distribute it personally to those absent. He could not afford to have his sermons printed so he purchased a small press and printed his own sermons and tracts.

Ryle the preacher

There was a strong personal quality about Ryle the preacher. He had a dignified presence and an earnest manner, and spoke in plain, simple English. He avoided long, complex sentences and his short, pithy utterances were remembered long after. Examples abound in his writings; 'What we weave in time, we wear in eternity;' 'Sin forsaken is one of the best evidences of sin forgiven;' 'It matters little how we die, but it matters much how we live,' 'He that begins with prayer will end with praise.' 'One thief on the cross was saved, that none should despair, and only one, that none should presume.'[5] These terse, epigrammatic utterances were typical of his style.

Such incisive, robust and forceful preaching, addressed to the heart and conscience of his hearers, was characteristic of the man. But it was not always so. When he was first ordained he regarded the preparation of a sermon as a serious literary production and took the learned Henry Melville, minister of Camden Chapel and a Canon of St Paul's Cathedral, also affectionately known as 'the evangelical St Chrysostom', as a model of good preaching style. When a student at Oxford he had heard Melville preach several times and he admired tremendously his gift of pulpit oratory. As a curate at Exbury he had tried to emulate Melville's eloquent pulpit delivery, but soon realised that he only mystified his parishioners. 'I felt', he admitted, 'that I was doing the country people in my congregation no good whatever. I was shooting over their heads; they could not understand my imitation of Melville's style, which I thought much of, therefore I thought it my plain duty to crucify my style and bring it down to what it is now.'[6] With a great deal of grace and common-sense he determined to cut out the rhetoric, the florid style and grandiloquence, in favour of plain homely words and a simple style. Gone for ever were those long, involved sentences which added nothing to the clarity of thought. Instead Ryle began to concentrate on a sincere, plain, practical style which his congregation could understand and follow. Nevertheless, he did sometimes include in his sermons some Latin tag which could not have been appreciated by his rural congregation.

Ryle readily acknowledged his debt to many preachers, orators, and authors who had influenced his preaching and writing. At Eton and Oxford he had studied the ancient classics and read widely the great English writers, including the Anglican divines. Among those who helped to improve his preaching ability was John Bright, the Quaker orator. When as a young man Ryle had had ambitions of a career in politics he had studied closely the speeches of John Bright and came to regard him as a master of plain English. This opinion was confirmed after he met the politician on his occasional visits to Helmingham Hall. Others he paid tribute to were William Corbett, the radical politician; Thomas Guthrie, the Scottish

preacher; John Bunyan, the Puritan writer; Matthew Henry, the
Bible commentator; and William Shakespeare, the dramatist. But
above all, the greatest influence on his style was the Authorised
Version of the English Bible. His constant reading and study of it
moulded his thought and helped to produce that strength, dignity
and clarity of language which was so characteristic of his
preaching. The time Ryle had spent in a lawyer's office gave him
a training in exactness, logic, and order which he never forgot. He
believed that one of the demands of preaching was to present the
message of God in a clear and orderly manner. A study of his
sermons and addresses reveals that he took great care over their
preparation and always made full use of divisions and headings to
break up the thought and concentrate the mind. In this he was
influenced by John Bunyan and other Puritan writers. He found
that headings gave direction to his preaching, made it easier for
his hearers to follow and enabled him to rely on brief notes. In
some of his addresses we find a three-point structure, with an
introduction and application at the end. But he did not limit his
sermons to three points; in one he preached on 'Regeneration', he
listed six characteristics of those who are born again.[7] Perhaps the
most remarkable example of Ryle's love of ordered structure is
the address he gave to the Church Congress at Southampton when
he received a great ovation from the audience as he concluded his
seventeenth and final point and sat down.

The content of his sermons
The content of Ryle's sermons was grounded firmly in the
evangelical mould. He made much of the Bible, did not hesitate
to condemn the sinfulness and guilt of man, pointed sinners to the
atoning death of Christ on the Cross and to the power of the
resurrection. Neither did he overlook the work of the Holy Spirit
in convicting men of sin and transforming their lives from within.
These were the constant themes of his preaching. Above all, his
preaching was Christ-centred. For example at the conclusion of
his sermon on 'Only One Way of Salvation', he stated:

If there is no salvation excepting by Christ we must not be surprised if ministers of the gospel preach much about Him. They cannot tell us too much about the name which is above every name. We cannot hear of Him too much. We may hear too much about controversy in sermons, we may hear too much of works and duties, of forms and ceremonies, of sacraments and ordinances, but there is one subject which we never hear too much of, we can never hear too much of Christ.[8]

Sermon illustrations

Ryle liked to illustrate scriptural or theological truth with a suitable story or anecdote. So his tracts and sermons contain a profusion of illustration, word-pictures, metaphors and quotations, drawn from a wide variety of sources, including the Bible, nature, literature, history, science, personal observation and human situations. One who heard him preach commented on his use of such aids, 'Mr Ryle gives full scope to his facility for illustration.... He does not appear however, to hold this power under control. We say that he takes an illustration, it would often be more correct to say that the illustration takes him'.[9]

Parish visiting furnished him with many illustrations for future sermons. He recalled that 'a humble country clergyman was once asked whether he studied the fathers [meaning the Early Church Fathers] to which the worthy man replied that he had little opportunity of studying the fathers as they were generally in the fields when he called. But he studied the mothers more because he found them at home and could talk to them. Wittingly or unwittingly, the good man hit the nail right on the head. We must talk to our people when we are out of church if we would understand how to preach to them when they are in church.'[10]

After attending a service at Helmingham, G. Herbert Wright, a freelance journalist, wrote in his Suffolk Notes:

The sermon was one of the longest we have met with, but the earnestness of the preacher's manner and ever ready flow of ideas, the simple yet forceful language and the wonderfully apt and forceful illustrations made the time pass very pleasantly, and we, who for that time at least had no pudding to be spoiled, were almost sorry when he concluded.[11]

For almost forty years Ryle was the incumbent of country parishes and he was mindful of the challenge of ministering week in and week out to a rustic congregation. Experience taught him the excellent pulpit maxim he often passed on when a bishop to younger clergy. 'Be awake yourself, if you want to keep your people awake.'[12]

A good strong voice, a lively presentation and a simple and direct message was his method of keeping tired farm workers awake in church on a hot Sunday afternoon. In all his preaching he preached 'to arouse, to awaken and to stir careless souls'.[13]

Ryle's sermons and addresses never ran out of steam or ended indecisively, but always on a practical note of exhortation to his hearers to be 'doers of the Word'. For example, in a collection of papers he called *Practical Religion*, he drew his sermon on 'The Best Friend' to a close by saying:

> If Christ is your friend, you have great privileges, and ought to walk worthy of them. Seek every day to have closer communion with Him, who is your Friend, and to know more of his grace and power. True Christianity is not merely believing a certain set of dry abstract propositions; it is to live in daily personal communication with an actual living person – Jesus the Son of God. 'To me,' said Paul, 'to live is Christ' (Phil. 1:21). Seek every day to glorify your Lord and Saviour in all your ways.

The importance of preaching

In the second half of the nineteenth century some were tending to treat preaching in its traditional form as outdated. Some argued there was too much preaching in Anglican churches, much of it of a low standard, and it was suggested that only those who held the bishop's licence to preach should be allowed to do so. Ryle believed there was no more important function in a clergyman's ministry than the preaching of the Word of God, yet he agreed that many preachers were dull and uninspiring. 'It is vain to shut our eyes to the fact that there is great room for improvement in the preaching of the Church of England. At present it is certainly below the mark. Neither in manner, nor in style, nor in delivery does our pulpit come up to the requirements of the day.'[14]

Ryle believed there were several reasons for the decline in effective preaching. First, an extraordinary amount of vague and woolly thinking about theology. 'We have hundreds of jelly-fish clergyman who seem not to have a single bone in their body of divinity. They have no definite opinions; they belong to no school or party; they are so afraid of extreme views that they have no views at all.'[15] The ministry of the Word is a demanding and responsible calling and he deplored the want of distinctive doctrine in many sermons. 'The absence of a certain sound, the want of a sharply cut, well-defined doctrine in sermons is one of the worst and most dangerous symptoms of the present day', he maintained.[16] Such indecision and vague preaching he felt was all the more inexplicable because every clergyman in the Church of England is a minister of the Church which has declared her mind about doctrines, most distinctly in that noble confession, the Thirty-Nine Articles.[17]

Secondly, younger clergy were not adequately trained in sermon preparation and pulpit skills. Of his own efforts when a curate he wrote, 'Nobody ever told me what was right or wrong in the pulpit. The result was that the first years of my preaching was a series of experiments.'[18] And this experience was not unique. 'Few men I believe ever go into orders with any clear idea of what a sermon ought to be or how to set about making one. "Alas master, it was borrowed" would be the true comment on many a clergyman's sermon.'[19] He believed standards could be improved if the Universities and the new Theological Colleges gave instruction in sermon preparation and the bishops included in their Deacons and Priests examinations questions on sermon content and composition.

Thirdly, he felt that the Catholic revival in an increasing number of churches emphasised liturgical and sacramental worship and overshadowed the proclamation of the Word. But in the reformed Church of England the ministry of the Word has a priority over the ministry of the Sacraments. 'If,' he pointed out, 'we had only to read services and administer sacraments, to wear a peculiar dress and go through a round of ceremonies, bodily exercises, and gestures and postures, our position would be comparatively light. But this is not all. We have got to deliver our Master's message, to keep back nothing that is profitable, to declare all the council of God.'[20] This was a priority he found underlined in Scripture: 'I can find no record of the church assemblies in the New Testament in which preaching or teaching orally, does not occupy a prominent position.'[21] It was his considered opinion that 'the minister who exalts the sacraments and forms of the church above preaching may be a zealous, earnest, conscientious and respectable minister but his zeal is not according to knowledge. He is not a follower of the Apostles'.[22]

Fourthly, the standard of preaching had declined, Ryle believed, because of the increasing demands made on a clergyman's time and energy. Clergy of all parties were getting more involved in parochial activities. Two or even three services on Sundays were becoming customary, plus one or more services or meetings in mid-week. There were far fewer absentee clergy than before, and most conscientiously worked their parishes. However, there were few gifted preachers and few, if any, able to preach a hundred or more inspiring sermons each year. Ryle regularly preached two and often three sermons on Sundays and sometimes he could be very dull. Moreover the gradual spread of general education and literacy after 1870 meant that congregations began to expect something worth hearing whenever they went to church. It was not enough, as Ryle told Convocation at York on one occasion, 'to bring forth old truths over and over again as old friends that our hearers get thoroughly accustomed to, but we should bring out new things as well as old.'[23] He knew how demanding sermon preparation could be, but considered it so great and important a duty that he urged his fellow clergy to wrest time from other occupations in order to produce better sermons.[24]

Ryle had strong and deep evangelical convictions, and never seems at any time to have experienced doubts about his faith. His preaching was that of a man whose heart was right with God and whose spiritual experience confirmed the truths he proclaimed. He often used the metaphor of the trumpeter to illustrate the importance and significance of the preacher, a metaphor he borrowed from the Book of Ezekiel in the Old Testament. The trumpeter sounds his trumpet to awaken the soldiers, to direct them, to encourage and unite them, and it is the duty and responsibility of the Christian preacher to arouse careless souls, to guide them and show them the way they must go. The trumpeter who gives an uncertain sound causes confusion in the ranks and this should be a warning to the preacher to be clear and definite in his message. He must never forget he is a trumpeter in the army of Christ and take heed that his trumpet gives no uncertain sound.[25] He believed that he was entrusted as a Christian minister with what the Reformers called the 'ministerium verbi divini' and without over-stating any doctrine, he kept nothing back which was profitable to salvation, whether it pleased or not.

In 1887 Ryle was invited to give a lecture on preaching to the Homiletical Society in St Paul's Cathedral. It was typical of him to entitle his lecture *Simplicity in Preaching*. His humour won over his audience immediately on this occasion as he told them, 'I would rather preach before the University of Oxford or Cambridge or the Temple or Lincoln's Inn or the House of Parliament than I would address an agricultural congregation on a fine, hot afternoon in August. I have heard a labourer who enjoyed Sunday more than any other day of the week, "Because", he said, "I sit comfortably in church, put up my legs, have nothing to think about and just go to sleep"'.[26] In order to arrest and keep the attention of a congregation Ryle's advice to the preacher was to have a grasp of the text, to use plain words with a simple and homely style, to speak to the heart and conscience and to use abundant anecdotes and illustrations. He would often say that to have a warm church, 'the stove must be in the pulpit'.[27] The lecture, later included as a chapter in *The Upper Room*, is in reality a full-length portrait of Ryle himself as a preacher.

The influence of preaching

Though he believed preaching to be the prime responsibility of the Christian minister, he had no grandiose illusions about the sermon's influence on the congregation. In his own ministry, he admitted, he did not often see the results he desired. It was some encouragement to him on resigning from his curacy in Exbury to know that his brief ministry had been appreciated by his parishioners. He was cheered when someone turned to Christ, a backslider repented or a believer determined to live a more holy life after hearing a sermon, but he was aware of the power of sin and Satan in holding back sinners from enjoying the benefits of God's great salvation. 'I have learned by the painful experience of a third of a century that people may go for years attending God's house and yet never feel their sins, or desire to be saved....They go away as thoughtless and unmoved as the marble busts which look down on them from the monuments on the walls.'[28]

The lack of response saddened him, but he did not despair. In a sermon he preached in the nave of Chester Cathedral in 1878, he told the congregation that 'that grand bell in St Paul's Cathedral, London, had struck the hour for many years. The roar and din of traffic in the streets have a strange power to deaden its sound, and prevent men hearing it. But when the daily work is over, and desks are locked and doors are closed, and books are put away, and quiet reigns in the city, the case is altered. As the old bell at night strikes eleven, and twelve, and one and two and three, thousands hear it who never heard it during the day. So I hope it will be with many an one in the matter of his soul. Now, in plentitude of health and strength, in the hurry and whirl of business, I fear the voice of your conscience is often stifled and you cannot hear it. But the day may come when the great bell of conscience will make itself heard, whether you like it or not.'[29]

His ministry had taught him patience, and he accepted that when the seed of the Word is faithfully sown it may take a long time to germinate and bear fruit in the heart and life.

Beginning of Ryle's written ministry

In Victorian England, publishing sermons and addresses was a popular and lucrative extension of a parson's ministry. Evangelicals saw publication as a cheap and effective means of spreading the gospel, while the Tractarians wrote to further the Catholic revival and instruct the faithful in Church doctrine. The *Tracts for the Times* written by Pusey, Newman, Keble and others became powerful weapons in the early days of the Oxford Movement, and initially Evangelicals were impressed by them because of their orthodox teaching on the Bible and the Prayer-book. With the mass production of cheap literature people were becoming more literate and began to read avidly everything that came to hand. Tracts as well as novels with religious and moral themes became increasingly popular. Ryle saw the potential of inexpensively produced tracts and began to adapt his sermons with suitably striking titles, 'Have you a Priest?' 'Do you want a Friend?' 'Are you Happy?' Titles such as these made Ryle's name widely known both in Britain and throughout the world.

Ryle had a passionate concern throughout his ministry to make known the gospel through both the spoken and the written word. His first tract had a tragic origin and was literally 'a tract for the times.' On 9 May 1845 a large crowd had gathered for the official opening of a new suspension bridge in Great Yarmouth. The bridge suddenly collapsed during the ceremony and over a hundred people were thrown into the water and drowned.[30] The disaster shocked the whole country and Ryle took the opportunity to write a pamphlet on the theme of life's uncertainties and God's sure provision of salvation in Christ. The tract was published anonymously, though it bore the distinctive style and message of J. C. Ryle, and thousands of copies were sold. The publication of his tract was the beginning of a long association between Ryle and his publisher, William Hunt of Ipswich, a relationship which made Ryle 'The Prince of Tract-writers'.[31] Hunt published the bulk of Ryle's work during the time he was in Suffolk, but unfortunately, in 1883 the firm went bankrupt and Ryle transferred his work to Charles J. Thynne in Lincoln's Inn.

Despite the success of his first printed tract Ryle declined the invitation of his publisher to edit an Evangelical Magazine, largely because of his domestic circumstances. He instead proposed that Evangelicals should publish a series of Ipswich Tracts, 'if his brethren in the ministry would contribute their aid.'[32] The idea did not meet with much enthusiasm so Ryle decided to undertake the task on his own and launched a steady flow of inexpensive gospel literature. Among the two hundred or so titles on a variety of Christian themes, every one written with his favourite quill pen, was one entitled *Living or Dead?* which went into 26 editions

and sold over 110,000 copies. Another, *Do you Pray?*, sold over
130,000 copies. They sold singly for one or two pennies per copy,
a little cheaper in bundles of a hundred for widespread distribution.
With the success of the pamphlets, various tracts originally
published in paper covers, and bound by his publisher under the
title *Home Truths*, became popular reading and were reissued time
and again. More than twelve thousand of Ryle's tracts were printed
altogether, and several were translated into over a dozen languages.
The *Repository Tracts* written by Hannah More appealed to an
earlier generation and the Oxford Tracts focussed on a different
readership, but neither had the phenomenal success of Ryle's titles.
The Times commenting on Ryle's appointment as Bishop of
Liverpool noted that 'he had carved a niche for himself as a
pamphleteer'.[33] *The Record* claimed, 'His terse, direct and vigorous
style, so characterized by his strong individuality that every
sentence recalls the tone and accent of his spoken addresses, has
given to the "tracts" an influence and position in literature it did
not possess before.'[34] John Ruskin thought highly of Ryle's firm
convictions and commended his writings to his friends, 'as all
profoundly doctrinal, but chiefly exhortative, the doctrine,
however, comes in incidently, very pure and clear.'[35]

Many tributes were paid to Ryle for blessings received through
his tracts. At the Swansea Church Congress in 1879 after he had
addressed the gathering on 'The Evangelical Aspects of the
Church', Canon W. J. Knox-Little, a leading Anglo-Catholic priest,
stood up on the platform and testified to the help he had received
through reading one of Ryle's pamphlets. 'While I was groping in
the dark', he said, 'a tract of Canon Ryle brought to my soul what
I wanted, and as I have never before seen my spiritual father I am
glad to have the opportunity of thanking the good canon'. Then to
the intense delight of the large audience, the two canons shook
hands most warmly. Another remarkable tribute was paid to Ryle
in a sermon by the Rev J. W. Bardsley, incumbent of St Saviour's,
Falkner Square, Liverpool. He said, 'One little booklet called *True
Liberty* was translated into Spanish. It came into the hands of a
Dominican friar who had been sent to stamp out the reform
movement in the church in that part of Mexico. As he read the

tract the scales fell from his eyes and he entered by faith into the true liberty of the sons of God. He began to build up the church he meant to destroy. That church grew in half a century from a tiny remnant of a few believers into a flourishing church of some fifty thousand members'.[36] Frances James Chavasse, who succeeded Ryle in 1900 as the second Bishop of Liverpool, said he received many letters during the early years of his episcopate addressed to 'The Bishop of Liverpool' and thanking him for his helpful tracts.[37]

A wider reputation

Ryle's reputation as a preacher and publisher of evangelical pamphlets soon led to invitations to preach more widely. He was delighted at this opportunity, saying, 'I was ready to go anywhere to speak and preach for Christ, and never refused, however great the inconvenience or fatigue... often driving fifteen or twenty miles home.'[38] Frequently he was offered hospitality before making his journey home, but he was not an easy social mixer and as a bachelor often felt embarrassed in the company of women he did not know. His apparent aloofness quickly earned him the reputation of being 'unsociable, distant and indisposed to encourage friendship', and unfortunately left a bad impression.[39]

Through his wider ministry Ryle became acquainted with many of the leading evangelicals in London and counted among his ministerial friends such men as Daniel Wilson, vicar of Islington; William Pennefather, vicar of Christ Church, Barnet; Harry Blunt, vicar of Holy Trinity, Sloane Square; Thomas Dale, vicar of St Pancras; William Dealtry of Clapham; and William Cadman, rector of St George's, Southwark. He was invited to preach in several notable evangelical churches and reckoned that he had preached in no less than sixty London churches.[40] He was at a loss to know why he was such a popular preacher 'for I am certain that my preaching was very inferior to what it was after I was turned fifty. But I was always bold and aggressive and downright, and I suppose was very unlike what London congregations generally heard, and therefore was popular.'[41] Such was his reputation that he was offered several livings in the City, but he was not drawn, because 'he never liked London as a ministerial sphere'.[42]

Ryle was also a popular preacher on the platform at Exeter Hall in the Strand. This was a favourite meeting place for evangelical gatherings, and Christians gathered there from all over the country for rallies, annual missionary meetings, Protestant assemblies and Temperance gatherings. A popular series of bright services on Sunday evenings intended to attract the non-churchgoing working-classes, were addressed by all the well-known evangelical preachers, including Hugh McNeile, Hugh Stowell, William Cadman and John Cale Miller. On one such occasion Ryle spoke to a congregation of four thousand with 'a force and earnestness which have been rarely equalled and which riveted the attention of a vast audience from commencement to finish'.[43] Bishop Tait, the Bishop of London, described the initiative at Exeter Hall as 'one of the best works that had been undertaken since he entered upon his office'.[44] Invitations to speak on behalf of the Church Pastoral-Aid Society, the British and Foreign Bible Society and the Church Missionary Society took Ryle to distant parts of the country. Bishop Handley Moule recalled that as a boy he heard Ryle preach to large and attentive congregations. Henry Venn, the secretary of the Church Missionary Society, was present at a clerical conference in Weston-super-Mare in 1858 when 'Ryle preached a noble sermon... which was listened to with deep attention for an hour and a half.'[45] F. J. Chavasse, Principal of Wycliffe Hall, Oxford, recalled he 'listened to such masters as Pusey, Goulburn, Liddon, Trench and J. C. Ryle.'[46] On one occasion when Ryle returned to Cheshire to preach in Gawsworth church, only a few miles from Henbury, he was delighted to meet again Isaac Eaton, his first teacher, who though now old, had taken the trouble to go over to Gawsworth to hear his former pupil preach.

Chapter Five

Years of singular trials

Shortly after his move to Helmingham Ryle felt his circumstances had improved to the point where he could seriously consider marriage. Since he became a Christian he had been most cautious about his relations with the opposite sex, realising how important it was to share his life with a lady of good standing, a true believer, and one who would be a support in his ministry. He had read the lives of some of the early Evangelicals and seen how unhappy marriages had marred the witness of both John and Charles Wesley and George Whitefield, and he was determined that he would only marry a lady of like mind and Christian faith.

Matilda

Ryle may have met his future bride and her parents as guests at Helmingham Hall. Her father was John Pemberton Plumptre, the Tory Member for East Kent, who had been converted to Christ under the evangelical preaching of Daniel Wilson when a law student at the Inns of Court. He became an energetic Evangelical with pronounced Protestant views, unafraid to speak up in the House in favour of stricter Sabbath laws and in opposition to what he considered 'Papal Aggression'.[1] His eldest daughter, Matilda Charlotte Louisa, was an attractive twenty-two-year-old, well educated and a committed Christian. Ryle found himself attracted to her since she combined all the qualities he hoped to find in his future wife. 'The great thing I always desired to find was a woman who was a Christian, who was a real lady, and who was not a fool. Whether I was successful or not, others must judge better than I can, but I call God to witness these were the three points I always kept steadily in view.'[2]

Ryle and Matilda married on 29th October 1845. From this time on, his years at Helmingham were a mixture of highs and lows, great joys and great sorrows. He records in his memoirs that after his marriage 'he lived very quietly with his wife at Helmingham Rectory, and indeed could not afford to live any other way, as we had barely £700 a year between us'.[3] He considered himself 'a poor man' and usually dressed in worn jacket and trousers and lived a frugal life. We can only suppose that out of his stipend he was making a considerable contribution to reducing his father's debts.

Within a year of the marriage baby Georgina was born. The confinement went smoothly, but a few weeks later the mother was taken seriously ill. When the doctor informed them that he could do no more, Ryle engaged two consultants to examine her, and she was diagnosed as suffering from puerperal mania. He was advised to take her away from the parish. She went to stay in a rented house in Tunbridge Wells under the care of her mother, and Ryle visited her for a few days every three weeks. Gradually her mind was restored and the family returned to Helmingham. At this time the baby was baptised Georgina Matilda – Georgina after Georgina Tollemache, a gracious Christian lady and friend, and Matilda after her mother's name.

With the coming of winter, however, Matilda caught a chill, and when she did not respond to treatment Ryle took her up to London to see a specialist. She was shown to have a weak right lung and was advised to go to the seaside. The family, along with a parlourmaid and nursemaid, stayed at Ventnor on the Isle of Wight from December until May the following year. This was not a wise choice, since it was a cold and foggy winter and one 'felt cut off from the world'.[4] When she was clearly not improving she returned to her parents' home at Fredville Manor, where she died on 18th June 1847 and was buried in the family vault at Nonington Church, a few miles south-east of Canterbury.[5]

Her death was a bitter blow to Ryle, after a marriage lasting so short a time and leaving him with the responsibility of a little daughter. At his study table sometime later he wrote these poignant words in his Expository Thoughts on the Gospels, 'Nothing cuts so deeply into a man's heart as to part with a loved one, and lay them in the grave.'[6] He went back to his parish a melancholy man, leaving Georgina in the care of her grandparents and travelling to

Kent each month to see her. Though bereavement made him feel sad and lonely, he was upheld by his trust in the risen Saviour and by the consolation of Christian friends, especially the Harcourts, who were staying at the Hall.[7]

In addition to the anxieties arising from his marriage, Ryle suffered a number of family and personal bereavements during these years. Although he had never been close to his brother Frederick, his sudden death in May 1846 was a terrible shock. Only a few months before Frederick had been inducted into the district church of Elson, near Gosport. He was now buried beneath the chancel window. Within a few years his mother and his younger sister Caroline had also died, along with several other close relations and friends. Georgina Tollemache also died unexpectedly and Ryle felt this, too, as a personal loss:

> She was always most kind to me and I believe really delighted in my ministry; had she lived it might have made a great difference to the course of my later life. When she died I soon saw Helmingham was no longer the same place it had been.... Her loss to my wife was also very great; she was a wise and most kind adviser to young women, and just such a one as my wife needed. I take occasion to say that, taking her for all in all, she was the brightest example of a Christian woman I ever saw... she was a wonderful woman.[8]

Ryle never forgot the huge congregation which attended Mrs Tollemache's funeral. He conducted the service and preached a stimulating Christ-centred sermon, focusing on the significance of the Cross and the Resurrection.[9] Her sudden death was a great shock to everyone in the village, and 'to her husband it was an irreparable loss, and he was never the same man again in religion.'[10]

Jessie
Ryle was now a widower, domiciled in a lonely country rectory, and the father of an active little daughter who needed a mother's love and care. Fortunately he knew someone who would make him a good wife and be willing to look after Georgina. She was Jessie Elizabeth, the eldest daughter of John Walker of Crawfordton House, near Moniaive, in Dumfries-shire. Jessie had

been a close friend of both Mrs Tollemache and Matilda, and was Georgina's godmother. He ventured to propose, was accepted, and the marriage took place on 21 February 1850.[11] Once more the Rectory was a happy home. Jessie was a wonderful Christian companion to her husband, and they looked forward to a happy life together of fruitful ministry.

Their hopes were, however, not to be fulfilled. Within six months of their marriage, Jessie's health began to cause anxiety, and for the next ten years she was never really well for more than a few months at a time. Ryle had the heavy duty of caring for a sickly wife, and he recalled in later life:

> Few can have any idea how much wear and tear and anxiety of mind and body I had to go through for at least five years before my wife died. I very rarely ever slept out of our own house, in order that I might be in the way if my wife wanted anything. I have frequently in the depth of winter driven distances of twelve, fifteen, twenty or even thirty miles in an open carriage to speak or preach, and then returned home the same distance immediately afterwards, rather than sleep away from my own house. As to holidays, rest and recreation in the year, I have never had any at all; while the whole business of entertaining and amusing the three boys in an evening devolved entirely upon me. In fact the whole state of things was a heavy strain upon me, both in body and mind, and I often wonder how I lived through it.[12]

In addition to an uncomplaining trust in the Lord and much prayer, a busy life helped him to overcome his difficulties. During the years of his wife's ill-health he often occupied himself writing gospel pamphlets and preparing his *Expository Thoughts on the Gospels* for publication.

Because of Jessie's poor health Ryle felt it necessary to take her up to London for all her confinements, so that she might have the finest medical attention. This meant that he was absent from his parish for considerable periods of time, never less than two months and on one occasion six months. Sometimes they stayed with the Walkers in Onslow Square, and once rented a house in nearby Onslow Crescent. Ryle acknowledged that without Mr

Walker's kind assistance he would not have been able to meet all the heavy expenses. He says his father-in-law was 'the most unselfish, generous man I have ever met and was always helping us.'[13]

His periodic visits to London gave Ryle the opportunity of meeting many of the leading evangelical clergy and laity in the City, from whom he received numerous invitations to preach and speak. These engagements helped to relieve him of some of his anxieties and he delighted to go off on a Sunday morning to preach Christ in one of the many evangelical churches in the capital. He was a popular preacher and could easily have moved to a London parish.[14] But at heart he was a northerner with no desire to take on a city church, and when his wife's confinements were over he was always glad to return to Helmingham.[15]

Jessie's physical condition gradually grew worse and eventually she died of Bright's disease on 19 May 1860, aged thirty-eight. For a second time the shutters were closed in the silent rectory, and as the church bell tolled a grieving young family saw their mother's coffin borne to the churchyard. Many years later Herbert recalled watching his mother's cortège and funeral procession from the attic window of the rectory. Ryle was deeply moved by his loss and wrote afterwards, 'I was once more left a widower with five children, the eldest only just thirteen, and altogether more disconsolable and helpless than ever.'[16]

Relationship with the Squire

Another difficulty of these years was Ryle's deteriorating relationship with Squire Tollemache. He appears to have got on well with him while Georgina Tollemache was alive. The two men had much in common. They were both fervent Evangelicals and militant Protestants. Both were keen sportsmen and often could be seen riding together on the estate, and both were strongly self-willed. A fad which particularly annoyed Ryle was Tollemache's habit of standing up in his pew below the pulpit and holding his gold hunter watch in his hand when he considered the Rector had preached long enough.[17]

The friendly relationship between the Rector and the Squire

seems to have come under strain, however, after Georgina's death. Ryle believed that Tollemache felt he owned all the servants on the estate since they were all tenant-farmers or estate workers who occupied the tied-cottages and lived 'in a state of servile subjection to Mr Tollemache'.[18] Yet there are many examples of his concern for their welfare and when any of them became ill when he was resident at the Hall, he would make a point of visiting them. It was after such a visit to a sick labourer on his estate at Peckforton Castle in Cheshire, in the depth of winter when he was eighty-five years of age, that he caught the chill from which he died.

For the last two or three years of his incumbency at Helmingham, Ryle admits there was 'a complete suspension of all friendly relations' between himself and John Tollemache.[19] Severe altercations between Squire and country parson were not uncommon in Victorian England. The seriousness of the rift is felt in a remark Ryle once made to a daughter-in-law of Tollemache, whom he surprised by saying to her, 'The Tollemaches are very good lovers, and very good haters too.'[20] Ryle offered no explanation of the cause of this breakdown in relations and it was probably due to a clash of temperaments. It is sad that two strong Christians could find no way of reconciliation. So it must have been with a deep sense of relief that Ryle opened a letter from the Bishop inviting him to consider a move to another parish in the diocese. He had known great happiness and great sadness at Helmingham, but for the sake of his young family he felt the time had come to leave the familiar surroundings, and early in 1861 he moved to Stradbroke.

Chapter Six

Not the man to stand still

In the mid-nineteenth century Stradbroke was a small market town with a population of about fourteen hundred. Pleasantly situated in the Suffolk countryside it was really a large village, the largest in the county, with the houses built along three main streets. All Saints, the parish church which stands at the junction of two main streets, is an imposing structure with a fine fifteenth century tower, visible for miles around. Herbert Ryle said of All Saints, there are 'few fairer specimens of a village church', and inside there is 'a wonderful sense of space combined with singular beauty of proportion'.[1]

A growing family

Ryle was in his prime at Stradbroke. Free from those domestic anxieties which had dogged his married life in his previous parish, he was able to devote himself wholeheartedly to the work of the ministry. It was a great delight to all his parishioners and friends when he announced that he was soon to be married. He had been a widower for less than eighteen months, but he longed for the sustaining companionship of a good Christian woman and a wife who would lovingly mother his family of young children. Ryle's choice of a third wife fell on Henrietta Amelia Clowes, a lady of good birth, highly respected, well educated and a woman with a strong personal faith. The couple had known each other over many years and they were married on 24th October 1861 in Kersal Parish Church, Salford. Henrietta was the eldest daughter of Lt-Colonel William Legh Clowes, of Broughton Old Hall, a distant relative of Ryle by marriage and the head of a respected evangelical family in Lancashire.[2] Henrietta seems to have been a very sensible and practical woman and to Ryle's relief, a wife who enjoyed good health. She was an accomplished musician and an expert in the new vogue of photography.

Stradbroke, unlike Helmingham, had no imposing, autocratic Squire, and indeed, there were only two professional gentlemen in the whole village. Another benefit of the move meant that his days of cheese-paring were over. He was now the incumbent of one of the richest livings in the diocese and received an income of £1,050 per annum.

As a youngster Ryle had received a privileged education, and now he was in a position to give his sons the same benefits. His stipend enabled him to send his three sons to preparatory schools and on to Public Schools and Universities. Reginald and Herbert went to Mill Hill, a private school in Wadhurst, Kent. It was run by the Rev R. H. Wace, a scholarly evangelical, a disciplinarian and a staunch supporter of Reformation principles, and Ryle was confident that his sons were in good hands. He accompanied the two boys to their new school at the beginning of term, and the next day wrote to his wife telling her about it:

> I left the boys at Wadhurst last night. Poor little Herbert cried most bitterly at the parting. Reginald was more quiet. Herbert's life from natural disposition has been so easy and happy hitherto that he naturally feels his first wrench. And he has been so accustomed to look up to me and be with me, ever since he can remember anything, that the separation strikes him more. It is sad work, and nothing but the sense of positive duty and the wisdom of it would make me go through with it.[3]

From Wadhurst Reginald went on to Repton School before entering Trinity College, Cambridge in 1874. He graduated with an excellent degree, and with his father's approval and delight decided to follow a career in medicine. He studied at Guy's Hospital in London and practised first in Barnet before moving on to Brighton. He specialized in sociological problems and published a number of learned articles in medical journals. He married Catherine Scott, daughter of a Brighton surgeon, and they had five sons and five daughters. As an adult he felt unable to maintain the Christian beliefs he had been taught as a child, and when he died in 1922, Herbert said of him, 'He could not accept a faith, but his conduct was an example of fidelity, devotion and love.'[4] Herbert, who outlived his brothers and sisters, went on to say, 'The last of the five, I remain, having had two such loving brothers as few men ever had – never a quarrel, always affection and confidence.'[5]

There was a particularly close affinity between Ryle and his second son Herbert, and when he went to sit the entrance examination at Eton, his father went with him. After more than thirty years it gave him a great thrill to return to his old Public School, and he made a point of returning as often as he could while his boys were there. Herbert passed the examination without difficulty and entered Eton as an Oppidan for the first year before moving into residence as a Colleger. It was less expensive to live in, and though Ryle had a good stipend it was a costly business sending three sons to Public Schools. However, he felt no sacrifice was too great. To help provide the fees he sold his horse and carriage, and dismissed his coachman and gardener. Visitors to the Vicarage could not help but notice the Vicar's patched trousers and threadbare jacket, carefully darned by Mrs Ryle to make them last longer, But few realised they were evidences of Ryle's self-denial on behalf of his sons' education.

Herbert's moral courage was put to the test at Eton in the first few weeks of term. At the daily service in chapel it was customary for the whole school to turn east for the creed. For the first few days Herbert stood his ground and was greatly embarrassed. He wrote home asking his father's permission to do as the other boys did, and consent was readily given in the circumstances. Herbert was a bright scholar and in 1875 he was awarded the Newcastle Scholarship which his father had failed to achieve. However, he was bitterly disappointed when he went up to Cambridge and missed the Bell Scholarship. He found it difficult telling his father, but received an encouraging letter in return:

> I am glad you have written so fully. If anything like coolness or want of confidence ever arose between us it would break my heart. No one can ever love you more than I do. Dismiss from your mind all idea that I am annoyed by your failure for the 'Bell'. Of course, my dear fellow, I should have been pleased if you had got it. But I have had so many failures in my life and seen too many, to dwell on failures long. It is no use crying over spilt milk. Go ahead![6]

In a letter home Herbert described a recent visit to the School by Sankey and Moody, the American evangelists. He was not impressed. 'I do not know that I was very much struck by either "Soody" or "Mankey",' he told his mother. "Soody" preached not much different from what father would have done, except with slightly more coarseness, without heads and with rather longer stories and illustrations. "Mankey's" singing would sound better in a building than a garden, and otherwise, I did not think much of it. As a whole, I doubt if it would do much good. But really I am sick of the names of Moody and Sankey now.'[7] To Ryle's disappointment there were hints in the letter that Herbert was turning away from what he considered the too narrow principles of evangelicalism to the acceptance of a liberal theology.

Herbert went up to Cambridge in 1875. Ryle regretted his son had not gone on to Christ Church, Oxford, as he had done, but Herbert had set his mind on King's College Cambridge. His father could see the advantage that Reginald and Herbert would be together in the same University, and away from the influence of the High Church and Tractarian traditions so prevalent in Oxford.

Herbert was a serious scholar and was awarded numerous prizes for his academic achievements. Sport and recreation took up only a small part of his time, though he did participate in cricket, football and athletics. In his last year at Eton he was selected to play in the School XI at cricket, and at Cambridge he received his colours for football. Unfortunately he sustained a bad injury in playing the game which prevented him from sitting his final examinations, and he had to be content with a aegrotat degree. He was disappointed, but his pride was restored later when he obtained a First in the Theological Tripos examinations in 1881. The same year he was elected a Fellow at King's College, and the following year to his father's great joy he was ordained. He became a distinguished theologian and eventually he was appointed to the See of Exeter before being translated to Winchester. Finally, he became Dean of Westminster and died in 1925.

Ryle's third and youngest son, Arthur Johnson, was described by Herbert as 'one of those happy, kindly souls, who carry brightness with them wherever they go'.[8] He was educated at Eton and New College, Oxford, and early developed a talent as a landscape artist, perhaps being influenced by the Gainsborough and Constable country near his home. Before the end of the century he was an accomplished artist with studios in London and Dornoch in Scotland. Many of his works were exhibited in the Royal Academy and in several galleries in the provinces. He, too, was unable to share his father's beliefs, but in Herbert's words he was 'the closest, most unselfish and loving brother'.[9]

Little is known about Ryle's two daughters. Georgina was born in 1847 and following her mother's death was brought up by her grandparents in Kent.[10] She eventually returned to Helmingham and nothing more is known about her. Isabelle was educated at home in domestic duties and the social graces like most other daughters in middle-class Victorian homes. She never married, and on the death of her stepmother she devoted herself to the Bishop's needs, looking after the home and acting as his personal secretary. Outside the home she took an active interest in the Women's Bible Mission, the Seaman's Orphanage, the Temperance Society and the Nurses' Institution.

It was in the middle period of his ministry at Stradbroke that Ryle began writing notes on his life so 'that my children may possess some accurate account of my history of life, after I am dead'.[11] His sons and daughters were at an age when they might be interested in this detail of family history. The memoir outlined his life and family background from his childhood in Macclesfield to the death of his second wife shortly before he left Helmingham. In his account he makes much of his conversion to Christ when an undergraduate. It was 'the greatest change and event in my life'.[12] And the opposition from some of his family and friends which followed, he says, made him work through the tenets of the Faith and think through the reasons for his beliefs. It was a testing period in his life but a triumph of faith over adversity

Ryle's ministry at Stradbroke

Ryle was a dedicated pastor and minister of the gospel. His conscientious work left no one outside his pastoral care. Dressed in the typical clerical garb of the day, a long, single-breasted black coat and a tall, stove pipe hat, he regularly visited his parishioners, including the sick and poor, in their homes. At a time when open-air meetings were considered a novelty he led gospel services twice a week. He superintended a well-attended Sunday School and regularly taught the Scriptures and Prayer-book in the day school. Following the publication of *Spiritual Songs*, his first collection of hymns for use at cottage meetings, he compiled two more collections, *Hymns for the Church on Earth*, selected for the use of the sick and lonely, and *The Additional Hymnbook* for general use. In the Preface to this collection he writes: 'I strongly hold that holy thoughts often abide for ever in men's memories under the form of poetry, which pass away and are forgotten under the form of prose.' He also comments on the increasing popularity of hymns in Christian meetings, saying, 'I regard with deep satisfaction the growing taste for hymn singing and praise, as an essential part of Christian worship. It is the healthiest signs of our times.... Nothing is so likely to heal "our unhappy divisions", and to make us of "one mind," as an increased spirit of praise as well as prayer.'

A contemporary wrote of Ryle's ministry at Stradbroke:

> In parish work he was practical and thorough, taking great interest in the temporal as well as the spiritual welfare of his parishioners. Three services on Sundays, meetings during the week at different places. Well-attended, bright and hearty congregational singing, service plain and forcible, rarely concluded without some words to boys and girls in the congregation. Ryle urged parents to bring young children. Some twenty or thirty years ago (Stradbroke was one of the worst places in the neighbourhood) a respectable person could hardly ride through without being insulted or very likely his hat would be knocked off his head. Now a quieter and more orderly parish is hardly found.[13]

The tall, manly figure of the Rector was held in considerable awe by all the youngsters in the parish. It was due to his insistence on discipline in the school, the church and the neighbourhood that the behaviour of the village children changed beyond all recognition.[14] He considered it the prime duty of parents to bring up their children in a godly and disciplined manner. He was sure 'no school will make such deep marks on character as the home' and 'the best schoolmaster will not imprint on their childrens' minds as much as they will pick up at the fireside'.[15] The lessons he had learned in bringing up his own children he passed on to other parents in a series of pamphlets. He said the parents should teach their children a knowledge of the Bible, the habit of prayer and to regularly attend the House of God. They must also be taught always to speak the truth and be obedient. For their part parents must be loving and kind, but disobedience must be punished 'seldom, but really and in good earnest'.[16] He warned parents that 'if you do not take trouble with your children when they are young, they will give you trouble when they are old'.[17]

Archdeacon James, one time headmaster of Malvern, and a school friend of Reginald and Herbert, recalled one of his visits to Stradbroke Vicarage during the school holidays, and his youthful impressions take us to the heart of the Ryle home:

> Mr Ryle, with his gigantic and stentorian voice, was perhaps rather formidable to a youthful visitor, but he was very kind and hearty, and I soon felt at home.... The atmosphere of the home was, like that of my own home, devotional, daily Bible readings, somewhat lengthy family prayers. and a good deal of religious talk. But it was all quite wholesome and unpretentious, and I don't think any of us were bored, much less cavil at the regime, at any rate at that time.[18]

The village school

When Ryle arrived in Stradbroke the little village school was in the charge of a seventy-seven-year-old teacher who lived in a tiny garret in the workhouse a little way out of the village. Before education was made compulsory, it was left entirely in the hands of the local inhabitants and often the teacher had no qualifications except a desire to teach the three 'Rs'. Fifteen boys attended the school. They had no text books but learned by rote and by reading from old books and newspapers. The school building was in a poor condition with little light and ventilation, and had only one primitive outside toilet. Any improvement depended entirely on the initiative of the parson and Ryle decided that a new school should be built.

He had been involved in the building of a new school in his previous parish and he knew what he wanted. He saw the school not only as an instructor of the young but also as a valuable adjunct of the church, believing that 'a church without a school is like a man with only one arm'.[19] He was thus opposed to W. E. Forster's Act of 1870 to provide Board Schools, being convinced that 'the Church which only cares for souls and the State which only cares for educating minds, are both making vast mistakes'.[20] Within two years of arriving in the parish he had raised the necessary £1,300, supervised the construction and opened a new school for 250 children. Typical of many schools built at the time, the single storey building was divided into two and the playgrounds between them divided by iron railings. One school was reserved for the sons of local farmers and tradesmen and the other accommodated one hundred and twenty boys and girls of poorer families. The school was maintained by voluntary subscriptions and a grant from the National Society. Ryle believed that education was worth paying for and he was opposed to the proposed free State schools. After school ended for the day Ryle would often meet the boys and girls on their way home and glean from them information about any sick and needy in the parish. He claimed that he ruled the parish by the sweets he gave away.

Restoration work
In the second half of the century both bishops and clergy were more active in their dioceses and parishes, and some clergy saw a need to thoroughly renovate their church buildings. The younger generation of Anglo-Catholics seized the opportunity of introducing the stations of the cross and confessional boxes into their churches and began to develop Catholic liturgy through art and music. Evangelicals protested against these innovations, and when they renovated their churches they removed the box-pews and introduced evening Communion. Many churches which had been in a state of decay for years with rotten timbers and broken windows were restored to their former glory. All Saints had been partly restored in 1820 and now Ryle saw that major repairs were required. To meet the cost, which he estimated would be far more

than the parish could afford, he appealed for funds on the inside cover of a tract entitled, *Are You Fighting?*

'After standing probably four hundred and fifty years,' he wrote, 'almost every part of this noble fabric requires more or less repair and renovation.... It is quite impossible for the inhabitants of Stradbroke to raise such a sum as £2,700. Stradbroke is a large straddling parish on a clay soil and seven miles from a railway station. There are no resident landlords or gentry and the population is made up of farmers, labourers, tradesmen and three professional men. It is quite evident that without help from kind friends unconnected with the parish the work cannot possibly be done...I am bold to express a hope that many unknown friends in Great Britain and Ireland, who have for twenty years read and approved the writings of the Vicar of Stradbroke, will now kindly remember the church in which he preaches and generously aid him in the heavy work he has undertaken.'

Ryle was delighted with the response to the appeal and work on the restoration began in faith. It was a major undertaking. For many weeks the church had to be closed while repairs were carried out on the roof and main beams and the stone work was restored. The box pews were removed and new oak pews installed to accommodate a growing congregation. The stone floor was relaid and the Jacobean pulpit replaced with a small oak pulpit. When the pulpit was in place, Ryle asked one of the craftsmen to carve a text around the top ledge where the preacher could not fail to see it. The text he chose had been painted on the wall beside the pulpit in Helmingham, 'Woe is me, if I preach not the gospel'. When the carving was finished he borrowed the chisel and cut a deep groove under the word 'not' in order to give it emphasis in the eyes of the preacher.[21] Following the example he had set at Helmingham he arranged to have a number of carefully selected texts painted on the roof beams. £250 was still outstanding when the work of restoration was completed, and again he penned a few words inside a popular gospel tract, *Have You a Priest?*, asking for more gifts from Christian friends. He was not disappointed and the money came in from all parts of the country. It was a great achievement to carry out such an extensive and costly renovation, and fitting that at a special service on 3 April 1872 in the presence of a large congregation, Dr Pelham, the Bishop of Norwich, should rededicate All Saints to the glory of God.

The chancel had not been touched, and a few years later Ryle again appealed for funds to complete the final phase of the work. He adopted the same method. On the back of a tract entitled *If Any Man*, he stated that he had personally contributed £500 to the cost of the new roof and a further £500 was required to finish the work. The appeal simply stated:

> Time is short and life uncertain. Before the connection of the present Vicar of Stradbroke with his parish is ended he is anxious to leave every part of his church in such complete order that no fair excuse may be left to any succeeding Vicar for introducing ornaments or fittings of an un-Protestant character. He wishes, in short, to leave his church a complete pattern of what the house of God ought to be in the Reformed Church of England.

The message touched hearts and pockets, and donations poured in to replace the organ, renew the choir stalls and install a new east window depicting St Paul's description of the whole armour of God for the Christian. The restored chancel was dedicated in memory of Ryle's father who had died in 1861. In all, the work of restoration took eight years and cost a total of more than four thousand pounds.[22]

The Farm Labourers Union

Stradbroke was the centre of an agricultural community and so one day Joseph Arch, the leader of the national Farm Labourers Union, arrived in the village and addressed a crowded meeting in the Corn Hall. Arch had begun working on the land when he was ten years old. Eventually he became a hedge-cutter and ditch drainer and earned his living by contract work. A Primitive Methodist, he had taught himself to read and write so that he could study the Bible and prepare sermons, and was often invited to speak at revival meetings. Concerned about the poor conditions and low wages of the workers on the land, he started a movement to improve their lot. His first meeting was in a field in

Warwickshire and within a short time 100,000 workers had joined the Union. Arch became a national figure and eventually a Liberal Member of Parliament.

Although Ryle felt aggrieved at the servile conditions imposed upon farm labourers, he refused to support Arch when he came to the parish, because he believed that the rural parson should avoid taking sides between farmers and workers. He had no wish to see unrest in his parish and was apprehensive about the growth of the Unions. He did not agree with the radical talk about equality:

> 'Universal equality' is a very high-sounding expression, and a favourite with visionary men. Many in every age have disturbed society by stirring up the poor against the rich, and by preaching up a popular doctrine that all men ought to be equal. But so long as the world is under the present order of things this universal equality cannot be attained. Those who disclaim against the vast inequality of men's lots will doubtless never be in want of hearers, but so long as human nature is what it is, this inequality cannot be prevented.[23]

He believed that social reforms were the responsibility of the State. He admired the labours of Lord Shaftesbury, the evangelical reformer, who had brought in the Ten Hours Act and abolished child labour in the brickyards and as chimney-sweeps. He admired, too, the labours of William Wilberforce, the philanthropist, who eventually effected the abolition of the slave trade through the Emancipation Act of 1833. These were changes the State could achieve, but the task of the Church was primarily a spiritual one. Addressing the Croydon Church Congress on 'Church and State' in 1877, he said:

> If the country clergyman will only live the life he ought to live and preach as he ought to preach, he will find as good friends amongst the poor as in any class in the land. I have no fear whatever for the Church of England in rural districts if the clergy are only faithful to their ordination vows and to the Word of God. The poor are not such bad judges as some people think and in the long run I believe they will not think the Chapel better than the Church if the clergy only do their duty. But in the matter of Unions, my sentence is that the clergy had better not interfere with them. Let them mind their own business and remember that business is to live and preach the Gospel.

So he refused to meddle in such matters as did the majority of bishops and clergy in the nineteenth century. He felt he could do no more than exhort the farmers to treat their farm-hands fairly and the labourers to be content with their wages.

The reforming Ryle

Ryle was a man of his time, whose outlook was largely governed by the conventions of the day. In some areas however he was ahead of his time and on occasions he was inspired with a prophetic voice and a reforming zeal. From the vicarage in Stradbroke he wrote several letters to the *Record* drawing attention to glaring anomalies and weaknesses in the Church's organisation and suggesting ways of improvement. In 1870 he published a series of papers on Church Reforms, written originally for a London newspaper and later published in a cloth cover. In this he outlined his proposals for making the National Church more efficient and effective in her work and witness. The areas in which he pressed for reforms included the uniting of the Canterbury and York provinces, smaller dioceses, more bishops, a slimmed-down Convocation with fewer ex-officio members, dynamic Cathedrals, shorter services and a greater use of the laity. Some of his bold ideas shocked more conventional churchmen, yet many recognised how sensible and practical they were. In characteristic manner he described the Established Church as:

> Stiff and rigid like a bar of cast iron, when it ought to be supple and bending like a whalebone. Hence its machinery is continually cracking, snapping, and breaking down. Churchmen talk and act as if a system which did pretty well for five millions of Englishmen two hundred and fifty years ago, when there were very few Dissenters, must needs be perfectly suited to the thirty millions of today.[24]

In the course of his address on this subject to the Church Congress in Hull, he insisted that 'Church reform was the answer to those critics of the Church of England who advocated disestablishment so strongly'. He believed that a Christian country should be seen to be governed by Christian principles by having an Established Church. The Church of England possessed many good qualities, and he urged that the Liberationist Society campaign to disestablish and disendow the Church must be resisted. However reform of the Church along scriptural principles was needed. It was an anomaly for the appointment of spiritual leaders in the Church to be in the hands of the Prime Minister and the Crown, and he proposed that a bishop should be nominated by two clerics and one lay person, with the final choice made by the sovereign as Head of the Church of England. He believed that most dioceses were far too large and should be reduced in size to make them more manageable. The present state where the bishop was out of touch with most of his clergy and people was one he believed 'St Paul and St Peter would neither understand nor commend'. The creation of smaller dioceses would enable the diocesan bishops to be more efficient in their spiritual oversight.

No one appreciated the greatness of our heritage in the Prayer-book more than Ryle. He loved the scriptural and reformed pattern of liturgy and worship. He did however recognise its weaknesses and imperfections. The services were generally too long and in parts the language was difficult to understand. There was agitation from time to time during the nineteenth century that the Prayer-book should be revised and the Ritualists actually produced their own books of devotion. Ryle was opposed to any wholesale changes and particularly any change in doctrine, but had no objection to a limited revision. He believed that the Church must be continually reforming herself. Indeed, as he pointed out, Thomas Cranmer in his Preface to the Prayer-book supposes that his work will not last for all time and there must be future revisions.

Ryle's final proposal in his address was a return to New Testament principles relating to the use of the laity in the Church. He recognised that selected lay men and women could become Scripture readers, Sunday School teachers and parochial visitors and serve Christ faithfully in his Church, but he wished to see the laity generally have a more responsible role:

> In our Established Church it will never do to try to man walls with officers and let the rank and file sit idle in the barracks. Clergy and laity must learn to work together. We must have not only an apostolic succession of ministers, but an apostolic succession of laymen, if our Church is to stand much longer.[25]

Ryle saw that the Church, and the Evangelical wing in particular, was losing ground because the laity were not being employed and treated seriously. He foresaw that the way forward was in a partnership between clergy and laity and laid down the principle that 'nothing ought to be done without the laity'.[26]

From the late 1850s onwards Ryle became widely known for his uncompromising evangelical stance, his expository preaching and platform utterances, his gospel tracts and larger publications. Evangelical ordinands leaving University and theological college were anxious to gain parochial experience under his direction. It was considered a privilege to be appointed a curate at Stradbroke, and during his long ministry in the parish he had no fewer than seven curates. Having a curate enabled him to hand over some of his parochial responsibilities, gave him greater freedom to accept preaching and speaking engagements outside the parish, and allowed him more time for writing and the preparation of manuscripts for the printer. The major part of his literary work was completed during this period of his ministry at Stradbroke.[27]

He had already published three biographical lectures on Latimer, Baxter and Whitefield under the title *The Bishop, the Pastor and the Preacher*. This he now enlarged with chapters on Bishop Hooper and the Puritans, Samuel Ward and William Gurnall, and reissued it as *Bishops and Clergy of Other Days*. The volume was added to yet again in 1890 and published with the new title *Light from Old Times*. In 1868 he published a series of biographical studies on the early evangelicals called *The Christian Leaders of the Last Century*. For twenty years he had waited for someone to write an account of their work, and tired of waiting he wrote the articles himself. Evangelical leaders like Whitefield, Wesley, Grimshaw and Romaine were his spiritual heroes, though he was mindful of their failings. In his Introduction he confessed his high regard for these evangelical stalwarts:

> I am an enthusiastic admirer of the men whose pictures I have sketched in this volume. I confess it honestly. I am a thorough enthusiast about them. I believe firmly that, excepting Luther and his Continental contemporaries and our own martyred Reformers, the world has seen no such men since the days of the apostles. I

believe there have been none who have preached so much clear scriptural truth, none who have lived such lives, none who have shown such courage in Christ's service, none who have suffered so much for the truth, none who have done so much good. If any one can name better men, he knows more than I do'.[28]

Stirred by the growing strength of the Ritualist movement in the Church, Ryle published a series of papers in 1874 with the intriguing title *Knots Untied*. The subtitle describes the volume of five hundred pages as 'Plain Statements on Disputed Points of Religion from the Standpoint of an Evangelical Churchman', and the nineteen papers give a clear insight into the controversial subjects which occupied the Church in Victorian times. These included the Thirty-Nine Articles, the Church, the two Gospel Sacraments, Baptismal Regeneration, the Real Presence, Confession, Worship and the Sabbath. It is generally agreed that this book is Ryle's 'magnum opus' and assured him of a lasting reputation among Evangelicals. The character of theological debate has moved on since Ryle wrote his papers, but it is evident that they were written by a man who knew what he believed and where he stood. 'In the faith of these opinions,' he maintained, 'I have lived for 55 years, and have seen no reason to be ashamed of them, however rudely they may seem to be assailed.'[29]

Knots Untied received an appreciative response from Evangelicals, assuring that it went into many editions. Not a few Dissenters also valued its scriptural insights, but the Ritualists were highly critical. A leading Anglo-Catholic said of the author: 'He unties knots only to produce a tangle. The book teems with theological misconceptions and unproven assertions.'[30] Perhaps there can be no greater praise than that lavished on the volume by Canon Alfred Christopher, vicar of St Aldates, Oxford, who described *Knots Untied* as 'one of the most intensely interesting and instructive books published in recent years'. It was a book he took with him on holiday every year for thirty years.[31]

Ryle's next volume was *Old Paths* or 'Plain Statements on some Weighty Matters of Christianity', published in 1877. The first chapter is an important paper on 'Inspiration' and the whole book deals with matters 'essential to salvation'. 'They are doctrines which I find wear well, and in the faith of them I hope to live and die.'[32] The same year he published *Holiness*, an outspoken criticism of the type of 'Perfectionism' expounded by some of the revivalist preachers of his day. In 1878, the last collection of papers by the vicar of Stradbroke appeared entitled *Practical Religion*, or 'Plain Papers on the Duties, Experiences, Dangers and Privileges of Professing Christians'. The volume is typical of Ryle's style and full of practical advice on Christian living. There are challenging chapters on Prayer and Bible-reading, Going to the Lord's Table, Zeal and The Family of God, though parts are now dated.

During the thirty-six years he spent in his two Suffolk parishes he was a prolific writer, producing evangelistic tracts, devotional commentaries, historical and biographical accounts, works on doctrinal and controversial subjects, papers on Christianity and prophecy, all unashamedly written from the standpoint of a convinced Evangelical and Protestant Churchman.

Chapter Seven

The one Book

From the moment Ryle believed God spoke to him through his Word in an Oxford church he was convinced that the Scriptures hold the Divine Revelation of God's saving grace and 'containeth all things necessary to salvation.' It seemed to him that the need of the hour was to recognise in the midst of uncertainty and confusion the truth and authority of God's written Word. Constantly he exhorted believers to 'prove all things by the Word of God, all ministers, all teaching, all preaching, all opinions, all practices...weigh all in the balances of the Bible.'[1]

In Suffolk, Ryle witnessed the liberal assault on the plenary inspiration and ultimate authority of Scripture, a controversy which lasted well into the twentieth century. The rise of biblical criticism in England in the 1830s was seen by many as an attack on traditional beliefs which could only lead to an increase in scepticism. The publication in 1860 of a slim volume, *Essays and Reviews*, by six Anglican clergy and one layman, shook the conservative faith of Victorian England and caused a serious crisis in the Church.[2] Modern liberal criticism had its origin in the seminaries of Germany, and since Christians in this country were not ready for such radical opinions the book received a cool reception. The two Archbishops, eleven thousand clergy and an even larger number of laity signed petitions confirming their faith in the divine inspiration of scripture and the doctrines of the Church of England. Evangelicals and High Churchmen even joined forces in an alliance to suppress the book.

In an attempt to allay the fears of devout Christians troubled by the critical comments of liberal scholars, Ryle wrote several tracts and papers which achieved a wide circulation. He wrote at the popular and practical levels with a desire to inform and encourage ordinary believers rather than attempt to rebut the arguments of the academic theologians. He left it to others to produce scholarly works expressing the Reformed and Evangelical position. One who did so was William Good, who wrote three closely argued volumes entitled *The Divine Rule of Faith and Practice*.[3] Ryle was uncompromising in his condemnation of biblical criticism, which he saw as an attack on the authority and trustworthiness of the Word of God. He wrote forcibly because he felt deeply. He described the exponents of the modern views as 'spiritual robbers, who fain would take from us the bread of life, and they do not give us in its place so much as a stone'.[4] He felt that the darkness and obscurity the critics professed to find in the text of the Bible were often in their own hearts.

In an age which became increasing sceptical about the traditional doctrines of the Bible, Ryle held resolutely to his belief in the divine inspiration, infallibility and authority of the Word of God. He was prepared to be unpopular and ridiculed in the cause of truth. Believing that the best form of defence is attack he set out to confront error with truth. He challenged the liberal critics to defend their position:

> We have a right to ask them how they can possibly explain the origin and nature of the Bible, if they will not allow that it is of Divine authority? We have a right to say, 'Here is a book, which not only courts enquiry but demands investigation. We challenge you to tell us how that Book was written. How can they account for this book standing so entirely alone, and for nothing having ever been written equal to it, near it, or fit to be compared with it for a minute? I defy them to give any rational reply on their own principles. On our principles we can.[5]

The absolute supremacy of Holy Scripture

'The first great principle of Evangelical religion,' he maintained, 'is the absolute supremacy it assigns to Holy Scripture.'[6] He was following in the steps of the early Evangelicals who were men of the one Book:

> The Bible, whole and unmutilated, was their sole rule of faith and practice. They accepted all its statements without question or dispute. They knew nothing of any part of Scripture being uninspired.... They never flinched from asserting that there can be no error in the Word

of God, and that when we cannot understand or reconcile some part
of its contents, the fault is in the interpreter, and not in the text. In all
their preaching they were eminently men of one book. To that book
they were content to pin their faith, and by it stand or fall.[7]

This was Ryle's position too. As a convinced Evangelical he felt
he could hold to no other view of Scripture. He firmly believed in
'the plenary inspiration of every word of Holy Scripture.'[8] To
him the divine authority of Scripture was not a cold doctrine, but
a truth verified by experience. He knew that at the time of his
spiritual awakening God had spoken to him through his Word
and he was 'born again, not of corruptible seed, but of incorruptible,
by the Word of God' (1 Pet. 1:23). He considered one of the greatest
achievements of the Reformation was to dethrone tradition and
enthrone Scripture as the supreme and sole authority in religion.
Those who urged believers to go to the Fathers or to primitive
tradition or to the voice of the Church or to the Prayer-book for
spiritual direction were false prophets.[9] And he warned believers
not to be deceived by the high-sounding phrases about the Church
Fathers and Catholic tradition or the verifying light within.[10] He
was adamant that 'It matters nothing who says a thing in religion,
whether an ancient Father, or a modern bishop, or a learned
divine.... What saith the Scripture? That is the one rule, measure
and gauge of religious truth.'[11] He stood unmovable, firm as a
rock, in his belief in the final authority of Scripture. If Ryle was a
dogmatist, as some asserted, it was because in an age of doubt
and intellectual speculation he possessed an unshakable faith in
the truth of God's Word and because he refused to be moved 'by
the cuckoo cry of "controversy".'[12]

Rival voices were heard in the nineteenth century claiming to
be the ultimate authority in matters of religion. Broad Churchmen
insisted that human reason must decide what is spiritual truth.
Tractarians maintained that the tradition of the early Church
Fathers along with the Creeds and liturgies were co-equal with
the Scriptures, and Roman Catholics and High Churchmen claimed
that the Church through the episcopacy is the guardian of truth
and the final authority in all matters of faith and practice.
Evangelicals rightly saw the supposed authority of the Church,

Tradition and Reason as rivals contending to usurp the enthroned Word of God, and Ryle strenuously denied the validity of these subjective claims. He insisted that when there were so many conflicting voices then a sure standard of truth was even more necessary and desirable. 'We have a written volume,' he claimed, "which is able to make us wise unto salvation",' and the believer has no need of 'man's tradition and Catholic teaching' to guide him.[13]

Ryle's spirited defence of the supremacy and sufficiency of Holy Scripture was greatly appreciated by evangelicals throughout the country. His arguments strengthened them and enabled them to hold fast the faith. Though not in the forefront of biblical scholarship he contended earnestly against 'an old enemy in a new dress'.[14] Modern opinions about the Bible he dismissed as simply 'the cold shoulders of mutton dressed up again in a new style'.[15] He saw no reason why he should change his tried beliefs, beliefs taught by our Lord and his Apostles, for the so-called 'assured results' of modern philosophers. 'We need not be afraid of all the assaults that criticism brings to bear upon the Bible. From the days of the apostles the Word of the Lord has been incessantly "tried" and never failed to come forth as gold, uninjured and unsullied.'[16] His strong faith and convictions fortified believers shaken by critical opinions. He assured them there was no real cause for alarm.

> The ark of God is not in danger, though the oxen seem to shake it....The startling novelty of many objections to Revelation, no doubt, makes them seem more weighty than they really are. It does not follow, however, that hard knots cannot be untied because our fingers cannot untie them, or formidable difficulties cannot be explained because our eyes cannot see through or explain them.[17]

Of course, the reader needs the illumination of the Holy Spirit to bring the truth to light. No one, he insisted, can reach a right understanding of the Word of God without prayer and the guidance of the Holy Spirit, who is both the Author and the Interpreter of God's Word. The meaning of Scripture is not always self-evident and the help of the Holy Spirit is needed in interpreting it aright. It is the Spirit alone who 'can apply truth to our hearts, and make us profit by what we read'.[18] Unless the Spirit reveals the truth to us 'we must not wonder if we find the Bible a dark and difficult book'.[19] It is the special ministry of the Holy Spirit to use the Word of God 'to illuminate the soul, to open the eyes of understanding, and to guide us into all truth'.[20]

Until the eighteenth century it was generally accepted that the Bible is the inspired Word of God. This traditional belief rests on the teaching of Scripture, has support in the writings of the Church Fathers and is written into the formulas of the Orthodox Churches. In the nineteenth century, however, many liberal-minded people held that the Bible is just an ordinary book, lacking divine authority and full of flaws and contradictions. So in an age which was becoming more and more perplexed by unorthodox opinions in religion, Ryle refused to give ground to sceptics. His own convictions on the inspiration of Scripture were firmly held. 'The whole of the Bible is given by inspiration of the Holy Spirit... all is inspired completely, not one part more than another, and... there is an entire gulf between the Word of God and any other book in the world.'[21] In his excellent paper *Inspiration*, he affirmed his belief in the verbal inspiration of the Bible in every part: 'every book, and chapter and verse, and syllable of the Bible was originally given by inspiration of God.'[22]

The special gift of the Spirit was 'bestowed on about thirty people out of mankind, in order to qualify them for the special task of writing the Scriptures'.[23] He accepted that the mode of inspiration was a miracle and remains a mystery and cannot be fathomed by the intellect. All that one can say about the writers of the Old and New Testaments is that 'the Holy Ghost put into their minds thoughts and ideas and then guided them in writing them'.[24]

Evangelicals were sometimes criticised for holding 'the dictation theory' of inspiration, which suggested that the personality of the biblical writer was suspended by the Holy Spirit during the period of inspiration. Ryle denied there was a mechanical process and that the authors were mere amanuenses:

> I do not admit for a moment that the writers were mere machines holding pens, and like type-setters in a printing office did not understand what they were doing. I abhor the 'mechanical' theory of inspira-

tion. I dislike the idea that men like Moses and St Paul were no better
than organ pipes employed by the Holy Spirit, or ignorant secretaries
or amanuenses who wrote by dictation what they did not understand.[25]

He believed the Spirit made use of the writer's reason, memory, style
and temperament, for the personality of each writer is recognizable
through his writing, yet his freedom of expression did not permit him
to make mistakes.[26]

In reply to those critics who argued that since there are so many
variant readings in the text of Scripture we cannot be sure which
is original, he gave this assurance:

> No doubt we have lost a few of the original words. We have no right
> to expect infallibility in transcribers and copyists, before the invention
> of printing. But there is not a single doctrine of Scripture which
> would be affected or altered if all the various readings were allowed,
> and all the disputed or doubtful words were omitted.... There is no
> ancient book which has been handed down to us with so good a text
> and so few various readings as the Bible.[27]

The Bible for the people

Ryle had a deep affection for the Authorised Version of the Bible.
He acknowledged that it had some 'faults, weak points and
defects',[28] and he was not in principle opposed to revision, but
what he had seen of modern attempts to revise the Bible did not
promise a better version, and his counsel to Christians was to 'let
well alone for the time being'.[29] Among the gains achieved at the
Reformation none was greater in his opinion than the restoration
of the Bible to the people.

The study of the Bible by the Reformers led them to condemn
'the corrupt system under which they had been born and brought
up, private judgment made them cast off the abominations of
Popery, and circulate the Bible among the laity'.[30] In spite of the
examples in history where men had been led astray by the misuse
of private judgment, Ryle believed that a man's right to read and
study the Word of God, and interpret it for himself without
reference to the teaching of the Church, was an incalculable
blessing. A fundamental principle of the Reformers was the
'perspicuity' of the Scriptures or the conviction that God will reveal

his truth to everyone who comes to the Scriptures humbly, prayerfully and in reliance on the Holy Spirit to make plain the message of God.

Before his conversion Ryle hardly ever opened his Bible, but after he became a Christian he formed the habit of daily Bible study, which continued without a break for more than half a century. He rose early each morning so that he could study the Word without interruption. Words and verses of special significance to him were carefully underlined in his large black-bound Bible. Every page from Genesis to Revelation showed evidence of painstaking study. He often said there are 'no gains without pains'.[31] His parish visiting and conversations with people led him to conclude that there had been a serious decline in the practice of Bible reading in his day, so he preached and wrote tracts urging believers to read their Bibles, assuring them that 'no book in existence contains such important matter as the Bible'.[32] Moreover, 'the man who has the Bible and the Holy Spirit in his heart, has everything which is absolutely needful to make him spiritually wise.'[33]

The beginning of Expository Thoughts

Always anxious to help others discover the treasures of God's Word, Ryle decided to share with a wider circle than his family and parish the fruits of his own Bible study through the printed page. The first volume of his *Expository Thoughts on the Gospels* was published in 1856, and in the Preface to his comments on St Matthew's Gospel, he briefly explains his purpose. The volume was published for 'family and private use'. He divided the text into short passages and expounded it in 'picked and packed' words, emphasizing just two or three points in the text. So the account of the Rich Young Man in Matthew 19:16-22, who came to Jesus 'to inquire about the way to eternal life', he subdivides as follows:

> We see from the case of this young man
> A person may have desires after salvation and yet not be saved.
> An unconverted person is often profoundly ignorant on spiritual subjects.
> One idol cherished in the heart may ruin a soul for ever.

For the benefit of the reader, he says, 'I have tried to place myself in the position of one who is "reading aloud to others", and must arrest their attention, if he can.' His comments from Matthew 11:28 are a fair example of his aim. He considered there were few passages in the four Gospels more important than this passage.

> We should mark who they are that Jesus invites. He does not address those who feel themselves righteous and worthy: He addresses 'all that labour and are heavy laden, 'It is a wide description: it comprises multitudes in this weary world. All who feel a load on their heart, of which they would fain get free, a load of sin or a load of sorrow, a load of anxiety or a load of remorse – all, whosoever they may be, and whatsoever their past lives – all such are invited to come to Christ.

The notes on St Matthew originally appeared in parts shortly after they were written and only later when their success was assured were they published in book form. The first volume received favourable reviews in the evangelical press, and it was evident that there was a readership for this kind of commentary. Readers appreciated the terse and lucid style, the devotional, homiletical and practical comments in his exposition. His was not a creative mind but he did possess a mind of extraordinary clarity and was able to expound the Scriptures in a way which ordinary believers found helpful.

The second volume containing his *Expository Thoughts on St Mark* appeared the following year. In a short Preface he refers to the minor criticisms levelled at the earlier volume and maintains that it was not intended to be 'a learned, critical commentary', but 'a continuous series of short practical expositions' intended for use in family prayers, to read to the sick and poor, and an aid in the private study of the Bible. In conclusion, he mentions his wife's indisposition and describes how the work was 'written under the pressure of many public duties and amidst many interruptions'.

In his Thoughts on the healing of Peter's mother-in-law in Mark 1:21ff, we can sense the empathy he felt with those near to the sufferer. 'We learn,' he writes, 'to what remedy a Christian ought to resort first, in time of trouble. He ought to follow the example of the friends of Simon's wife's mother. We read that when she "lay sick of a fever" they "told Jesus of her".... Let us know what to do, when sickness, or bereavement or cross or loss or disappointment breaks in on us like an armed man. Let us do as they did in Simon's house in Capernaum. Let us at once "tell Jesus".'

In 1858-59 he published his *Expository Thoughts on St Luke* in two volumes. While he disclaimed any deep learning in his expositions he did include some scholarly notes on hard and difficult texts after his own devotional comments. The Notes are invaluable for throwing light on the meaning and significance of some difficult texts, as for example his Note on Luke 12:10: 'Him that blasphemeth against the Holy Ghost it shall not be forgiven.'

> The language of this verse is deep and mysterious. There are sins which are unpardonable. The distinction drawn between 'speaking against the Son of man' and 'blaspheming against the Holy Ghost,' ought not to be overlooked. The expression is probably something of this kind. The sin against the Son of man was committed by those who did not know Christ to be the Messiah in the days of his humiliation, and did not receive him, believe Him or obey Him, but ignorantly rejected Him, and crucified Him. Many of those who so sinned were pardoned, we cannot doubt; as for example, on the day of Pentecost, after Peter's preaching. The sin against the Holy Ghost was committed by those, who after the day of Pentecost, and the outpouring of the Spirit, and the full publication of the Gospel, persisted in unbelief and obstinate impenitence, and were given over to a reprobate mind. These especially grieved the Spirit and resisted the ministrations of the Holy Ghost. That this was the state of many of the Jews appears from several places in the Acts, and especially Acts 28:25-28. See also I Thess 2:15-16.

In studying his Bible Ryle took the trouble to carefully note and compare the comments of great scholars, both ancient and modern, and in some of the later volumes his own fuller comments along with the gleanings from the commentaries of others sometimes run to several pages and enhance the value of his *Expository Thoughts* for the modern reader.

When he began work on his *Expository Thoughts on St John's Gospel* in the autumn of 1858, he acknowledged it was 'no light matter to publish an exposition of any book of the Bible', and the Fourth Gospel he found to be 'a peculiarly serious undertaking', and 'full of things hard to be understood' (2 Pet. 3:16). One reason being that John's Gospel 'contains a large portion of our Lord Jesus Christ's doctrinal teaching... and I can truly say that I have commented on many verses in this Gospel with fear and trembling'.[34] Commenting on John 7:37-39, words which he says deserve to be written in gold, 'If any man thirst, let him come unto me and drink', he elucidates the passage under three simple headings:

> A case supposed, 'If any man thirst.'
> A remedy proposed, 'let him come unto Me and drink.'
> A promise held out, 'He that believeth on Me, out of his belly shall flow rivers living water.'

After the publication of the first few chapters of *St. John* Ryle was unable to give any more time to the project and the first volume was not completed until February 1865, when he had moved to Stradbroke. In an extended Preface he explained the extenuating circumstances which had caused the long delay in publication.

> The first four chapters went through the press when sickness unto death was in the house. The proof sheets were corrected under pressure of much sorrow and mental distress.

However, with a happy marriage and a more settled home life Ryle was able to complete his *Expository Thoughts on the Gospels*. He was delighted to have time to continue writing his notes on St John's Gospel, and published the first of his three volumes of *Expository Thoughts on St John* in February 1865. In a postscript at the end of the Preface he explained the circumstances which had caused delay in the publication, 'Death, domestic anxieties, illness and change from one residence to another, have had much to do with it. The principal cause has been my removal to my present parish. It has been resumed in a widely-scattered parish of 1,400 people, requiring almost the whole of my attention.' The needs of the parish came first and, he acknowledged, 'it is not one of the primary duties of a parochial clergyman's office to write commentaries.' The second volume on chapters 7–12 was not published until 1869 and the final chapters in 1873. The whole work on the four Gospels had occupied sixteen years of his ministry and was published in seven volumes. It had been painstaking and a labour of love.

Ryle had looked at the comments of many commentators in the preparation of his own work and his estimate of their worth is interesting. The writings of Calvin he quotes with approval and the commentaries of other Reformers he felt were 'greatly underrated and neglected'.[35] On the other hand, he thought the comments of the early Fathers were greatly overrated, notwithstanding the deference paid to them in the nineteenth century. The German commentators, with one or two exceptions, left him disappointed. 'What people can mean by telling us that we have much to learn from modern German writers on Scripture passes my comprehension.'[36] The Continental divines who lived immediately after the Reformers, who wrote vast tomes either in Latin or Greek, he found most edifying. 'There is nothing like them,' he claimed. 'Later commentaries rarely contain any good thoughts which are not to be found in these and... they say many excellent things which have not occured to later writers at all.' He was surprisingly magnanimous in his praise of some Roman Catholic commentators, whose works 'often contain much that is useful, and little that is objectionable. Happy would it be for the Church of England if all her clergy knew their Bibles as well as such men as Ferus and Toletus.'[37] The Scottish and English commentators do not excel, and of the older writers, Rollock, the Scottish divine, is incomparably the best.[38] After years of studying many commentaries, he came to the conclusion: 'I trust none of them unreservedly, and I expect nowhere to find perfection. All must be read with caution. They are good helps but they are not infallible. They are useful assistants, but they are not the pillar and cloud of fire. I advise my younger readers to remember that. Use your judgment prayerfully and diligently. Use commentaries, but be slave to none. Call no man master.'[39]

Ryle's evangelical response to the liberal onslaught on the

supremacy, sufficiency and authority of Scripture as the sole rule of faith and practice for the believer was indicative of his unquestioning belief in the Bible as the inspired Word of God. Throughout his ministry he held firmly to his belief in the divine inspiration, infallibility and ultimate authority of the Word of God. His spirited defence of Scripture was greatly appreciated by fellow evangelicals and his commentaries encouraged believers to read, learn from and live by the Word of God.

Chapter Eight

Doctrines which wear well

Evangelicals in the nineteenth century were often the subject of derision and ridicule, and Ryle contended that no party in the Church of England was 'so thoroughly misunderstood and so frequently misrepresented'.[1] They were said to be unlearned and ignorant men: 'that they do not interpret the formularies honestly and naturally, that they are more like Dissenters than Churchmen, that they are narrow Calvinists, that they despise the Sacraments, and are Zwinglians, that they do not understand Catholic views and corporate privileges, that they are not, in a word, true Churchmen, and are out of their proper place. All this and similar language Evangelical Churchmen have long had to bear.'[2]

Ryle was not one to let such notions pass without reply. As an 'Evangelical Churchman' he held positive and distinct beliefs which he had not found wanting over a lifetime, and it was his practice in all his preaching and teaching to emphasize those doctrines which Evangelicals have always regarded as supremely important. He answered the critics by setting out in the clearest terms 'what Evangelical Religion is' under five simple headings: the Scriptures are the supreme rule of faith and practice; all men are sinners needing forgiveness; God graciously offers salvation through the death and resurrection of his Son Jesus Christ; the blessing of justification is the gift of grace through faith; God continues his work of grace in our hearts by giving us the gift of his Holy Spirit, and by manifesting the 'fruits of the Spirit' in our daily lives.[3]

The Scriptures are the supreme rule

The first and fundamental doctrine of Evangelicalism is 'the absolute supremacy it assigns to Holy Scripture as the only rule of faith and practice'.[4] From a dogmatic belief in the supremacy and final authority of the Word of God, Evangelicals derived all

the principles of Evangelical religion. In controversies concerning
the faith we must ask 'What saith the Scriptures?' The Word of
God is infallible wisdom and the only sure standard by which
questions of doctrine and conduct can be judged.

All men are sinners

From his immovable stand on the rock of Scripture he accepted *in
toto*, contrary to the liberal views of the day, the biblical account
of man's creation and his fall from grace. An important constituent
of evangelical religion is 'the depth and prominence it assigns to
the doctrine of human sinfulness and corruption'.[5] Man was created
by God 'in his own image', but through disobeying God's
command he lost his original righteousness and became sinful
and corrupt. Sin separated man from God and the former
relationship between God and man was broken. Consequently all
men are now inclined to sin and stand guilty before the Holy God.
He believed this 'ignorance of the extent of the fall, and of the
whole doctrine of original sin, is one grand reason why many can
neither understand, appreciate, nor receive Evangelical Religion'.[6]

God graciously offers salvation

He saw that this emphasis on man's corrupt nature and his state of
guilt was a necessary prerequisite to understanding the great
salvation God has graciously provided for us in Christ. So another
distinctive mark of evangelical religion is 'the importance it
attaches to the work and office of our Lord Jesus Christ and to the
nature of the salvation which He has wrought out for man'.[7] More
than anything else man needs a Saviour, so at the appointed time
God sent his Son into the world to be our Redeemer. It was on the
Cross that Christ achieved for man what he could not achieve for
himself, and without which he would be lost for ever. The Cross
was a Divine necessity. The defeat of sin and death could only be
achieved at great cost, and in self-giving love and perfect obedience
to the Father's will Jesus laid down his life that sinners might be
redeemed and reconciled to God.

There were those in the Church who ridiculed the idea of the
penal suffering of Christ to take away sin as unworthy of a God of

love and mercy. But Ryle was steadfast in holding to a substitutionary view of the atonement. He acknowledged that theologians offered different interpretations of this doctrine, but he was satisfied that the substitutionary exegesis was the one most in accord with the teaching of Scripture.

> At the Cross the Lord Jesus Christ offered himself as a sacrifice for us, and allowed the wrath of God to fall on his own head. For our sins, as our Substitute, He gave himself, suffered, and died, the just for the unjust, the innocent for the guilty, that he might deliver us from the curse of the broken law, and provide a complete pardon for all who are willing to receive it.[8]

Ryle made no apology for Evangelicals making much of Christ's death on the Cross, but he believed that even Evangelicals sometimes overlooked the importance and significance of the Resurrection of Christ in their preaching: 'I do not say that we dwell too much on the sacrifice and blood of Christ but I do contend that we dwell too little on his resurrection.'[9] He believed that the resurrection was a vital part of God's saving plan and the completion of his work of redemption. The resurrection 'proved that the ransom was accepted, and the victory over sin and death obtained'.[10] It is also the ground of the believer's final hope, and the assurance of his resurrection to eternal life.

Ryle firmly believed that the work Christ accomplished by his death and resurrection for our salvation was sufficient to save the whole world, but each one must appropriate for himself the benefits of Christ's redeeming sacrifice. There was a prevalent liberal belief in the country that God is the Father of us all and we are all his children whether we have faith or not. Ryle insisted that Scripture clearly teaches that faith in Christ justifies the sinner and makes him a child of God. We are saved not by being earnest, not by a little church-going, not through the sacraments, not by good works, but by the grace of God and our simple trust in Jesus. Faith justifies, and even the weakest faith is enough to join a soul to Christ and secure salvation. It is a delusion to think that we are all the children of God, whether we have faith in Christ or not.

Justification by faith

Ryle saw the Reformation doctrine of justification by faith alone as a foundation truth of the gospel. Our redemption and reconciliation to God rests solely on the saving merits of Jesus Christ. 'Everyone that believes on the Son of God and trusts his soul to him,' he boldly affirmed, 'is at once pardoned, counted righteous, reckoned innocent, and freed from all liability to condemnation.'[11] A wonderful transaction takes place. Christ's righteousness is reckoned to the believer in exchange for his sins. 'Christ's righteousness is placed upon him, and his sins are placed upon Christ. Christ has been reckoned a sinner for his sake, and now the sinner is reckoned innocent for Christ's sake.'[12] Justification is not a reward for 'good works', but 'good works' which should follow on the sinner's redemption are evidence of justification.

And this is not all. The sinner who trusts in Jesus Christ for salvation is saved eternally. Ryle saw that the doctrine of assurance is established in Scripture and is meant to be the believer's right. It is 'a positive gift of the Holy Ghost... which every believer in Christ ought to aim at and seek after'. [13] Christian assurance is the divine conviction that God by his Spirit is abiding and working in the heart of the believer for time and eternity. Assurance is simply taking God at his word and trusting in his promises. Sometimes the doctrine may be misunderstood, which leads to presumption, or misinterpreted, which leads to pharisaism, but properly understood assurance, after all, is no more than than 'a full grown faith, a masculine faith that grasps Christ's promise with both hands'.[14] This assurance of salvation is the title-deed of all the elect, for salvation is all of the sovereign grace of God.

The work of the Holy Spirit

Christ is the author and finisher of our faith, but it is the Holy Spirit who makes Christ and his salvation effectual in our lives. Another distinct doctrine of evangelical religion is 'the high place it assigns to the inward work of the Holy Spirit in the heart of man'.[15] Ryle in his preaching and teaching made much of the person and work of the Spirit in the believer. When a sinner repents of his sin and receives Christ as Saviour, the Lord does two things. 'He washes him from his sins in his own blood and gives him a free pardon, this is justification. He puts the Holy Ghost in his heart and makes him an entirely new man, this is regeneration, or new birth.'[16] To be justified by faith in Christ marks the beginning of the Christian life.

It is then the continuing work of the Holy Spirit in our lives to enable us 'to grow in grace' and become more and more like Christ. Evangelical religion is marked by 'the importance it attaches to the outward and visible work of the Holy Ghost in the life of man'.[17] 'The Spirit within is the distinctive mark of every Christian believer, and he makes his presence known by the effects which he produces.'[18] It is no profit to say that we have been redeemed if there is no visible evidence that we have been renewed. The Spirit will always 'make his presence known'.[19] It is the Spirit's work in our hearts to convict of sin, to draw us to Christ, to sanctify our hearts, to increase our love for the brethren, to open to us God's Word and to teach us how to pray.[20]

The one true Church

These five essential marks of evangelical faith, in Ryle's judgment, are not intended to be a complete and comprehensive list of evangelical doctrines, but the first and foremost principles on which evangelical religion is grounded. They relate only to the personal aspects of religion, not because Evangelicals think corporate religion irrelevant, but because Scripture treats personal faith as of primary importance. Ryle was at pains to refute the notion that Evangelicals discount the Church, the ministry or the sacraments.

It is said that the great discovery by the Church in the nineteenth century was the discovery of herself. The Tractarians revived a fresh interest in the theology of the divine society and aroused public awareness about it through their *Tracts for the Times*. Ryle thought that High Churchmen were extravagant in their language and appeared to exalt the Church above Christ. He concluded that there was much confused thinking in his day about the Church which ought to be clarified. He boldly asserted that 'Evangelical

Religion does not undervalue the Church, or think lightly of its privileges'.[21] However, in common with his fellow Evangelicals he insisted that there is but 'one true Church, out of which no man can be saved'.[22] This true Church is founded upon Christ and its members are all those who have repented of their sins, received Christ as Saviour, and been born again of the Spirit. They do not all belong to the same denomination or worship God in the same way, but they are all united in 'the mystical body of Christ, which is the blessed company of all faithful people'.[23] 'The mystical body of Christ' is invisible and distinguished from the visible manifestation of the Church as 'the kernel is from the husk'.[24] 'The mystical Body of Christ' is the whole body of believers of every age and tongue and people. It is a Church composed of all who are washed in Christ's blood, clothed in Christ's righteousness, renewed by Christ's Spirit, joined to Christ by faith, and epistles of Christ's life; it is the Church of which every member is baptised with the Holy Ghost, and is really and truly holy; it is the Church which is one body; all who belong to it are of one heart and one mind, hold the same truths, and believe the same doctrines as necessary to salvation. It is the Church which has only one Head, that Head is Jesus Christ Himself.[25]

The visible or denominational churches, on the other hand, are mixed bodies of converted and unconverted people, yet God uses them to carry out his mission in the world. They are useful guardians of the Scriptures for maintaining a regular ministry of preaching, and preserving order in the Christian community. No particular church can claim a monoply of the truth in doctrine, worship, government or any other mark of the true Church. The best example is the one 'which adds most members to the one true Church, which most promotes "repentance towards God, faith towards the Lord Jesus Christ" and good works among its members'.[26] Membership of the Church is not identical with membership of Christ. Yet 'there is a sense in which the true Church is eminently visible to those who have eyes to see it. Its members, like its Master, cannot be hid. Their holy lives and characters will always show whose they are, and whom they serve, and where they are going when they die.'[27]

Ryle also insisted that evangelical religion does not undervalue the Christian ministry.[28] He valued the Christian ministry as a scriptural institution and he believed that 'episcopacal government, rightly administered, is the best form of church government'.[29] He believed that for the regular preaching of the Word and the administration of the sacraments no better plan could be devised than setting apart an order of men to devote themselves to Christ's work. But he was opposed to the notion that Anglican ministry is a sacerdotal ministry and that her ministers are a sacrificing priesthood. There is nothing either in the New Testament or the Articles to support such an idea. 'It is nowhere written, "God hath set some in the Church, first apostles, then priests" ' (1 Cor. 12:28).[30] On the contrary, the chief work of the Christian minister is to 'preach the Word' (2 Tim. 4:2). The proclamation of God's Word, Ryle says, 'appears to me to be the chief instrument by which the Holy Ghost not only awakens sinners, but also leads on and establishes saints'.[31] He firmly believed that the preaching of the Gospel had always been the main instrument God uses in offering men the gift of salvation.

The Sacraments

A persistent criticism levelled against Evangelicals in Victorian times was that they treated the sacraments with indifference. Ryle insisted that the charge was entirely without foundation and that Evangelical Religion 'does not undervalue the Sacraments of Baptism and the Lord's Supper'.[32] 'We honour them as holy ordinances appointed by Christ himself, and as a blessed means of grace, which in all who use them rightly, worthily and with good faith, "have a wholesome effect and operation".'[33] The two sacraments of the Gospel are signs and symbols of God's favour toward us, and when they are received in faith they become to us effectual means of grace. But where faith is absent they are then a mere form and convey no real and lasting blessing.

Baptism

In the second half of the last century both sacraments were the subjects of bitter controversy in the Church. The controversy surrounding baptism came to a head in the Gorham case which attracted a great deal of publicity around 1847. Henry Philpotts, the Bishop of Exeter, accused the Rev G. C. Gorham of 'unsound doctrine' in a legal action because he did not accept the Catholic interpretation of baptismal regeneration. The dispute led prominent evangelical bishops and clergy to write open letters to the *Record*, *The English Churchman* and *The Christian Guardian* denying the doctrine of 'baptismal regeneration'. Ryle, too, published some pamphlets on the evangelical understanding of the doctrine of baptism in order to strength the laity and point out the dangers of unscriptural beliefs.

He began by declaring that the practice of baptism has dominical authority, and in the Apostolic Church it was the rite of initiation into the Christian community and a sign of belonging to the body of Christ. It is 'expressly named in the New Testament about eighty times', [34] and though it is not 'absolutely necessary' to salvation, it is 'an ordinance on which we may confidently expect the highest blessing, when it is rightly used'. [35] The mode of baptism he treats with indifference. Immersion or 'dipping' are both valid in Christian baptism, but 'so long as water is used in the name of the Trinity, the precise mode of administering the ordinance is left an open question'. [36] To those who insist that baptism must be by complete immersion, he pointed out that the Greek word to baptise ($\beta\alpha\pi\tau\iota\zeta\omega$) means, 'to wash or cleanse with water, but whether by immersion or not must be entirely decided by the context.' [37] To illustrate the point he turned to Luke 11:38, 'The Pharisee marvelled that he (Jesus) had not first washed before dinner', and comments:

> It may surprise some readers, perhaps, to hear that these words have been rendered more literally, 'that he had not first been baptized before dinner'. Yet it is evident to common sense that the Pharisee could not have expected our Lord to immerse or dip himself over head in water before dining! It simply means that he expected him to perform some ablution or to pour water over his hands before the meal. [38]

In support he quotes with approval some words of Witsius: 'A little drop of water may serve to seal the fulness of Divine grace in baptism as well as a small piece of bread and the least tasting of wine in the Holy Supper'.[39] He accepted that the New Testament references to baptism relate to the baptism of adults, though he believed it was possible that young children were included in the baptised households. Although there is no direct evidence to support the practice of infant baptism in the Apostolic Church, he held that the attitude of Jesus toward little children (Mark 10:13-16) shows that infants are capable of receiving some benefit from our Lord, that the conduct of those who would have kept them from him was wrong in our Lord's eyes, and that he was ready and willing to bless them when they were too young to understand what he said or did.[40] The historical evidence from the third century onwards confirms the practice of infant baptism in the early Church.

Not all Evangelicals were of one mind in their understanding of the doctrine of baptism and the efficacy of infant baptism in particular. However Ryle, and probably the majority of Evangelicals, were attracted to an interpretation rooted in covenant theology. In the biblical covenants God makes a promise to his people Israel, who respond in faith, and God seals the promise with a sign. Having drunk deep of covenant theology in the writings of the Scriptures and the tomes of the Puritans, Ryle found a close parallel between the acceptance of young children into Israel through the covenant rite of circumcision in the Old Testament and the reception of infants of believing-parents into the Christian Church by baptism in the New Testament. The covenant promise is 'to you and your children' (Acts 2:39). He contends that 'Children were "admitted into the Old Testament Church by a formal ordinance," from the time of Abraham downwards. That ordinance was circumcision. It was an ordinance which God himself appointed, and the neglect of which was denounced as a sin.... Now if children were considered to be capable of admission into the Church by an ordinance in the Old Testament, it is difficult to see why they cannot be admitted in the New. The general tendency of the Gospel is to increase men's spiritual privileges and not diminish them.'[41]

The Tractarians made much of sacramental grace in their

teaching. They believed that the sacrament of baptism conveys the grace of God to the soul *ex opere operato*. They were convinced that they rightly interpreted the teaching of Article XXVII and the Prayer-book Service of Baptism in their references to 'regeneration and new birth'. So their encouragement to parents to have their children baptised was based on the belief that in the sacrament of baptism infants received remission of their sins and spiritual rebirth. In objecting to this interpretation Ryle took a pragmatic stance. 'Parents bring their children to the font without the slightest sense of what they are doing. Sponsers stand by and answer for their children in evident ignorance of the nature of the ordinance they are attending, and as a mere matter of form.'[42] He rejected out of hand the notion that

> the grace of the Holy Spirit invariably accompanies the administration of the ordinance, that in every case, a seed of Divine life is implanted in the heart, to which all subsequent religious movement must be traced, and that all baptised children are, as a matter of course, born again and made partakers of the Holy Ghost.... Multitudes of our worshippers have not a spark of religious life or grace about them. And yet we are told that they must be addressed as regenerate, possessors of grace, because they have been baptised. It is a dangerous delusion.[43]

The Sacraments are an 'outward and visible sign of an inward and spiritual grace', but they do not exert their influence *ex opere operato*. To say that everyone who is baptised is thereby a child of God is contrary to Scripture and plain fact.

On the other hand, Ryle believed that 'the men who drew up the Baptismal Service held that there was a connection between baptism and spiritual regeneration, and they were right. They knew there was nothing too high in the way of blessing for the child of the believer.'[44] Baptism signifies a change of state, bringing the child within the realm of grace, but it does not signify a change of nature. 'Whether any particular child was actually and really regenerated in baptism they left to be decided by its life and ways when it grew up.'[45] However, 'there was much misunderstanding over the language of regeneration in the Baptismal Service, which he believed could be resolved by the Prayer-book principle of 'charitable' assumption. On this principle, the only formula on which Christian worship can be arranged, it is assumed that the parents and sponsers who bring their children to be baptised do so as believers, and 'as the children of believers the infant when baptised is pronounced "regenerate" and thanks are given for it'.[46] The baptised child is the recipient of a rich inheritance of blessings which, when he comes to an age of understanding, he is to claim for himself by faith and prove in personal experience.

The Lord's Supper

With the rise of the Oxford Movement High Churchmen tended to exalt the sacrament of the Lord's Supper above everything else and give it an importance unwarranted by Scripture. It is mentioned only four times in the whole of Scripture, once each in the synoptic gospels and by St Paul in 1 Corinthians, and Ryle believed it was never intended to be 'the first, foremost, principal and most important thing in Christian worship'.[47] Nevertheless, Evangelicals honour the Sacrament of Holy Communion for it was ordained by Christ and commanded to be observed in remembrance of his offering on Calvary. Ryle loved it as a divinely appointed means of grace and believed the Church would be the poorer without it. 'You will rarely find a true believer who will not say that he reckons the Lord's Supper one of the best helps and highest privileges. He will tell you that if he were deprived of the Lord's Supper he should find the loss of it a great drawback to his soul.'[48] At a time when the sacrament was neglected it was the Evangelicals who introduced the practice of early morning and evening Communion services, and took infinite care in preparing the communicants before-hand.

Sadly, the Communion Service which was intended to unite believers and be a sign of love among the brethren became a focus of acrimony. Evangelicals became alarmed when they saw in the revival of Catholic theology an attempt to reinterpret the sacrament in terms of the Eucharistic Sacrifice and the Real Presence of Christ. Ryle repudiated the idea that the Lord's Supper was a sacrifice in any sense other than an offering of ourselves to God in response to Christ's offering for our salvation at Calvary. He argued that the sacrifice of the Mass dishonoured the finished work of Christ; it contradicted the plain teaching of Scripture, and it threatened the whole structure of the Protestant Reformation. He insisted, 'The last literal sacrifice, we are repeatedly told in the Epistle to the Hebrews, is the once for all finished sacrifice of Christ on the cross.'[49]

The Catholic wing of the Anglican Church took literally Christ's words of Institution, 'This is my body', 'This is my blood', and insisted that they are 'proofs that Christ's body and blood, in some mysterious manner, are located in the bread and wine at the Lord's Supper after their consecration'.[50] Ryle firmly believed in the spiritual presence of Christ in the Communion, but he denied that the priestly act of consecration made the actual Body and Blood of Christ really, though invisibly and supernaturally present, under the form of bread and wine. Ryle readily accepted that the consecration of the elements changed their function, but not that it changed their substance. The elements remained bread and wine. It seemed to him that there could be but one true interpretation of the words of institution. 'Those who heard the words, "This is my body," and "This is my blood," and were accustomed to our Lord's mode of speaking, understood them to mean, "This represents my body," and "this represents my blood".'[51] The bread and wine are 'emblems' of his body and blood. Clearly the words were understood in a figurative sense and the disciple would never have dreamed of taking them literally. As for the Catholic interpretation of the Real Presence of Christ in the Sacrament, Ryle rejected this on three counts: There is not a word of Scripture to support such an idea; the rubric at the end of the Communion Service denies it; and the notion threatens the whole doctrine of Christ's true manhood. 'Once admit that Christ's body can be present at God's right hand and on a communion table at the same moment, and it cannot be the body which was born of the Virgin Mary and crucified on the cross.'[52] Scripture clearly teaches that the real bodily presence of Christ is in glory and the real spiritual presence of Christ is in the heart of the believer.

Many thought Ryle too dogmatic and narrow-minded in his

beliefs. His answer was that a faith without doctrine or dogma is like a body without bones and sinews.[53] His aim in the ministry was at all times to be 'as broad as the Bible, neither less nor more'.[54] He was not a great or profound theologian, and the subjects he wrote about were often well worn, but in all his teaching he was unashamed to uphold the first principles of evangelical doctrine and practice.

Chapter Nine

Scriptural holiness

A revival of evangelical religion in Great Britain in the mid-nineteenth century touched thousands of individuals who joyfully surrendered their lives to Christ. The revival not only changed lives, but also led to a new interest in and support for missionary work overseas and Christian social work among the poor at home. The beginnings of this religious revival may be traced to Hamilton, Ontario, where towards the end of 1857 'a gust of Divine power' swept through the Methodist congregation and hundreds were converted.[1] Within a few months thousands were attending prayer gatherings at all times of the day and night in New York and other towns on the east coast of North America. Evangelistic and prayer meetings multiplied and the spirit of revival spread westwards to the prairies.

Revival comes to Britain

Relations between the USA and Ireland were close and reports of the religious revival in North America stirred Christian believers in Ulster to start praying for a similar outpouring of God's Spirit on his people in Ireland.[2] Prayer was answered and in Belfast revival meetings were held in churches and chapels, the Music Hall and on the streets of the city. In the same year, 1859, the influence of the American revival reached South Wales and thousands of men, women and children came under a deep conviction of sin, and, after repenting, felt the liberating power of the Spirit fill their lives. That September, *The Times* reported under the heading, 'A Religious Revival', that Newcastle-upon-Tyne 'has become the scene of a religious "Awakening," which bids fair to rival anything which has occurred either in America or Northern Ireland'.[3] The awakening in Ulster also provoked great interest in Scotland and by the summer of 1860 many churches in Glasgow, the Western Isles and the Northern Highlands had experienced the quickening power of the Holy Spirit.

Dr and Mrs Walter C. Palmer, American Methodists, had both been stirred by the revival in Hamilton, and became the leading exponents of the new message.[4] Phoebe Palmer was the more influential and her teaching greatly impressed Pearsall Smith and other revivalists. When they came over to Britain prayer meetings were filled morning, noon and night, hundreds of men and women were converted, backsliders were restored, drunkards took the pledge and criminals became honest citizens. As a result of the revival the following year, the Britannia, the Garrick and the Sadler's Wells theatres were opened for Sunday evening revival services led by evangelical clergy and ministers. Special services to attract the middle-classes were also held in St James' Hall and Exeter Hall in the West End, and in the nave of St Paul's Cathedral and Westminster Abbey.[5] Such evangelistic outreach was needed. Thousands of professing Christians were content with a nominal 'churchianity' and knew nothing of the saving power of Christ or the experience of the Spirit-filled life. The revival left no part of the Kingdom untouched. There was no town or country district where at least some of the inhabitants had not felt 'the showers of blessing'.

During the Revival, evangelists, both men and women, were raised up to preach the gospel in the power of the Spirit. In Liverpool, Reginald Radcliffe, a greatly respected solicitor in the town, felt the call of God to evangelize and in the autumn of 1861 he began a series of Sunday evening meetings in the Concert Hall, which attracted large audiences.[6] He was dedicated to open-air preaching and was listened to attentively by miners at the pit heads and stevedores at the docks. On one occasion he was imprisoned by the magistrates at Chester for conducting an open-air meeting on the race course. Radcliffe became a prominent preacher in the revivalist movement and with a fellow evangelist he started the East End Mission, which gave employment to women sewing garments. Reginald Radcliffe joined forces with Thomas Shouldham Henry, son of the president of Queen's College, Belfast, to conduct a series of mission services in Ipswich and throughout Suffolk. Ryle was in favour of any movement to deepen the spiritual life of God's people, provided it was based on sound, biblical principles, and he invited the missioners to address a meeting in the Corn Hall, Stradbroke.[7] Their message made an impression and several parishioners entered into a deeper spiritual experience.

Holiness teaching in the Anglican Church

About this time, William Edwin Boardman, a zealous American businessman, published a slight book entitled *The Higher Christian Life*, which became a best seller among Christians and made a considerable impact on those seeking a deeper religious experience.[8] The thesis of the book was simply that entire sanctification was an immediate gift of God to be enjoyed by all who had faith in Christ. Christians were exhorted to enter into the experience of 'the higher life' by faith alone. To enter into the rest of faith was to cease to struggle against sin, the world and the devil, and to enjoy constant peace. Evan Hopkins, a young evangelical clergyman, was greatly influenced by the book, and both he and his wife entered into the promised blessing by faith alone. He invited a group of his evangelical friends who had shown interest in holiness teaching to a gathering convened to discuss the deeper spiritual life and how they could make it known to a wider audience. The main speakers were Robert Pearsall Smith, a Presbyterian, and his wife Hannah, a Quaker and author of *The Way of Holiness*, from the United States.[9]

Smith had been converted at one of the camp-meetings in the mid-West. He gave up his business as a glass manufacturer and without any theological training became a well-known Holiness preacher on both sides of the Atlantic. In 1870 he published the book *Holiness Through Faith* in which he declared that the blood of Christ cleansed the believer 'not only from the stain of sin, or the punishment of sin, but from sin itself, and that sanctification, like salvation, is the gift of faith alone'.[10] Persuasively the book showed that Christians may know something better than a nominal Christian faith so frequently beset by temptations and sin, for God offers believers a life of constant joy and victory over all sin through simply trusting in Jesus. After a preaching tour among the pietists in Germany, where the message of inner quietism was readily accepted, the revivalists came to England. Lord Mount-Temple invited Pearsall Smith and his wife to address a six day religious convention in July 1874 for invited guests in a large marquee on the lawns of his estate at Broadlands, near Romsey.

At Broadlands, both Pearsall Smith and his wife testified to their experience of God's dealings with them, and how he had revived and blessed their Christian experience through simply abiding by faith in Christ.[11] At the camp meetings in America they had learned the blessed truth of justification by faith alone and rejoiced in it for years, but they had stopped at that point in their Christian experience and failed to make any progress in Christian living. Then God showed them the necessity of committing themselves daily to the Lord; as they obeyed he gave them deliverance from the power and dominion of sin, and they began to enjoy victorious Christian lives. From that time they ceased to struggle against temptation and began to rest in faith in the promises of God and thus entered into a new spiritual experience of full salvation. The revivalist message offered not only deliverance from past sins, but also from the presence and power of sin in their daily lives.

The addresses captured the imagination of the audience, and such was the persuasive power of Pearsall Smith's message that a thousand believers, including many evangelical clergy, attended follow-up meetings for the Promotion of Scriptural Holiness in Oxford the following September to learn more about the teaching of 'full salvation' and 'the rest of faith'.[12]

Among those evangelical clergy who were dissatisfied with their own spiritual condition and longed to know more about the sanctified life were Evan Hopkins, the vicar of Holy Trinity, Richmond, who became a leading figure in the new movement; E. W. Moor of Brunswick Chapel; G. R. Thornton, vicar of St Nicholas, Nottingham; D. B. Hankin, vicar of Christ Church, Ware; and Canon T. D. Harford-Battersby, vicar of St John's, Keswick.[13] They broke step with the majority of Evangelicals and were won over by what they heard at the revival meetings. Canon Harford-Battersby was at first sceptical of the movement and attended the Oxford meetings intent on criticising 'Higher life' theology. After hearing the address and having further prayer and discussion with Evan Hopkins, however, he came away convinced that the holiness movement was of God and the message one that the Church urgently needed. Consequently, he decided to invite some of his friends to join him in the Lake District in July for a series of convention meetings on the theme of 'Holiness', in a marquee on the vicarage lawn.[14] The gathering in 1875 was the first of the famous Keswick Convention meetings which have continued annually, almost without a break, for more than a century. The Convention has maintained a close association with speakers from across the Atlantic, but after Handley C. G. Moule, a fellow of Trinity College, Cambridge, became a regular speaker from 1886 onwards, 'Keswick teaching' took on a more balanced scriptural form.[15]

Ryle's reaction to holiness teaching

Ryle had generously sponsored Reginald Radcliffe, the revivalist preacher, and wholeheartedly welcomed Dwight L. Moody and Ira D. Sankey when they came to these shores from the States. However, he became suspicious about the scriptural basis of some teaching gaining popularity in the Holiness Movement which had grown out of the Revival and Awakening of 1859. His friend George T. Fox of Durham had published a scathing review of Pearsall Smith's book *Holiness Through Faith* in the *Record* on 7th November 1870 and had written a rejoinder in his book *Perfectionism*. Ryle was in general agreement with Fox, and felt that many rash statements being made about holiness could not be substantiated by the Scriptures. It seemed to him that some 'holiness preachers', by the emphasis they placed on 'entire consecration', 'victory over sin' and 'the gift of inward peace', taught a doctrine of sinless perfection which was both unscriptural and harmful.[16] He saw nothing in Scripture and found nothing in his own Christian experience to lead him to believe that Christians may claim 'perfection' in this life.

Other evangelical leaders joined Ryle in raising questions about the scriptural basis of this new teaching on 'holiness by faith alone', which they felt could so easily degenerate into a pernicious doctrine of 'sinless perfection'. Francis Close, Dean of Carlisle; Hugh McNeile, Dean of Ripon; and Handley Moule, who later became the Bishop of Durham, all stalwart Evangelicals, wrote lengthy letters to the *Record*, airing their concerns over the fundamental beliefs of the movement.[17] Such was the impact of the Revivalist movement on the Church that it was debated year on year in Church Congress and at evangelical conferences.

In spite of a spate of letters to the Church press and the hostile publicity criticising the 'higher life' movement, around five thousand believers each day attended another great convention in Brighton in June 1875, seeking a deeper spiritual experience.[18] The Corporation offered the use of the Dome, the Pavilion, the Corn Exchange and the Town Hall free of charge for the services. Pearsall Smith was the main speaker at the Convention, but during the meetings he appeared to suffer a recurrence of a previous brain disorder. He became 'rambling and wild' in his speech and eventually was unable to continue. His wife Hannah, also a gifted speaker, took over from him and declared to an attentive audience that Jesus not only delivers believers from the guilt and power of sin, but also from the very presence of sin in this life – instantly. All that they had to do to experience a life free from the thraldom of sin was to rest in Jesus. Simply lay all on the altar and believe in Him.

Many left the meetings claiming that they had entered into a new religious experience. Others were not so persuaded, and after the Convention more letters began filling the columns of the *Record*, critical of the Brighton meetings and Mrs Pearsall Smith's teaching on holiness. In the debate which ensued, Ryle contrasted the biblical teaching of Moody, at the time engaged in a successful evangelistic campaign in London, with the unsound, exaggerated and unscriptural teaching at the revivalist meetings, arguing that 'the difference between Moody's theology and that of "the Oxford Conference" is the difference between sunshine and fog'.[19] Christians all over the country were shocked when the Pearsall Smiths suddenly returned to the United States. Shortly after the Brighton Convention they had been quietly advised by Christian friends, among them William Cowper-Temple and Lord Radstock, to leave Britain immediately. Apparently Smith was guilty of the indiscretion of talking 'in antinomian terms with his arm round the shoulders of a young woman'.[20] At the end of December 1875 the *Record*, which had constantly been criticising Smith's theology, published a series of articles on 'The Collapse of Smithism', more or less bringing to an end this particular phase of holiness teaching in this country.[21]

Ryle was ready to give support to any movement to deepen spiritual life and encourage personal holiness, but only if it was based on sound, biblical principles. He viewed the increase of what were called 'Higher life' and 'Consecration' meetings with some concern. 'Sensational and exciting addresses by strange preachers or by women, loud singing, hot rooms, crowded tents ... all this kind of thing is very interesting at the time, and seems to do good. But is it good, real, deep-rooted, solid, lasting?'[22]

He was particularly troubled over the widespread teaching in the holiness movement that a sanctified life is attained by nothing more than faith; audiences were urged to simply trust and rest in Jesus. Believers who did so could then live the 'victorious life' over all sin and temptation. Simply by believing in Jesus and 'laying their all on the altar' in total consecration, so the revivalists taught, they would experience deliverance from all 'inbred sin' and 'carnal desires.' He questioned the claim that an absolute literal perfection and total freedom from sin is possible in this life, and doubted the assumption that Paul's teaching in Romans 7 supported this interpretation.[23] There was much vague talk in the meetings about attaining perfection simply by resting in Jesus, but Ryle found nothing in Scripture to support such a belief.[24] He admired the place the revivalists gave to Christ in their preaching and teaching, but felt that by overemphasizing the doctrine of Christ in us, they were in danger of neglecting the equally important work of the Spirit in sanctifying believers.[25] Finally, he felt that all too often revivalists made exaggerated statements to support their views, misinterpreted Scripture, and sank to abusive attacks on fellow Christians who did not agree with them.[26]

His book *Holiness*

Ryle's concern about these matters was the origin of his book *Holiness*. He followed up his letters to the Church press criticising the 'Higher life' movement by publishing a series of papers entitled *Holiness: its Nature, Difficulties and Roots*.[27] After the success of the first small work published in 1877, he added several more chapters and the enlarged volume ran into many editions. In a long introduction to the original work, Ryle admitted that Christian standards had been falling and there was more worldliness and less holiness among believers than there used to be. He believed the Spirit was grieved by the low standards of so-called Christian behaviour and insisted that for a true Christian holy living is an evidence of the reality of our faith.[28] It was a reproach that an Evangelical might be 'sound' in Christian doctrine and yet live by careless and 'worldly' standards. He admitted that the need for practical holiness in daily life had been absent from much preaching and teaching, and felt that one of the 'wants of the times' was a thorough revival of 'Scriptural holiness'.[29]

To the surprise of many readers who turn to *Holiness*, the first chapter is devoted to a careful study of 'Sin' and its meaning in Scripture. 'I make no apology,' Ryle says, 'for beginning this volume of papers about holiness by making some plain statements about sin.'[30] The subject was deliberately chosen because he believed that sin is a great enemy which can deceive unbelievers into thinking that they do not need salvation and Christians that they do not need sanctification. Man is a mixture of good and evil, and such is the power of evil that it can flatter him into thinking he is far better than he really is. Ryle believed that the ready acceptance of perfectionist theories against the plain teaching of Scripture clearly revealed the power and 'the deceitfulness of sin'.[31] Scripture tells us that 'if we say that we have no sin, we deceive ourselves, and the truth is not in us' (1 John 1:10), and the daily Prayer-book service begins with a confession of sin, reminding us that we are all sinners needing pardon. Christians will only attain a higher standard of holiness as they become aware more fully of the sinfulness of sin. Ryle's purpose in this chapter was clearly to rectify an inadequate and deficient understanding of the doctrine of sin.

Ryle declared that sanctification is God's will for every true believer (1 Thess. 4. 3).[32] It is part of his gracious work of salvation to turn a pardoned sinner into a godly man. 'The moment a person begins to be a justified person, he also begins to be a sanctified person. He may not feel it, but it is a fact.'[33] It seemed to Ryle that the teaching of the 'Higher life' movement confused the doctrines of Justification and Sanctification. In some respects they are alike – both are the work of God, both take place simultaneously, and both are necessary to salvation.[34] However, they differ in other important respects.[35] Justification is reckoning a pardoned sinner righteous, Sanctification is actually making him inwardly righteous.[36] Justification is clearly a finished work which cannot be added to; sanctification is an imperfect work and continues through the whole of our Christian life as we gradually conform to 'the image of Christ'.[37] The believer can never be more justified than when he first trusted in Christ, but more sanctified he certainly will be as he grows in grace. There are degrees in sanctification but not in justification.[38] Furthermore, contrary to those who taught that by simply believing in Jesus we may know constant rest and peace, Ryle insisted that though Scripture clearly teaches that we are justified by faith alone, nowhere does it say we are sanctified by faith alone.[39] We are justified by faith; we are sanctified by the Spirit through prayer, and by overcoming temptation and striving against sin in Christ's strength.

Holiness is the practical outworking of sanctification in our lives. Practical holiness is intended to be seen in our everyday behaviour and in our relationships in the home, in the church and in our places of work. Holiness is aiming to please God in our daily lives; avoiding sin and overcoming temptation; dealing honestly and speaking the truth, and being faithful in all the duties and relations of life.[40] Holiness is worth little indeed, 'if it does not bear this kind of fruit'.[41] Holiness is not being religious, pious or sanctimonious; it is striving to be 'like the Lord Jesus Christ' in our daily lives.[42] Saving faith and real converting grace will always produce some conformity to 'the image of Jesus'.[43] Family likeness is the only firm evidence that we are really born again and truly children of God.

Ryle insisted we have to work at our faith if it is worth anything, a truth often overlooked by the revivalist preachers. Large numbers 'came to Christ' in the revival meetings and for a time experienced the promised peace and joy. But often within a short time, when all the excitement began to fade, they found there is a cost to pay, a cross to bear, and returned to their old ways. Ryle believed that essential to our growing in grace is diligence in the use of private means of grace through prayer and reading the Scriptures.[44] Then our sense of sin will become deeper, faith stronger, hope brighter, love more extensive, and spiritual-mindedness more marked.[45] Essential also is 'carefulness in the use of public means of grace' provided by the ministry of the church.[46] God's people are meant to be a holy people and we neglect the means of grace he has provided at our peril.

Some holiness preachers appeared to have a blind-spot about the many exhortations in the New Testament to Christians to 'wrestle' and 'fight' against sin (Eph. 6:12; 1 Tim. 6:12) and to 'put on the whole armour of God' (Eph. 6:11) if they would be holy.[47] So the Christian who longs to be holy, said Ryle, may be known by his inward warfare as well as by his inward peace.[48] Many professing Christians whose spiritual life is nothing more than attending a formal religious service once or twice a week know nothing of this warfare against sin, the world and the devil. They have not counted the cost of being a true Christian. Ryle could find no evidence in the Bible that faith alone brought the believer rest from inner conflict. On the contrary, his study of the Scriptures, Church history, the lives of the Puritans and his own experience, led him to believe that the normal pattern of sanctification by the Holy Spirit is a gradual process and not an instant experience. It does not prevent the believer knowing a great deal about inward struggle against temptation and sin. He could find no warrant in Scripture for the doctrine of 'imputed sanctification' and instant perfection.[49] Sanctification is not accomplished without a great deal of inward spiritual conflict and struggle, between the flesh and the spirit, the old nature and new. In the desire to please the Lord and live a holy life the Christian is faced with a constant battle against Satan and must expect 'a great deal of conflict'.[50] Nevertheless, those who take up the cross and 'fight the good fight of faith' are assured of being more than conquerors through Christ (Rom. 8:37).

Ryle's *Holiness* challenged nineteenth century Christians to weigh seriously the imperatives of Scripture through Christ's power to forsake sin, and with the aid of the Holy Spirit grow in grace and Christlikeness and live holy and sanctified lives. In the late twentieth century the renewal movement has swept through the Church, and *Holiness* remains a challenge to charismatics today to examine some aspects of their faith in the light of Scripture.

Keswick teaching
Ryle's book on holiness was generally well received. However, those Evangelicals who were loyal to 'Keswick teaching' were not entirely won over. Evan Hopkins, who after the death of Canon Harford-Battersby became the chairman of the Keswick Convention, wrote a classic exposition of New Testament holiness, *The Law of Liberty in the Spiritual Life*, which went some way towards answering Ryle's criticisms of the so-called 'Higher life' teaching. The book helped to clarify 'Keswick teaching', as it was becoming known, and won over many Evangelicals who had hesitated about accepting its theology. Keswick supporters were often maligned for attending the annual Convention in much the same way that Ryle and his Evangelical colleagues had been criticized in the previous decade for attending the Church Congress meetings. A contemporary wrote what it felt like to be a Keswick supporter: 'We went up to Keswick more or less with a feeling that we were losing our reputation to do so, especially if it happened to be a ministerial reputation. We were speckled birds. We were associated with those who were looked down upon, to a considerable extent, and our doctrines were much criticized, as well as ourselves.'[51]

Though Ryle was outspoken in his criticism of those beliefs which he considered did not have any credential in Scripture, he remained magnanimous and charitable towards those who differed from him. To his friends in the opposing camp, he wrote:

Do they think that a higher standard of Christian living is needed in the present day? So do I. Do they think that clearer, stronger, fuller teaching about holiness is needed? So do I. Do they think that Christ ought to be more exalted, as the root and author of sanctification as well as justification? So do I. Do they think that believers should be urged more and more to live by faith? So do I. Do they think that a very close walk with God should be more pressed on believers, as the secret of happiness and usefulness? So do I. In all these things we agree. But if they want to go further, then I ask them to take care where they tread, and to explain very clearly and distinctly what they mean.[52]

The same generous thoughts were expressed later in the Preface to his enlarged edition of *Holiness*:

Towards those who think holiness is to be promoted by the modern, so-called 'spiritual-life' movement, I feel nothing but charity. If they do good, I am thankful. Towards myself and those who agree with me, I ask them to feel charity in return. The last day will show who is right and who is wrong. In the meantime, I am quite certain that to exhibit bitterness and coolness toward those who cannot conscientiously work with us, is to prove ourselves very ignorant of real holiness.[53]

Ryle made several friendly gestures towards his Keswick friends. He never lost touch with his friends Handley Moule and Webb Peploe, and on the Sunday before the start of the Keswick Convention in 1879, he preached for his friend Canon Harford-Battersby in St John's Church, though he did not attend any of the meetings in the marquee during the week. Again, after his holiday in the Lake District in 1892, he sat on the platform at a meeting specially convened to hear Dwight L. Moody preach, the Convention being ended. After leading the gathering in prayer, he 'listened with evident satisfaction' to the American evangelist proclaiming the gospel.[54]

Chapter Ten

I am the Bishop of Liverpool

As the acknowledged leader of the Evangelicals in the Church of England (a status he disowned) Ryle was frequently invited by fellow Evangelicals to preach or address meetings, and always delighted to respond. During the winter lecture season he was a popular speaker at conferences and missionary meetings in East Anglia, and regularly on the platform at the great annual rallies of the Home and Foreign Missionary Societies in London. The coming of the railway to Suffolk with connections from Harleston and Diss meant that he could attend meetings in Norwich, Cambridge and London without any difficulty. Often on the day of a speaking engagement he would be occupied with some parochial matter or sermon preparation, so that it was not until the very last moment that he set off for the railway station, leaving himself little time to catch the train. On these occasions he would hire a carriage to take him to the station and when pressed for time he would lower the window and boom out in a clear, deep voice, 'Garnham, we shall lose the train.' The coachman's reply was always the same, 'I can't go faster, Sir, unless the horses gallop.' Whereupon Ryle would again call out, 'Then make them gallop!' and through the streets of Harleston the horses would gallop at a pace that brought the people to their doors to see 'old Ryle late again!'[1]

Evangelicals in the Church

Ryle was an enthusiastic supporter of the Islington Clerical Conference. This important and influential gathering of Evangelicals from all parts of the country met annually in January to discuss theological and other issues facing the Church from an evangelical standpoint. The first gathering was convened by Daniel Wilson, the Vicar of Islington in 1827, and continued to flourish after his son, a prominent figure among Evangelicals in London,

123

succeeded his father. In 1860 Ryle was invited to give one of the addresses and he chose as his subject, 'How may a revival of spiritual religion be promoted among clergy and greater effectiveness be given to pulpit administration?' It was a subject close to his heart and the address evoked a warm response from a large audience. In 1877 he took part in the Jubilee celebrations of the Conference and gave a factual and thought-provoking paper on 'A comparative estimate on the condition of the Church of England in 1827 and 1877 in respect of its spiritual life and the balance of the parties existing at the two periods.' Among the conclusions he reached were that there were far more Evangelicals, both clerical and lay, in the late seventies; clergy were more active, taking more services, attending more conferences and supporting more missionary societies.

However, the strength and effectiveness of Evangelicals in the Church was questioned following the death of Dean Hugh McNeile of Ripon in 1879. *The Times* in an obituary notice stated that 'the death of Dean McNeile removes a striking figure from the dwindling band of men who still represent the old evangelical tradition of our Church in the midst of a generation who has sought other faiths than theirs. He belonged to a school who are now few and far between, to a party whose influence has almost ceased to count in current controversies.'[2] This sceptical conclusion was not shared by Ryle and his friends, who wrote to correct this statement. Ryle maintained that the distinctive doctrines of Evangelicalism were now believed and preached in five times as many churches in England and Wales as had been the case fifty years earlier; Evangelical Societies were well supported and there had been a healthy growth in the number of Evangelical conferences and conventions. History confirms that Evangelicals were probably at their most active, most resilient, most serious and most influential in the nineteenth century around the 1860s. Ryle, in the first edition of *The Churchman* which replaced *The Christian Observer*, gave his own candid appraisal of his party in 1880, saying: 'No doubt the faults and infirmities of the Evangelical body are not a few, and it does not need a Solomon to discern them. No doubt we are only a minority in the Church of

England. We never were anything else, and probably never shall be. But the Evangelical Party with all its faults shows no sign of decay. We shall live and not die, if we are only true to our principles, if we will only work and watch and pray and read and understand the times.'[3]

A distinctive characteristic of Evangelical religion has always been to show an active interest in and support for evangelism at home and overseas. Several missionary societies were founded around the turn of the century by enthusiastic Evangelicals with a concern for those who had not heard the gospel. The Society for Missions to Africa and the East was founded in 1799, becoming better known when the name was changed to the Church Missionary Society. The same year the Religious Tract Society was launched, which in turn gave rise to the British and Foreign Bible Society in 1804. In 1836 the Church Pastoral-Aid Society was established 'for the purpose of benefiting the population of our country by increasing the number of working clergymen in the Church of England, and encouraging the appointment of pious and discreet laymen as helpers to the clergy in duties not ministerial'.

These were some of Ryle's favourite societies which he supported wholeheartedly by prayer, gifts and practical encouragement. In 1862 he was invited to preach the annual sermon in St Bride's Church, London, on behalf of the Church Missionary Society, an honour regarded as 'the blue ribband of the evangelical pulpit'.[4] Basing his words on Acts 17 he spoke about St Paul's witness in the heathen city of Athens. It was an apposite address in the wake of the liberal controversy following the publication of *Essays and Reviews*, a year or two earlier. Eugene Stock, who wrote the official *History of the Church Missionary Society*, said of the sermon, 'It is needless to say how easy the application was to broad views that were beginning to become fashionable.'[5] At the annual May Meeting of the Society in 1864 he was again the main speaker and sat alongside Samuel Adjai Crowther, shortly to be consecrated Bishop of the Niger Territories. Crowther was a native of Sierra Leone, where the CMS had established a diocese in 1853. Through the work of its missionaries, Crowther, a former slave, was converted to Christ and became the first African convert to be consecrated a bishop. In the course of his address Ryle spoke of the pioneer work of the Society. In a dramatic moment he turned round on the platform and pointing his finger at Samuel Crowther, challenged the liberal Broad Church party to produce a like trophy of grace.[6] His words immediately brought forth a spontaneous round of applause from the appreciative audience. He frequently spoke at the local meetings of the Church Pastoral-Aid Society in the diocese, proudly declaring that he had been a friend and supporter of the Society for the past forty years and was more than ever disposed to support it. With his wide experience of ministry and a clear view of the parochial situation in England, his addresses on the Church Pastoral-Aid Society and Church Association platforms always drew an expectant and attentive audience at local meetings or at the annual gatherings in London.

The Church Congress
During his time at Stradbroke Ryle began to take an active interest in the recently formed Church Congress. This annual Congress was started to meet a growing demand among churchmen for a platform on which to debate problems of the day facing the Church. It brought together men of different schools of thought and, though lacking any legislative power, provided an opportunity for expressing opinions on controversial subjects. The Congress gathered in the chief cities of different dioceses and in 1866 convened in Norwich, where the Bishop, Dr Pelham, uncertain of its purpose and value, sent Ryle along to report. Ryle was not enthusiastic about the new assembly but decided to attend future gatherings in order to make an evangelical contribution to the symposium.[7]

Clergy and laity from the High and Broad Church traditions were quite enthusiastic about the three-day Congresses, but Evangelicals were generally opposed to associating with churchmen of other traditions. Only a tiny number of Evangelicals bothered to attend, and those who had the courage to address the assembly sometimes found they were shouted down.[8] By their absence Evangelicals virtually handed over control of Congress to others and gave rise to the belief that evangelicalism was a dying cause. Ryle, however, refused to be intimidated either by the strength of his opponents or the criticism of his friends.[9] He determined to go even though he knew that he would stand almost alone. It was his firm belief that 'in large assemblies of men convened to consider ecclesiastical and religious questions, we may confidently assume that there are always some present whose hearts are right, and who are willing to support the truth, even though they sit in bad company, and are for the present silenced and overawed. Gamaliel's conduct in Acts 5:34, is an illustration of this. There is no warrant for staying away from assemblies and councils merely because we happen to be a minority.'[10] So he felt it his duty to go and stand firm for evangelical principles. His friends Canon Hoare and Canon Garbett did support him in this, but Dean Close after attending one Congress, felt that 'he had no business to be in that atmosphere of cloudy, confused, misty compromise', and never attended another.[11] Even the saintly Handley Moule was censured by his fellow Evangelicals 'for going over to the other side' when he attended the Salisbury Congress.

Ryle was bitterly disappointed that he got so little support from his fellow Evangelicals in his efforts to consolidate evangelical truth in the Church's witness. To stir up interest he published the pamphlet 'Shall We Go?', setting forth persuasive arguments why Evangelicals should attend Congress. He also raised the matter at a Church Association conference. In 1872 he addressed the Islington Conference on the subject. The burden of his argument was that as Evangelicals:

> We ought to assert our right to take part in them, to be heard in them, and to prove that we are as good Churchmen as any in our pale. I am quite certain that men like Romaine and Venn and Cecil and Simeon would have come forward and taken part in them if they had had the opportunity which we have. If we let them fall into the hands of one restless, revolutionary school, and refuse to go anywhere unless we have everything our own way, I do not think we shall be doing our duty.[12]

However, the opposition grew stronger. *The Rock*, the voice of the ultra-Protestants, was most bitter in its attack and denounced Canons Hoare, Garbett and Ryle as 'Neo-evangelicals', because they mixed with ritualists and radicals. Criticism came also from C. H. Spurgeon, the eminent Baptist preacher, who described Ryle as

> An evangelical champion for whom we entertain a profound regard... yet...one of the bravest and best of men is found temporising in a way which grieves thousands even in his own denomination. Congresses in which Christ and anti-Christ are brought together cannot but exercise a very unhealthy influence even upon the most decided followers of the truth. We wish Mr Ryle would review his own position in the light of the Scriptures rather than in the darkness of ecclesiasticism; then would he come out from among them, and no more touch the unclean thing.[13]

On the Congress platform Ryle was a forceful speaker who demanded attention even though many disagreed with his point of view. It is said he 'at once proved himself to be a born debater. Quick, incisive, good humoured, never at a loss, he soon became one of the most popular of the Congress speakers...and the great audiences began to realise that there was an Evangelical point of view that deserved consideration.'[14] He frequently spoke plainly on matters generally left alone and passed over in silence. He never kept back the truth for the sake of personal reputation, or deference to others. He was particularly outspoken against practices in the Church which he considered contrary to her doctrines, but he always spoke in charity.

Ryle was a great advocate of Church reform and at the Congress at Southampton in 1870 he won for himself the permanent respect, if not the affection, of all parties. He was one of the principle speakers on 'Home Reunion' and he made a passionate plea for needful reforms. 'Repeal the Act of Uniformity,' he urged. 'Shorten the Services, use the laity, treat Dissenters kindly.' The audience warmed to him and he received loud applause when he said things would have been different in the Church of England if John Wesley had been made Archbishop of Canterbury instead of being denounced by the Church. In conclusion, he made a plea for all parties in the Church to support the Bible Society in its work of disseminating the Scriptures at home and overseas. At this point, the mood of the meeting changed dramatically, and there were cries of disapproval throughout the building. Ryle refused to retract. He argued that Nonconformists had recently been invited to assist churchmen in the revision of the Bible on the motion of Bishop Wilberforce, so 'since we may unite to revise the text, why not also to print and circulate it?' He won his point, and sat down to one of the greatest ovations ever accorded a Congress speaker.

Ryle attended the annual Congress regularly for some twenty years, during which time he left his antagonists in no doubt that Evangelicals had not ceased to think and speak on important issues facing the Church. The topics he spoke on included 'Church and State', 'Diocesan Synods', 'Comprehensiveness in the National Church', 'Internal Unity in the Church of England', 'The Church and the Working Classes' and 'The Laity.' After being raised to the Episcopate he became a vice-president and member of the Consultative Committee, which met at Lambeth Palace to draw up the agenda for the next Congress. Eugene Stock claims:

> The Congress platform not only introduced the Church generally to the chief bishops and other leaders, but also brought forward promising younger men. It spread the oratorical fame of Magee, it added to the influence of a Maclagan, and a Walsham How, it made J. C. Ryle and E. Hoare popular men.[15]

Vigorous and good humoured in all his addresses, Ryle moved a vote of thanks on the last day of the Croydon Congress in which he made a jocular apology for some of the hard things he had said about the bishops, 'I'm afraid,' he said, 'I have been rather severe upon them, but I meant it for their good.'[16]

For an Evangelical to attend Church Congress was rather like Daniel going into the lions' den, yet Ryle insisted that he came to no harm. He confessed:

I do not particularly like Congresses. I never expect them to do very much for the Church, or to add much to our stock of knowledge. I have attended them purely as a matter of duty. I have advised others to attend them for the same reason. Whether those who go to Congresses take much harm by going I do not know. But one good thing I am convinced they do. They help Churchmen to understand one another, and in this way they are useful. Personally I am not conscious of having imbibed any poison, or caught any theological disease. But whether any good is done to the cause of unity by our going, I feel no doubt at all. I believe some High Churchmen and Broad Churchmen have discovered for the first time that Evangelical Churchmen read and think, and are not always 'unlearned and ignorant men'. They have discovered that they love the Church of England from their standpoint as much as any, and that they are not dissenting wolves in sheep's clothing. They have discovered, not least, that they can talk civilly and courteously and considerately, and that they are not all unmannerly, rude, Johnsonian bears. And all this has come from meeting them face to face on neutral ground. Surely it did good.[17]

Samuel Wilberforce, the Bishop of Oxford, was ecstatic when he observed Ryle and Father Charles Lowder, an extreme Ritualist of St George's-in-the-East, London, walking arm in arm and in deep conversation. The incident was widely reported in the Church press and the reaction of the ultra-Protestants was very different. They castigated him and accused him of 'Treason'. His simple reply was that Evangelicals have no monopoly of grace, and the surest way to dispel religious prejudice was to put two antagonists together and let them look at each other face to face. He was convinced that 'if some of us could have a quiet walk or spend a quiet evening with some Churchmen we now dislike, we should be surprised when we got up next morning to find what a different feeling we had about him, we should say, "I like that man, though I do not agree with him." Great is the power of the face, the voice, the eye.'[18]

The *Church Times* was being mischievous when it asserted that 'Canon Ryle takes the colour of his company, and never imparts his own to it'.[19] He was always courteous but never kept back the truth as he saw it for the sake of a personal reputation or in deference to others. This was noted by Dean Magee who, presiding at the final gathering of the Congress in Dublin, was paying tribute to all the platform speakers. 'We have heard high Churchmen – very High Churchmen, we have heard Broad Churchmen, we have had at least one "pronounced" Evangelical Churchman address us. We thank not only the Bishop of Oxford and Lord Nelson, but the frank and manly Mr Ryle.'[20]

Recognition and preferment

Ryle's sterling work at Helmingham and Stradbroke was duly recognised when in 1870 the Bishop appointed him rural dean of Hoxne, with the pastoral oversight of twenty-five parishes. Some of his clerical neighbours may have been among those who spent much of their time hunting, shooting and fishing, whom he critically described as 'Nimrods, Ramrods and Fishing-rods'.[21] It was a common saying in Suffolk that if the sporting parson fell into a brook, he need not be rescued, since he would not be needed until next Sunday. Two years later Dr Pelham made him a canon of Norwich Cathedral for his fine work in the diocese. Twice he was appointed Select Preacher at Cambridge in 1873 and 1874 at the invitation of the Vice-Chancellor, and no less than five times at his own University between 1874 and 1880. Canon Alfred Christopher recalled how Ryle received the invitation from H. G. Liddell, his former tutor and now dean of Christ Church, to preach the University Sermon in St Mary's, the University Church of Oxford. Next day, he received another letter, saying, 'I find that you are only a BA. To preach before the University a clergyman must be an MA.' 'It was a curious fact,' wrote Canon Christopher, 'to see this stalwart veteran of 55 among the MAs taking his hitherto avoided degree.'[22] The sermon he preached in 1880 in Oxford, the city of the Protestant martyrs and the Tractarians, he called 'Foundation Truths',[23]

The growing reputation and respect with which Ryle was held by a large body of churchmen marked him out as a candidate for higher preferment. His name was known in Church and State, and on the death of Dean Henry Parr Hamilton, Dean of Salisbury for thirty years, the Crown nominated Canon J. C. Ryle to the Deanery.

Ryle was already sixty-three, and if he still had any personal ambitions of preferment they had begun to fade. On receiving the Prime Minister's overture, he said, 'I did not like it at all. I went to Salisbury and the more I looked at it, the less I liked it. I wrote to my friends and asked them what I should do, and they all said I ought not to refuse it. They said it was my plain duty to go and so, under pressure, I accepted.'[24] When he told his friends in the parish that he was leaving, he humorously described Salisbury as 'a quiet place, except on market days. They could fire a bullet down any of the streets and never hit anyone.'[25]

The Times, announcing Canon Ryle's nomination to Salisbury, stated that he was 'very far from resembling an extinct volcano. He had always kept his freedom of will and there was no time within the last twenty years when he could not have been equal to a Deanery.'[26] The *Church Times*, however, was rankled at the news and could only pour scorn on the appointment:

> We cannot understand why Mr Ryle should have thrust himself into it. It cannot have been 'a louder call' for he will receive rather less as Dean of Salisbury than he has as Vicar of Stradbroke. It would be insulting him to say he coveted the title 'Very Reverend'. It cannot be that he craved for a larger audience when he preached, and so we arrive at the only possible solution – either he is after all a Ritualist at heart, or he wanted to get into Convocation, and despaired of finding a constituency where he would have the least chance of being elected.[27]

It was a striking departure from tradition to nominate a parish clergyman, an Evangelical, and a tract-writer to a Cathedral close. When the appointment was announced many speculated as to how far the champion of Protestant and Evangelical principles would find a congenial field of service within the High Church tradition at Salisbury. Would Ryle be a success at Salisbury? Would the new Dean be able to work amicably alongside the Bishop and the Cathedral Chapter? Would he insist on making the Cathedral services a model of Protestant and Evangelical worship as he had advocated in his Cathedral reforms? Would he have the leisure time to produce a Library of Evangelical Doctrine comparable to the Library of Anglo-Catholic Theology, an ambition he once entertained? To these questions of the day we shall never know the answers for shortly after his appointment he received a summons to Downing Street. There a decision was made which closed the door to a Deanery and opened another to a Bishop's Palace.

Will you take the bishopric of Liverpool?
After receiving the telegram he caught the early train next morning up to London. He loved to tell the story of what happened:

> I never thought a man who has taken such a decided stand as a Protestant clergyman, as an Evangelical clergyman, would ever be called upon by the Prime Minister to take a different position. I always thought the quiet men, those who won't kick up a row, those who would be trusted to go quietly and gently, were chosen. But as you are aware, I was offered by Lord Beaconsfield, the Deanery of Salisbury, and the more I looked at it, the less I liked it (I felt like a dog with his tail between his legs). But although I did feel, and do feel incompatible, I felt it was my duty to go. But I was suddenly relieved by a telegram from Lord Beaconsfield asking me to go to London for an interview on a very important matter. I felt it my duty to go, and I saw Lord Sandon, the Member for Liverpool, who told me that they had sent for me for the simple purpose of asking whether I would accept the Bishopric of Liverpool? "Well," I replied, "you strike me all of a heap. I don't know what to say. It takes me unawares; it is a very serious matter. I am not so young as some people, and I am not a wealthy man to take a new bishopric." "We know all this," answered Lord Sandon. "We have made up our minds about that, the question is, will you take the Bishopric of Liverpool?" I said, "My Lord, I will go!" I thought it was a clear, plain call to duty. A variation on a saying of his evangelical hero George Whitefield then came to mind, 'I would much rather wear out as Bishop of Liverpool than rust out' as Dean of Salisbury. Well, I asked Lord Sandon several questions, which he answered, and this ended, I was taken in to Lord Beaconsfield, who gave me an interview, kind and courteous as one would expect from that wonderful statesman. He gave me excellent advice, which I hope I shall never forget. I told him I was not as young as I used to be, and I did not get younger. He took a good look at me from head to foot, and said, 'I think, sir, you have a pretty good constitution and I think you will have a few years yet.[28]

Ryle left Downing Street elated that he was going to be a bishop, and from the railway station sent a telegram to his wife telling her to expect some good news. When he arrived home in the evening he announced, 'I am the Bishop of Liverpool!' She like a good wife went and told the housekeeper, and in a few minutes all the people in the place heard about it.[29]

It was generally known that the Prime Minister, Benjamin Disraeli, Earl of Beaconsfield, disliked 'Rits and Rats,' his nickname for Ritualists and Rationalists, and Ryle was probably not his personal choice since he favoured moderate churchmen. However, with the defeat of his party in the recent General Election an appointment to the new diocese of Liverpool was urgent if it was not to fall into the hands of William Ewart Gladstone, the incoming Liberal leader and High Churchman. Disraeli was delighted to have an immediate reply from Ryle. Lord Sandon, an Evangelical, had done more than anyone to secure an Evangelical bishop for Liverpool. He was satisfied that he would now retain his Liverpool constituency and the new bishop could be relied on to strengthen the Protestant cause there. With only days before the Administration left Office, Disraeli wrote urgently to the Queen, who was on holiday in Baden Baden, saying:

> The people of Liverpool are very anxious about their new Bishop. The Tories subscribed the whole endowment and bought the "Palace". Lord Sandon says his seat for Liverpool depends upon the appointment being made by Your Majesty's present adviser. The whole city is most anxious that Your Majesty should appoint the present Dean of Salisbury, (Canon Ryle). He is known in Liverpool, and has a great following.[30]

On the face of it, Ryle became a bishop because of a remarkable episode in English politics.

Chapter Eleven

A committed man

In the closing decades of the nineteenth century Liverpool was the emporium of all the manufacturing towns of Lancashire and Yorkshire and was the largest port in the United Kingdom. Trade through the docks was double that of the London docks and served half of Britain's needs. Raw cotton, wool, tea, sugar-cane, meat, timber, and tobacco were some of the goods unloaded, while iron, steel, machinery, textiles and manufactured goods were exported to all parts of the world.[1]

The growth of Liverpool

The creation of the port and subsequent expansion of the dock system after 1851 had given employment to thousands of skilled and unskilled workers who flooded into Liverpool from all quarters of the United Kingdom. In the twenty years between 1861 and 1881 the population of Liverpool more than doubled in number; between 1881 and 1900 it increased from 553,000 to 685,000 inhabitants and several townships were brought within the city boundaries. In other towns of south-west Lancashire, Wigan, Warrington, St Helens, Widnes, and the surrounding districts, many more people were employed in the collieries, iron foundries, cotton mills, glass manufacturing and chemical works. Beyond the heavy industrial areas around Ormskirk, Sefton, Hale and Speke there was rich agricultural land and some very fine houses. Liverpool's self-confidence in the nineteenth century was expressed through its architectural grandeur. St George's Hall, constructed on the site of the old Infirmary was acclaimed as one of the finest buildings in the classical style in the whole of Europe. The fine block of buildings adjacent to St George's Hall included the William Brown Library and Museum opened in 1860, the Walker Art Gallery built in 1877 and the Picton Reference Library opened in 1879.

Liverpool had many wealthy benefactors who generously gave to improve the social, educational and cultural amenities of the town. Among these were the Earl of Derby, the Earl of Sefton, William Ewart Gladstone, leader of the Liberal party, William B. Forwood, shipowner, William Brown, cotton broker, Andrew Walker, brewer, William Rathbone, Liberal member for Liverpool, William Roscoe, banker and James A. Picton, architect. In addition to the fine libraries and galleries they built, the city had numerous drinking fountains, public lavatories, wash houses, equestrian statues and foundation stones depicting the liberality and public spirit of the wealthy benefactors. They also provided some magnificent parks, which being situated out of town were used mainly by the well-to-do. But there was a darker side to the city. Following the potato famine in Ireland in the 1840s, thousands of poor and destitute Irish came over to England seeking work and arrived through the port of Liverpool.[2] Some moved on, but the majority settled in the lower parts of the town near the docks where they existed in crowded, verminous and unhealthy conditions. Because of the overcrowding in the courts and cellars of the city, drunkenness, crime and prostitution were a constant social problem. In 1881 there were 89 brewers, 289 beer retailers and 1269 public houses. Not unrelated to these figures is the fact that there were no less than 196 pawnbrokers in the city.

A new diocese established

The rapid development of the seaport and the growth of the population on Merseyside in the second half of the century caught the church sleeping. Clergy and pastors were insufficient to minister to the human flood which swept into south-west Lancashire, and churches and chapels were not in the right places to serve the people. Liverpool was part of the ancient See of Chester, but commercially the town was far more important than Chester and many felt that the part of the diocese across the Mersey should form a separate diocese. Early in the century Chester diocese extended over the whole of Cheshire and Lancashire, West Yorkshire and the southern half of Cumberland. In 1836 Chester surrendered its Yorkshire territory and in 1847 the diocese was again sub-divided when Manchester gained ecclesiastical independence. Once more the diocese was reduced in size in 1856 when the counties of Cumberland and Westmorland were transferred to the diocese of Carlisle. The diocese of Chester, which originally had been created out of the vast diocese of Lichfield, had over the years been considerably reduced in area and now, because of the gravitation of thousands of workers to south-west Lancashire, it seemed reasonable to carve yet another diocese out of its expansive domain.[3]

After the diocese of Manchester was established, civic pride on Merseyside led to a determined effort to win support for a new episcopal See centred on Liverpool. By means of letters to the press, lobbying Members of Parliament and influencing friends in high places, churchmen sought to bring pressure to bear on the government to establish the new diocese. The Home Secretary, Richard Assheton Cross, considered this a feasible and common sense proposal and there was a confident hope that Cross would introduce the required Bill.

The first public meeting in Liverpool to discuss the project was convened by John Torr, member for Liverpool, in the Town Hall on Friday, 8 January 1875.[4] William Thomson, the Archbishop of York, had given his general approval of a further division of the diocese of Chester, and William Jacobson, the Bishop of Chester had also agreed. After a vigorous debate in a crowded meeting it was unanimously agreed that it was desirable for Liverpool to be separated from Chester, that the new diocese should be united with the diocese of Sodor and Man, and that this union would secure a large part of the endowment required. This scheme was strongly opposed by the Manx clergy and later modified. Cross proved himself a wise counsellor of Archbishops and a sympathetic advocate of episcopal extension. In March 1876 he informed the Archbishop of Canterbury that the government was ready to respond to a bill to establish several new bishoprics, and he had in mind Liverpool, Nottingham, a town in south Yorkshire, Newcastle and Birmingham.[5]

In 1877 Lord Beauchamp, the Lord Steward, introduced the first reading of the new bill in the House of Lords, proposing the establishment of four new bishoprics at Liverpool, Newcastle and Wakefield in the Province of York and Southwell in the Province of Canterbury. It was in the northern half of the country that the greatest deficiency was felt and the pressing claims of the industrial towns were given priority over south Wales and south London. In order to expedite the creation of Liverpool diocese, Earl Beauchamp informed the House of Lords that 'the people of Liverpool were anxious to have an independent See and there were liberal promises of funds which were expected to be forthcoming from subscribers as soon as the bill was passed.'[6] The new Bishopric Bill left the House of Lords with evident support, but in the Commons it was opposed at every stage by the Liberationists. 'The Liberation Society', supported mainly by Nonconformists, was opposed to the privileged position of the Established Church and worked tirelessly to liberate religion from State control. They opposed amendment after amendment in an attempt to delay the passage of the bill. Nevertheless, it was passed by sixty-two votes to twenty and the new Bishopric Act of Lord Cross was enacted on 16 August 1878.

The new dioceses created by the Act were Liverpool, founded in 1880, Newcastle in 1882, Southwell in 1884 and Wakefield in 1888. The Bishopric Act defined the borders of the new Liverpool diocese as 'the Hundred of West Derby in the County of Lancashire, with the exception of as much of the Hundred as is now in the Diocese of Manchester, and the whole of the ancient parish of Wigan'. In addition to the concentrated population in Liverpool, the area included the industrial and mining towns of Wigan and Warrington, the dock area of Bootle, the seaside resort of Southport, and the rural districts at the northern and southern ends of the diocese. Nearly two million inhabitants lived within the new diocese. Nine dioceses in England had larger populations than Liverpool, but in none except London were the inhabitants so crowded together.

Within a year of the Act being passed the people of Liverpool had raised the capital endowment of £100,000 to ensure the Bishop a minimum stipend of £3,000 a year. A fine house was purchased in Abercromby Square and designated 'the Bishop's Palace'.[7]

Securing the capital within so short a time was a great achievement and proved the enthusiasm of the people of Liverpool to have their own Bishop and diocese.

Reactions to Ryle's appointment
The announcement that Canon J. C. Ryle was to be the first Bishop of Liverpool came as a complete surprise to the majority of church people, because Ryle had recently been designated Dean of Salisbury and it was unusual to change one crown appointment for another. For weeks before the public announcement, rumours were circulating that Gladstone, the in-coming Prime minister, intended translating either Frederick Temple, Bishop of Exeter or James Fraser, Bishop of Manchester, to the new See on the Mersey. Other possibilities were Edward Bickersteth, the evangelical Dean of Lichfield or Canon James Fleming, vicar of St Michael's, Chester Square. Political motives had clearly played a role in Ryle's appointment, to which there was a mixed response. Evangelicals naturally were delighted and High Churchmen disappointed. The Rev Richard Hobson, vicar of St Nathaniel's, Windsor, Liverpool, claimed that the announcement was 'hailed with delight by every Evangelical Churchman throughout the world'.[8]

Perhaps the claim was exaggerated, but no doubt Evangelicals and Protestants in Liverpool were well satisfied. The *Record* stated that the appointment was one of the best things Lord Beaconsfield had ever done for the Church of England and that 'a better appointment could hardly have been imagined'.[9] A friendly correspondent in one newspaper described Ryle as 'one of the ablest, soundest and most practical clergyman in the Church of England'.[10] When a few weeks later Canon Ryle attended the May meeting of the Church Missionary Society in London, he received a warm and enthusiastic reception, and replied, 'I tried to hold the fort for Christ during the past 35 years in the comparative seclusion of Suffolk, and I hope by God's grace to hold the same fort in the giant city of Liverpool.'[11]

Few appointments to an important office meet with universal approval, however, and Ryle had many critics. Among them was

Lord Halifax who wrote in desperation to Henry Liddon at Oxford
on hearing the news: 'I must relieve my feelings, Canon Ryle
Bishop of Liverpool! As I told Lord Devon last night, I rejoice
beyond the expression of words that we have got rid of Lord
Beaconsfield, Lord Cairns, and all their works.... I declare I prefer
Bradlaugh to Lord Beaconsfield and I cannot say more.... I am
quite angry with Lord Devon... he is not angry about Canon Ryle.'[12]
Before any announcement was made *The Times* in prophetic mode
gave this warning: 'The clergyman who is appointed will be called
upon to prove not merely his personal competence, but the
advantages of the episcopate in general. Like many bishops he
will have his professed champions, and like many he will have
his serious antagonists.'[13] *The Church Times* was bitterly
disappointed that an Evangelical had been nominated, and asserted
that Lord Beaconsfield in 'a moment of political pique allowed
the local Orange leaders to substitute the prospective occupant of
Salisbury for the Dean of Lichfield, whom it is an open secret he
intended to promote to the See'.[14] *The Guardian* took a more
moderate view: 'Probably no man of his school of thought would
be so acceptable to High Churchmen, and there can be no doubt
that under his direction a higher tone of Churchmanship will be
realised than would have been possible under a Bishop of whom
evangelical clergy would have been jealous.... The new Bishop
has much offended ultra-evangelicals by condemning their
denunciations of clergymen who chant Psalms, turn east at the
Creed, and otherwise adopt moderate High Church practices.'[15]
Most caustic in its comments was *The Rock*, the journal of the
Protestant Low Church militants, which had been suspicious of
Ryle since he began attending the Church Congress. It denounced
Beaconsfield for nominating 'a neo-evangelical to the Protestant
See of Liverpool'.[16]

Ryle remained unmoved by acclamations or strictures alike.
The majority of his critics who knew and respected the stand he
took at the Church Congresses felt that there was no one in the
evangelical party whom they would more gladly tolerate on the
episcopal bench. On this point the *Church Times* guardedly said
of him: 'If a Puritan was to be appointed at all, we think that any

fair estimate of the leading men of the party, by whomsoever made, would have named Mr Ryle amongst the half dozen defensible nominations, along with, should we say, Dean Payne Smith, and Canons Miller, Garbett and Bernard...a man of much mother wit and shrewdness, with the gift of speaking in clear, idiomatic, forcible English, and not without some insight into the weaknesses and follies of that school to which he belongs'.[17] The position of Evangelicals in the Church in general and in Liverpool in particular was strengthened by Ryle's appointment. It was in a measure a tribute to their influence in the country long after the Evangelical Revival, as well as being a rebuff to the Ritualists.

On Wednesday 21 April, Canon Ryle took his wife and second son, Herbert, up to Liverpool, where the mayor placed his carriage at their disposal so that they could visit their new home up the hill, in 'the most aristocratic quarter of the town'. [18] He met the Bishopric Committee and addressed them at some length, telling them that he was 'a convinced Evangelical' and he held beliefs from which he could not move.

> You know my opinions. I am a committed man. It would be vain for me to make any statement at all as to what I feel with regard to the duties of a Bishop. I have nothing to withdraw or retract from the opinions I have expressed again and again. I come among you as a Protestant and Evangelical Bishop of the Church of England, but I do not come among you as a bishop of one particular party. I come with the desire to hold out the right hand to all loyal churchmen, by whatever name they are known. I am sure you would not want me to come among you as a milk and water bishop, a colourless bishop without any opinions at all.[19]

Lancashire is reputed to pride itself in respecting a man who speaks his mind and says clearly what he thinks. His frankness may at times have been mistaken for arrogance, but in his diocese he was understood and men were left in no doubt of his opinions.

> I hope at the age of 64 that I have learned to think, and never to expect to find men entirely of the same mind as myself, but I desire and expect to find loyal churchmen, and whenever I meet them I shall cordially work with them, and I confess from experience that I

have never found any difficulty in getting on comfortably and pleasantly with loyal churchmen of whatever school. It is my earnest hope that I shall never forget the principles which we contend for, the principles we fought for, too roughly sometimes, and that I shall be able to contend for the old Protestant principles of the Church of England, in which the Church was founded, in which the Church has lived, and without which the Church would entirely die. These principles I hope to maintain, kindly and consistently, but firmly, so long as God shall spare my life. I hope you will regard me as a friend to the clergy and laymen, a friend to the rich and working classes, and I cannot but express my earnest hope that when the enthronization takes place it may not be merely celebrated by a gathering of those who hold a high position in Liverpool, but that there may be a mass meeting of working men in the Philharmonic or St George's Hall, where I hope to meet them face to face, and where I can tell them that I have come to be their Bishop as well as the Bishop of the higher classes.[20]

A new bishop

The consecration of Bishop J. C. Ryle took place on St Barnabas Day, 11 June 1880. Two excursion trains from Liverpool conveyed the mayor and civic dignitaries together with hundreds of clergy and well-wishers to York for the service. The Minster was thronged and seventeen hundred people were estimated to be congregated in the nave. Canon Edward Garbett, Rector of Barcomb, and one of the Bishop's closest friends, preached on Acts 11:24, 'He was a good man and full of the Holy Ghost and faith.' Wearing a simple rochet, Ryle was consecrated by the Archbishop of York and the Bishops of Durham, Chester and Manchester.[21]

John Charles Ryle was every inch a Bishop, tall dignified, patriarchal, with a bearing as though born for high office. His face possessed a remarkable strength and dignity with a high forehead, a keen and discerning eye, and a long white beard. His University graciously conferred on him a doctorate by diploma, which pleased him, but he was not happy about other well-meaning gifts which were offered. A beautifully embroidered cope and mitre he returned immediately, saying that he had 'no intention of making a guy of himself.'[22] Another gift of a pastoral staff was courteously, but firmly declined. 'No staff for me', he wrote to the donor. 'If you send me a staff I shall lock it up in a cupboard and never see it again. A Bishop wants a Bible and no staff.' As a postscript he said he found 'no fault with other bishops who were happier with their staffs and croziers, but he was happier without them'.[23]

Before he left Stradbroke Ryle promised his parishioners that he would return for a few days after his consecration. He kept his promise and on Sunday, 20 June, attired in his episcopal robes, Ryle conducted both services in the parish church. Mrs Ryle took her customary place at the organ, and at the afternoon service the Bishop preached on Acts 20:32, 'And now, brethren, I commend you to God, and to the word of his grace, which is able to build you up, and to give you an inheritance among all them that are sanctified.' In the course of his sermon, he said: 'The old street down which I walked so often, the school which I often visited...my own little garden where I had quiet walks and communion with God, my own beautiful church in which I have often seen so many faces – all these things I am about to leave and leave for ever. I go, called by God, to the noise, bustle, smoke and confusion of a great seaport town.... Pray that I may be kept faithful, that I may be a true bishop of the reformed Church, and that I may not be a Popish bishop, or so broad that men cannot tell what views I hold, or so narrow as to exclude everyone from an interest in Christ, except my friends.'[24] On the Thursday evening in the Corn Exchange the parishioners presented farewell gifts of a silver flower vase to the Bishop and to Mrs Ryle a photograph album. The clergy of Norwich diocese also presented the Bishop with a beautiful set of communion plate.

Bishop Ryle's enthronement took place on 1 July in St Peter's pro-Cathedral in Liverpool. Vast crowds thronged the streets to witness the civic and church dignitaries process from the Town Hall to the Cathedral, and the bells of the churches in the city rang out in acclamation. The loudest cheers were reserved for the carriage carrying Bishop Ryle and the Dean of Chester. In the Cathedral Ryle was led to the Bishop's throne on the north side of the chancel. Because Bishop Jacobson of Chester was indisposed, Dean Howson preached on Acts 5:20: 'Go and stand in the temple and speak to the people all the words of this Life.' During the service the choir and Cathedral clergy turned east for the Creed, but many in the congregation noticed that the Bishop did not turn, and in fact it seemed that he deliberately moved forward so that it could be seen that he did not turn. After the enthronement service the Bishop was heard to say to some of his friends, 'I have changed my clothes, but I have not changed my coat nor my principles.'[25]

That evening the Lord Mayor gave a reception for the Bishop and Mrs Ryle in the Town Hall, at which the Bishop spoke of the opportunities for evangelism in the city. 'There is a vast work to be done in the great city of Liverpool, and in many parts of the new diocese, but I firmly believe that there is so much to be done by going back to apostolic principles and working as the old apostles worked by trying to send the right men to preach the old Gospel, of which St Paul was not ashamed, when he went to the great city of Rome. If St Paul was not afraid nor ashamed to go to the great city of Rome, how much cause have I not to be ashamed when I come to the city of Liverpool, where so much has been done, where so much is being done at the present day, and where so many clergy and laymen are ready to cooperate in every possible way.'[26]

His first tasks

Immediately after his consecration the Bishop set about the task of organising and administrating the new diocese. He had no illusions about the undertaking and was determined to create a strong diocese, resolutely evangelical in character and established on Scriptural and Reformed principles. Out of his wide experience and active participation in the affairs of the Church at national level he was confident that he could work amicably with all loyal parties within the Church. The *Church Times* expected him to fail. It wrote:

> No Evangelical bishop named in our times has been an administrative success. The downfall of the Low Church party began by the nomination of Dr John Bird Sumner to the Primacy, and was particularly hastened by the universal failure of the Shaftesbury promotions under Lord Palmerston, Wigram, Baring, Waldegrave,

Pelham, Bickersteth, Jeune, each and all proved incapable. Ryle, therefore, comes to his new work with all the precedents against his proving a success, and we must add, without any favourable report of his organising or pastoral powers, which are not likely to take a new spring at his time of life.[27]

The next twenty years were to prove this pessimistic view mistaken.

One of his first decisions was to place the diocese under the oversight of two experienced clergy. He appointed J. W. Bardsley, a friend and evangelical, his Domestic Chaplain and first Archdeacon of Warrington; the octogenarian J. H. Jones continued to serve as Archdeacon of Liverpool. He also appointed a number of honorary canons in order of seniority, which included High, Broad and Evangelical churchmen, but not Anglo-Catholics. Because of an 'unhappy oversight of Parliament' the Bishop had only four livings in his absolute patronage, and frequently he regretted that he had so little to offer worthy men for faithful service. Gradually, however, the number of benefices in which the Bishop had a voice in the appointments increased as vacancies occurred on various trustees. Ryle was familiar with the cut and thrust of debate in the Church Congress, and he initiated the creation of a Diocesan Conference of clergy and laity which met annually in St George's Hall. Diocesan Conferences were a recent innovation in the Church and not all bishops were in favour. Bishop Wilberforce declined to call a conference for many years, maintaining that 'when all goes well and smoothly, the laity will say, "How well we did it! If it should fail, they will say, "What a mess the Bishop made of it!" '[28] Ryle had no uneasy fears about chairing an assembly of clergy and representative laity. He was an eloquent platform speaker and a lively debater, and the Conference gave him the opportunity of keeping in touch with his clergy and expressing his views. He insisted that 'a bishop was never meant to be a figure-head, and an honorary member of all schools of thought. He ought to have decided opinions, and on suitable occasions to express them.'[29] On occasions when he did not please or persuade his audience, he would say that he was 'a big man getting on for sixteen stone, and he could not help treading

on people's toes'.[30] He had a broad back and was not the man to
take the 'huff' at being treated 'ruff'. Defeats were taken in his
stride, 'When a man gets to sixty-four years of age,' he would
say, 'his skin gets thick.'[31]

The Bishop was a pastor at heart. Every Tuesday morning it
was his custom to attend at the Diocesan Registrar's office, where
the clergy knew they could meet the Bishop without appointments
to discuss any aspect of parochial work and seek his advice.
Incumbents were ready to welcome the new bishop and he received
many invitations to preach in Liverpool and throughout the diocese.
He took time to consider where he and his wife might worship
when he was free from preaching engagements. The imposing
parish church of St Catherine in Abercromby Square was just
across the gardens from the Bishop's Palace, but he felt he would
not be happy with the ceremonial worship there. One Sunday
evening in March 1881, he preached on behalf of the Irish Church
Missions at St Nathaniel's Church, Upper Parliament Street, after
which nearly four hundred communicants partook of the Lord's
Supper. In the vestry after the service the Bishop told Richard
Hobson, the vicar: 'I make much of hands, and I conclude that
five out of every six of your communicants are working people.
St Nathaniel's is an answer to those who say the Church of England
is not suited for working people.' Then he added, ' I wish to preach
in this church every six months, only give me sufficient notice.' [32]
From that time on, the Bishop and his family made St Nathaniel's
their spiritual home. Two pews were assigned for the use of the
Bishop's servants, and Hobson offered his own pew to the Bishop
and his family. When free from episcopal duties he loved to attend
and participate in the simple, hearty service, and hear the pure
gospel preached by a faithful minister.

Chapter Twelve

The first and foremost business

Many civic and church leaders in Liverpool thought when the new diocese was created that it should have a great Cathedral worthy of a great seaport. In all the post-Reformation dioceses except Truro, cathedral status had been conferred on the parish church in the metropolitan city. In Truro the parish church proved too small and a new cathedral was built and consecrated in 1910. Although Liverpool had many fine churches, there were none that could accommodate all the proposed cathedral activities with ease.

The Bishopric Act had designated St Peter's Church as the pro-cathedral and mother church of the diocese. It stood in a prominent position in the centre of the town on Church Street, a busy main thoroughfare, and was surrounded by a pleasant churchyard. Inside there was seating for more than twelve hundred worshippers. A brass lectern for the Bible was presented to the cathedral by the clergy of Norwich to mark Canon Ryle's elevation to the Episcopate. However, St Peter's was not really suitable as a cathedral church, and Ryle disliked it intensely, describing it as 'the most unpretentious structure either in England or Wales that can boast Cathedral dignity'.[1] He proposed some improvements, but it was generally felt that Liverpool, which proudly claimed to be the second city in the Kingdom, should have a grand new Cathedral.

The priority – a cathedral?

After his consecration, Bishop Ryle told a gathering in York that he wished to see a new Cathedral in Liverpool, and was confident that the merchant princes of the city would finance it. In his Primary Visitation Charge delivered in October 1881, he spoke of 'the want of a Cathedral in Liverpool'. However, he doubted whether it would be built during his lifetime, as there were far more urgent demands in the diocese: 'I only know that my first and foremost business is to provide for preaching the Gospel, to souls now entirely neglected, whom no cathedral would touch.'[2] In his paper 'Can the Church reach the masses?', he admitted that there was a lot of church work going on in the diocese, additional services, weekday meetings, church bazaars, popular concerts, evening recreations, but it was not vital Christianity. It was not Apostolic ministry. When he went about Liverpool on preaching engagements he saw vast numbers of working men, who 'to all appearances live and die "without God".'[3] He was anxious that they should be reached with the good news, and believed 'the Church ought to provide facilities for an organized system of aggressive evangelism in her large parishes',[4] for 'there is far less preaching of the whole Gospel than there ought to be'.[5]

In spite of Ryle's ambivalence about it, the next Diocesan Conference in 1882 passed a resolution that Liverpool should have a new Cathedral. For the next few years there was something of 'a Cathedral fever' in the city.[6] It was agreed that it should be built on a scale befitting the capital city of the diocese and a great port which annually received thousands of travellers. The problem was to find a suitable site near to the city centre. So 'the battle of the sites' began. In all, twenty-three sites were considered by a large cathedral committee, which found it difficult to reach any agreement. Weary of the debates, the Bishop said in his second Charge, 'How many times that committee has met, and how much anxious discussion has been devoted to the matter, I will not attempt to say.' Eventually a decision was reached, though it was not unanimous, and the Liverpool Cathedral Act was passed on 25 June 1885, to erect a new Cathedral on St John's churchyard to the west of St George's Hall.

After the Cathedral Act received the royal assent, the committee needed to consider appointing an architect. They invited several notable church architects to submit plans, and awarded the work to William Emerson. He had tried to adapt his design to the spirit of the age by including cupolas and domes in his building.[7] Emerson confidently predicted that when the Cathedral was completed the acoustic qualities would be perfect and the congregation would be able to hear the preacher in every part of the building. The winning design, however, did not please everyone, and even the committee had second thoughts. A new competition was hastily arranged and Emerson was asked to submit another plan, but he refused on the ground that it was unfair 'to ask the winner of a race to compete a second time because the committee chose to change the shape of the cup'.[8]

The Cathedral Act of 1885 prescribed the powers under the Act should be exercised before 1 June 1888, but when no agreement could be reached over the plans the Act was allowed to lapse, and the project was left in abeyance. Speaking with his usual frankness about the breakdown of the enterprise, the Bishop admitted that 'the position of the scheme is humbling after such a large expenditure of time, talk and controversy, and not a little money on the subject. I am not surprised that churchmen at a distance who do not understand Liverpool, speak rather sceptically about us.'[9]

Ryle was known to consider cathedrals and cathedral clergy the weakest and most vulnerable part of the Established Church, and he had proposed reforms for improving the image of 'sleepy cathedrals'. Nevertheless, the failure of the project was a genuine disappointment to him. Sir William Forwood, MP, and a member of the cathedral committee, felt the Bishop himself was largely responsible for the half-hearted response to the project. 'The Bishop did not help the cause, for though he was anxious that a cathedral should be built, he frequently expounded his opinion, both in public and in private, that additional churches and mission halls could be more useful.'[10] This gave the impression throughout the diocese that the Bishop did not rate a new cathedral among his priorities.

The priority – more churches

The Bishop had carefully surveyed the situation since arriving in the city, and addressing the Diocesan Conference in 1885, he said:

> Around Liverpool, miles and miles of eighteen-pound houses are continually springing up. These houses are occupied as soon as they are built, and the difficulty of providing means of grace for the inhabitants is simply appalling. Without places of worship provided

by the Church of England, and without pastoral visitation, it is useless
to be surprised if the dwellers in these new districts are lost to the
Church altogether, and may never attend any place of worship at all.
Until the means of grace and living agents of the gospel are at least
doubled, Liverpool will never cease to be branded, blamed and held
up to public notice, as it was last year by Mr Gladstone, the High
Churchman, as a city remarkable for its numbers of non-worshippers
and Sabbath-breakers.

If the building of a new cathedral worthy of the city had to be
postponed for the time being it was only that the more urgent
need of more churches might be met. After all, the Bishop
concluded, 'a Cathedral is a luxury, and not a necessity. If this
thing is to be done, it will be done well.' In his Primary Charge
Ryle had surveyed the history of church building in the area
occupied by the new diocese and noted that John Bird Sumner,
Bishop of Chester from 1828-1848, had initiated the building and
restoration of many churches. But when serious discussions began
later in the century about a further division of the diocese, church
building across the Mersey had been curtailed. Ryle now proposed
setting up a 'Twelve Churches Fund', and asked the wealthy
citizens, shipping magnates and rich merchants of Liverpool, to
meet the cost of erecting and endowing these churches. William
Groves agreed with the Bishop's policy and gave a generous gift
of £10,000 since 'it was more important to provide pastoral
superintendence and spiritual instruction to those perishing
multitudes than to erect a material building, however splendid, to
justify the tastes and wishes of a few'.[11] The Bishop was
disappointed at the immediate response to his appeal, but reviewing
the work a few years later he observed with pride that since the
founding of the diocese twenty new churches had been opened,
three were in the course of erection, and many more were being
renovated and restored. In addition, there were fifty licensed
mission rooms, three of them in the charge of missionary curates.
The number of clergy had also risen and now there were two
hundred incumbents and almost as many assistant clergy in the
diocese.

Not all the churches built in the Ryle period were evangelical foundations, and a small number were built by private patrons whose sympathies were with either the Broad or High Church traditions. High Church benefactors preferred to build churches in the neo-Gothic style, while Evangelicals adopted a plainer design without elaboration and ornamentation.[12] In some parishes Ryle was happy to licence a temporary 'iron church', such as those manufactured locally by Isaac Dixon at his Windsor Iron Works. An advertisement described these structures as 'tasteful in design, economical, durable, made of the best materials, and erected in the most careful manner'.[13] The 'tin tabernacles' as they were affectionately called, were considerably cheaper than a brick building and could be easily taken down when the parish had money to build 'a proper church'. Roman Catholics and Nonconformists did not lag behind the Anglicans in providing more accommodation for their people. Between 1881 and 1900 Roman Catholic chapels in the city increased from 23 to 35 and Nonconformist places of worship from 139 to 179.

Ryle's episcopate was a fine achievement of church building. A church historian concluded that 'Ryle was a great builder of churches, and deserved praise rather than blame for having preferred finding church accommodation in Liverpool to pushing on too rapidly the scheme for building a Cathedral'.[14] A leader writer in the Liverpool Courier, said of the Bishop at the close of his episcopate: 'If he did not build a cathedral, he did something better and more practical, he encouraged the building of churches and mission-rooms, and his reign will be memorable for the completeness with which the spiritual needs of the populous districts have been covered.'[15]

Church attendances
In the second half of the nineteenth century there was intense interest throughout the country in the level of attendances at places of worship. The first and only official religious census had been taken in 1851 in connection with the decennial census in England and Wales. Its figures revealed that in Liverpool only one in ten of the inhabitants attended church on Census Sunday, of which the largest number went to Roman Catholic services. Ever since

the bill for Roman Catholic emancipation in 1829, fears of 'papal aggression' had strengthened Protestant opposition as Catholics became more assertive in their claims. This concern seemed justified when successive religious surveys revealed that the Roman Catholic Church was continuing to grow in numerical strength. Nonconformists were also interested in the census returns since they believed that statistically Nonconformists were as strong as Anglicans, although the census showed them slightly behind. In Liverpool Nathaniel Caine, a local Nonconformist, organized a census in 1853 to prove that Dissent was not a minority religion. The Liberationists in Parliament made capital out of the census returns and insisted that since the Church of England was no longer the Church of the people it should be disestablished.

On two Sundays in the autumn of 1881 the Liverpool Daily Post organized a religious census in the city. Notification was sent in advance to all the churches and chapels stating that a teller would attend the main service on Sunday morning, 16 October to count the attendance. The results were tabulated under denominations and individual churches and published in later editions of the newspaper. The survey revealed some interesting facts. There was accommodation for 32.2 per cent of the population and 26.5 per cent attended a place of worship at least once on a Sunday. It also showed that the majority of Anglican churches were far too large for the numbers attending. The largest Anglican attendance was 1,000 worshippers at St Chrysostom's church, Everton, and the largest Roman Catholic was recorded at St Francis Xavier church, where a congregation of 1,554 attended the main Mass of the day.

The accuracy of the returns was questioned, mainly by Nonconformist ministers, who argued that their people were mainly working-class and usually went to the evening services. The editor of the *Daily Post* replied that the figures were true in substance and that the enumerators appointed by the newspaper were less likely to exaggerate numbers than church-nominated tellers. Bishop Ryle was naturally disturbed when he read the results, though he was not surprised. He treated the findings as a challenge to the diocese to be more zealous in the work of evangelism. He believed that in a diocese where Nonconformity was so strong no more than one third of the population could be classified as belonging to the Church of England. Preaching in the pro-Cathedral prior to the second census in the evening of 6 November, he insisted that a count of church attendances on a Sunday morning in a great seaport was hardly a fair test of Christian allegiance. However, he was confident that given more preachers of the gospel and an ample number of mission rooms, a census taken five years later would reveal vastly different results.

The census conducted on Sunday evening, 6 November, showed that, with the exception of the Roman Catholics and Presbyterians, all the denominations had larger attendences at the evening services. The Church of England had an appreciable increase. The largest Church of England congregation was 1,211 at St Andrew's, Renshaw Street, with 1,196 at St Nathaniel's, Windsor, where the Bishop was preaching. The largest attendance of the day, 1,280, was again at St Francis Xavier.

Canon Abraham Hume, a sociologist, was critical of the newspaper's method of enumeration and the accuracy of its findings. He proposed to the Diocesan Conference that the diocese should conduct its own credal census. Each incumbent should appoint enumerators to visit house to house in the parish and glean the religious affiliation of each family. Hume believed that such a census would prove that the Church of England was stronger than the Daily Post survey suggested.[16] The Conference gave Hume the go ahead, and from this survey Hume concluded that the Church of England had a professed allegiance of 53% of the population in Liverpool, 'that the working-classes were not lost to the Church, and that nine-tenths of the population were well-disposed toward the Church.'[17]

Ryle accepted Dr Hume's report with some reservations, recognizing the weakness of a credal survey. In an effort to correct misconceptions and ascertain facts, the Bishop decided to initiate his own survey, selecting Trinity Sunday, 4 June 1882. The appointed date was kept secret until a few days before, when the clergy received a confidential letter from the Bishop informing them of the census and the method of emumeration. They were forbidden to bring pressure to bear on their parishioners to attend church, a criticism made by secularists against earlier surveys. The clergy were instructed to count the number of worshippers as they left the service. The numbers were to be treated as confidential, and only the collective figures would be published. The weather was inclement on the appointed day and undoubtedly affected the attendances, yet nearly 166,000 worshippers attended Church of England services in the diocese that day. 189 churches provided two services and 65 had three services. 59 churches offered early morning Communion services when over 1,200 communicants attended.

Ten years after its first survey, the Daily Post organized another church census on 18 October 1891, and published its findings a week later. Since the last census the population of Liverpool had risen from 553,000 to almost 630,000. 42 new churches and chapels had been opened, but eleven of these for various reasons were closed on census Sunday. The survey revealed that the Church of England alone among the denominations had increased attendances, while the Presbyterians, Baptists and Unitarians all showed a fall. The latest returns confirmed that the swing toward evening attendances continued and that the best attended churches were generally situated in upper and middle-class neighbourhoods. For the first time the census gave some indication of the strength of the Anglican parties in Liverpool: Forty-nine churches Evangelical, thirteen Moderate, eleven High Church, and eleven Advanced High or Ritualist.

The usual spate of critical letters appeared in the press following the publication of the census results. Among the correspondents was Mr Gladstone, a son of Liverpool and a devout churchman, who naturally took a personal interest in the religious life of the city. He expressed his profound dismay that the Church of England was so poorly attended in Liverpool and felt that the Bishop could do more to improve attendances. Ryle felt that Gladstone's criticisms could not pass unanswered, and wrote a strongly worded reply to the editor of the Liverpool *Daily Post*:

I frankly admit that the general results of your census are painful and unsatisfactory – only sixty-three thousand morning worshippers out of six hundred thousand people. I do not wonder that Mr Gladstone in his letter last Saturday calls it 'a dismal spectacle'. But it does not surprise me at all. Ever since I came to Liverpool as the first Protestant Bishop, ten years ago, I have repeatedly told the public that the Established Church in our city is like a ship quite undermanned, our parishes and parochial districts, as a general rule, are far too large. That eminent Scot divine, Dr Chalmers, said long ago that a town district of three thousand, five hundred souls, allowing for all denominations, would find work enough for one minister of the Establishment, if he would only do his duty as a preacher and pastor. Think of that, and look at Liverpool. We want more sub-division, more churches and more clergy. I gladly acknowledge the good work done by other churches and denominations. Where should we be without it? But I unhesitatingly assert that there is room enough and work enough for twice as many churches and clergymen in Liverpool as we have now.[18]

Living agents

On arriving in Liverpool Ryle had seen that the diocese was seriously undermanned and that an increase in the number of 'living agents', as he called them, was an urgent necessity. He firmly believed that the first and foremost business of the Church was to proclaim the Gospel, and for this ministry more men were required. He was struck by the sharp contrast in clergy numbers between Liverpool and his former diocese of Norwich. In Norwich more than 1,100 clergy ministered to 660,000 parishioners, but Liverpool diocese with over one million people had only 300 clergy. The Bishop did everything in his power to encourage ordinands to serve in the working class and industrial parishes of his diocese. He was a founder member of Wycliffe Hall Oxford, opened in 1877, and was also closely associated with Ridley Hall, Cambridge, a similar evangelical training college established in 1881. He used his influence in both to interest men in taking their titles in northern parishes. On the last occasion he was a select preacher at Oxford, shortly after his consecration, he said that 'he hoped some of his hearers would come to the new diocese of Liverpool'.[19] Ordination lists show that each year several men from Oxbridge colleges were ordained in the diocese, along with a constant number from St Aidan's Theological College, Birkenhead.

In addition to successfully completing their courses at University or theological college, the Bishop required his ordinands to sit the Deacons examination in the diocese, and he appointed three examining chaplains to supervise the admission of ordinands. H. C. G. Moule, Principal of Ridley Hall, Cambridge, C. H. Waller, tutor and later Principal of St John's, Highbury, and H. James, vicar of Livermore, Bury St Edmunds were all men of strong evangelical convictions.[20] Ryle took great care over his selection of men for the ministry. He set the highest standards and did not hesitate to refuse to ordain any man who fell short. In a letter to his son, Herbert, he wrote that he had been obliged to reject three men for Priest's Orders because of 'utter ignorance and inefficiency', and two deacons for 'unsound doctrine.'[21] At the Advent ordination in 1884 no less than six candidates were refused ordination on the advice of the examiners. Following Bishop Sumner's example at Winchester, Ryle invited candidates awaiting ordination to stay a few days at the Bishop's Palace, during which time they were interviewed by his chaplain. Each evening the Bishop addressed the young men from a large Bible on the dining-room table, and exhorted them to study the Scriptures daily: 'Read your Bible, young men, read your Bible', he would say.[22] Ordinations generally took place on Advent and Trinity Sundays in St Peter's pro-Cathedral, and after the service the deacon and priest with the highest marks in the examinations received a handsome variorum Bible from the Bishop. During the period of his episcopate Ryle ordained 553 deacons and 549 priests.

To help foster good relations with his clergy, to get to know them better and encourage them in their ministry, he called all the clergy in the diocese whom he had ordained presbyter to an annual gathering at St Nathaniel's Church, Windsor. No one was more aware than he of the incessant demands upon a clergyman's time and energy in a working-class parish, and the need for ministers to meet together periodically for prayer and spiritual encouragement. They came to look forward to the 'Bishop's Priests

Party', as the gathering became affectionately known among the younger clergy.[23] Canon Richard Hobson, the genial vicar of St Nathaniel's, whose ministry in that slum parish was so remarkable, records that the annual gathering always began in church with a service of Holy Communion, administered by the Bishop and assisted by the vicar. After the service the clergy adjourned to St Nathaniel's Jubilee Hall to hear addresses from leading evangelical speakers on some aspect of the minister's life and work. These gatherings continued annually until 1899, when prior to his resignation from the See, the Bishop told his clergy that 'it might be the last time' he would be with them. [24]

One of the glaring anomalies in the Church of England requiring urgent reform was the discrepancy in clergy stipends. Some clergy in small ancient parishes received far higher stipends than clergy in huge working-class parishes. Many stipends in Liverpool diocese were appallingly low and Ryle was determined to raise them. Thomas Chalmers had initiated a fund in the Church of Scotland which proved successful in raising the stipends of Presbyterian ministers, and Ryle in 1891 decided to open a similar Sustentation Fund in his diocese. Gradually the fund built up and raised the stipends of many poor and needy clergy. The aim was to pay incumbents with less than 5,000 parishioners a stipend of £200 a year, and those with more than 5,000 inhabitants an additional £35. By 1905 the diocese had raised clergy stipends in the towns to £300 or £275 with a parsonage, and clergy in rural parishes £275 pounds or £250 with a house. Unbeneficed clergy often received less than £100 a year, and the greater part of this was met by the incumbent out of his own stipend, though some grants were made by the Additional Curates Society and the Church Pastoral-Aid Society. The need of suitable residences for clergy and their families was an acute problem in Liverpool and other large towns, and the Bishop gave permission, where there was no suitable accommodation available, for the incumbents of a down-town church to live in a better district outside the parish. These clergy who travelled in to carry out their parochial duties were known with good humour and affection as 'tram-car clergy' by all Liverpudlians.

Before he became a bishop Ryle had campaigned for a greater use of the laity in the parishes. He believed that Christian laity were a potential asset whom the clergy overlooked and underused. They needed to be challenged to be more active and given the opportunity to be more useful in the service of Christ. He complained that:

> A mischievous habit of leaving all religion to the parson of the parish had overspread the country, and the bulk of Churchmen seem to think that they have nothing to do with the Church but to receive the benefits of her means of grace, while they contribute nothing in the way of personal active exertion to promote efficiency....Their only idea is to be perpetually receiving, but never doing anything at all. They have taken their seats in the right train, and they are only to sit quiet, while the clerical engine draws them to heaven, perhaps half asleep.[25]

In his first major address to the diocese in 1881, he asserted that 'The first thing needed is not buildings, but living men, men ordained, if you can get them, men not ordained if you can get no other agents; but in any case, men who have the grace of God and the love of souls in their hearts.' To assist the clergy in their work of evangelism and pastoral care he established the Liverpool Scripture Readers Society, whose members were licensed by the Bishop to lead services in mission rooms, superintend Sunday Schools and visit the sick, and whom he described as 'the right hand of the clergy'.[26] He also set up the Voluntary Lay Helpers Association in 1882. Each helper was admitted into the association at a special service in the pro-Cathedral and was listed as an accredited lay worker in his own parish. His duties included house to house visiting, sick visiting, speaking in working men's clubs and conducting mission services. By 1887 there were some five hundred 'Helpers' in the parishes. There was a place, too, for women helpers, and along with Mrs Ryle, the Bishop initiated the Ladies Parochial and Domestic Mission, in which a group of dedicated women visited the tenements and courts of Liverpool's 'down and outs', ministering spiritual sustenance and material comforts to families where the need and poverty were greatest.

Chapter Thirteen

Who breaks the peace?

The long controversy over the proposed site of the new Cathedral was not the only dispute to disturb the peace of the diocese. Ryle disapproved of the growing number of extreme High Churchmen entering the ministry. He considered them to be doctrinally unsound and in breach of the law by their ceremonialism, and it was not long before he found himself at odds with more than one incumbent in the diocese.

Anglo-Catholic trends

The Catholic trend in Anglican worship in the nineteenth century arose out of the Church teaching of Pusey, Newman and Keble, the founders of the Oxford Movement. Though the first generation of Tractarians showed no enthusiasm for elaborate ritual and were far more interested in the doctrine of the Church, Ministry and Sacraments, in the second half of the century the younger generation of Anglo-Catholics became fascinated by innovations in worship. They loved eucharistic vestments, lace and fine millinery, lighted candles and solemn processions. They adopted the eastward position at the mass, set up stations of the Cross and erected confessional boxes in their churches. They insisted that they were loyal members of the Church of England, intent only on restoring to the Church the ancient ceremonials and ornaments in use before the Reformation.[1] Ryle, however, discerned that the fine embroidered vestments and rich ceremonial concealed error and false doctrine, and began warning Evangelicals of the danger.

Not only Evangelicals but many Broad and High Churchmen protested against the excessive ceremonial Anglo-Catholics were introducing into church services. Some bishops tried unsuccessfully to restrain the more demonstrative ritualists until finally recourse had to be made to the Church Courts under the Church Discipline Act of 1840 in an attempt to bring the extremists to order. The recalcitrant clergy, however, refused to recognise the lay authority of the Courts and for the most part ignored the judgments of the Dean of Arches.

Queen Victoria was most unhappy about the increase in ritualism and wrote to Archbishop Tait urging him to take every measure available to curb Anglo-Catholicism in the Established Church. 'It is clear,' she told Tait, 'that... liberties taken and the defiance shown by the Clergy of the High Church and Ritualist Party is so great that something must be done to check it, and prevent its continuation.'[2] In support of the Protestant pressure in Parliament public rallies were held in the major cities and scores of letters were written to the press. Eventually Tait drafted a Bill which, after undergoing several amendments in a more Protestant direction, was passed in 1874 as the Public Worship Regulation Act. However the Act proved powerless and ritualism continued to gain a hold in the parishes and in every diocese.

The controversy over St Margaret's
Bishop Ryle had been in the diocese only a matter of weeks when his attention was drawn to a report in the Liverpool Courier of 21 July, 1880. This described a service in St Margaret's Church, Toxteth, in which lighted candles were flickering on the altar, incense was used and a cope and biretta worn by the celebrating priest. St Margaret's had always followed the Catholic tradition and Bishop Jacobson, then Bishop of Chester, had tolerated the ritualistic practices in spite of complaints from the Church Association and individual Protestants. Eventually the vicar, Charles Parnell, had been forced to resign and the church appointed the curate, Bell-Cox, in his stead. He, however, continued the ceremonial and ritual of his predecessor. Evangelicals considered that the ritual at St Margaret's contravened the so-called Ornaments Rubric in the Prayer Book, but extreme High Churchmen maintained that the use of vestments and 'other ornaments' and the restoration of the Catholic ceremonial did not negate lawful authority. Ryle found the rubric an obstacle rather than a help and told the Diocesan Conference in 1883 that as it stood it was 'the mother of all ecclesiastical mischief...which nobody can explain

as to satisfy all. Until that rubric is swept away, and replaced by a plain, intelligible substitute, there will be no peace in the Church of England.'

The Bishop could not ignore the newspaper report, however. He immediately wrote to the Rev. J. Bell-Cox, the priest in charge of St Margaret's, inviting him to 'the Palace... for some friendly conversations'.[3] When they met on 31 July the Bishop made no suggestion that he was failing in his pastoral duties or lacking in devotion. Rather he quietly appealed to Bell-Cox to give up his ritualistic practices for the sake of peace in the Church. Such a plea for moderation within the limits of the Church's law set the standard for the whole of Ryle's episcopate. Bell-Cox, however, would give no such undertaking. In August he replied in a letter to the Bishop, who was on holiday in Keswick, stating that his churchwardens maintained that:

> Ever since St Margaret's was consecrated, the full Ritual prescribed by the Church of England in the Ornaments Rubric, and elsewhere, has been in use, and since the ritual complained of had been practised at St Margaret's for the past eleven years and the ornaments had been presented by members of the congregation the Wardens felt it would be difficult to persuade the congregation to consent to any change in the accustomed ritual (especially as during the late Episcopate they had not been required to deprive themselves of it), and it would be, if not necessary, at least highly desirable to set before them some reasons for making the change at this moment.[4]

Bell-Cox received short-shrift from the Bishop when he returned home from holiday:

> The question I want you to consider is not what your Congregation likes or has been accustomed to, but what is legal.... As I told you in our interview, my attention was called to a paragraph in a Liverpool newspaper stating that, on a public occasion, in your Church, incense was used, lighted candles were on the Communion Table, when not wanted for Divine Service, and a cope and biretta were worn by the officiating minister. Now all these things have been declared illegal, and for that reason, I asked you to call upon me, and requested that they might be discontinued in future.[5]

The question of legality, however, was not one that Bell-Cox and his congregation cared to recognise. In company with other Anglo-Catholics he believed that the Queen's Court of Law and the Privy Council had no spiritual authority and they refused to acknowledge their decisions. Ryle on the other hand contended that though the laws and legal decisions may be imperfect in the eyes of some, as long as they are not repudiated or reversed they must be obeyed, otherwise there will be nothing left but chaos and confusion. 'The Court of Appeal,' he insisted, 'is at present the only authorized exponent in ecclesiastical causes, and as long as it is so, its decisions are the law of the land. Within the limits of the law I will not interfere, but you cannot expect a chief officer of the Church to allow the law to be broken without interfering.'[6] Ryle always respected the authority of law. He had studied civil law in London, administered it as a magistrate in Macclesfield, and now as a Bishop it was his duty to uphold the law in the Church.

Correspondence passed between the Bishop and Bell-Cox in which Ryle emphasized that since the Bishop had to obey the law of the Church it was reasonable to expect the clergy to do the same. Moreover, he reminded Bell-Cox that at his ordination he had promised obedience to his bishop in all things lawful. On this point, Bell-Cox's reply was brief and polemical: 'The obedience I have promised to pay the bishop is a canonical obedience, due only when acting in his spiritual capacity as bishop. Whenever a bishop takes action simply on the ground of a secular decision, the validity of which we cannot recognise, we are bound to repudiate the bishop's action.'[7]

The Bishop sent all his communications through his legal adviser and for the sake of peace in the diocese he requested that they be treated with the strictest confidence. However, news of the rift between the Bishop and the priest leaked out in a paragraph of the Liverpool Mercury and was immediately picked up by *The Church Times*. Against the Bishop's expressed wishes Bell-Cox then published the full details of the altercation in the church's own monthly magazine. Ritualists believed that their cause would be strengthened by the publication of such correspondence, as it would be seen that the accused priests were being unjustly persecuted for the faith. Bell-Cox was taken to task by the Bishop for breaking confidence, and now the controversy became public gossip. The ritual continued without restraint and Ryle was at a loss what to do next. The situation had reached stalemate.

Meanwhile, a reporter on *The Protestant Standard* attended a service at the church and concluded that 'the place is now as perfect a condition as it need be to receive the Pope's blessing. Enjoying peace and quiet and having no fear of being disturbed by Bishop Ryle, the affairs at St Margaret's are progressing most favourably in the Romeward direction....' This conclusion was stated most succinctly by someone who wrote on the church notice board, 'St Mary's station, change here for Rome.'[8] There is no denying that Bell-Cox was a dedicated clergyman with a passionate zeal for the work of the church, but he was ostracized by many of his fellow clergy and ridiculed by every Protestant in the city. Feelings ran high among those opposed to Anglo-Catholicism, and once Bell-Cox bitterly complained that he had been spat upon as he was passing St James' cemetery.

Matters came to a head in February 1885 when James Hakes, a Liverpool consultant and chairman of the local branch of the Church Association (a Protestant organisation established in 1865 to maintain the Reformed and Protestant character of the Church of England) wrote to the Bishop listing thirteen ceremonial acts in the services at St Margaret's, all of which had been declared illegal by the Church Courts, and threatening a prosecution if the illegalities were not stopped. Ryle again summoned Bell-Cox to his office and warned him that unless he curtailed the ritual at St Margaret's, he had no alternative but to allow the case to go forward to the court.[9] Bell-Cox stood his ground, 'because', he said, 'it would naturally appear that I yield, now that I am threatened by a prosecution by a mere outsider, to what for five years I have refused to one who asked it of me as "my Bishop and my friend".'[10]

Ryle was not in favour of litigation in such cases. In a debate on the Ornaments Rubric in the House of York Convocation in April 1881, he had said that 'prosecution in the present state of things would do more harm than good'. In one of his letters to

Bell-Cox, he had written, 'If you suppose that I am going to institute legal proceedings against you, you are quite mistaken.'[11] In a last effort to maintain peace in the diocese he sought the advice of the Archbishop of Canterbury. After the interview Archbishop Benson wrote in his diary how troubled Ryle appeared over the controversy,

> He was very earnest and oppressed by it, seems to have tried honestly his best to avoid it. But these people like B [Bell-Cox], who are excellent in the theory of obedience, never obey a bishop. The Bishop had behaved magnanimously in consecrating a church for them. Without any sense of honour, the man immediately adopts all manner of illegal practices.[12]

Reluctantly Ryle allowed the law to take its course. On 6 March 1885 he issued his Request of Letters to Lord Penzance, Judge of the Chancery Court of York, delegating his power of jurisdiction to the ecclesiastical court. He was aware that his action would please some and anger others, though he did not realise at the time how bitter the controversy would become. As a bishop he had the right of veto, giving him authority to halt a church prosecution. In those dioceses where Anglo-Catholic clergy were prosecuted under the Public Worship Regulation Act, most bishops exercised the veto. Ryle however chose not to use it since he believed he had no right to stop *in limine*, the application of a complainant seeking justice He felt that the use of the veto struck at the root of the first principles of the English constitution and deprived a citizen of his rights of justice. In his opinion 'a more mischievous argument, a more ingenious device for setting a Bishop at variance with one party in his Diocese, whenever a complaint of illegality is made, and for creating divided counsels among Bishops – one Bishop allowing suits and another forbidding – I cannot conceive'.[13]

When John Gamon, the Bishop's legal secretary, informed Bell-Cox that proceedings were to be taken against him in the ecclesiastical court, he replied direct to the Bishop insisting that 'If it was right to prosecute him now, it was right four years ago. There had been peace in St Margaret's for some years and there were no aggrieved parishioners. The number of communicants in one year was 9,235; there was an average of forty candidates for Confirmation each year, and the church without endowment was supported entirely by voluntary contributions.'[14]

A memorial was presented to the Bishop signed by one third of the clergy in the diocese, urging him 'to stay the proceedings if possible', and a simliar petition was presented by the laity. All was to no avail.[15] The case was already before the Provincial Court of York. The Bishop exonerated himself by saying, 'I have had nothing whatever to do with the institution of this suit. The only point which has come before me has been the decision whether or not to prevent it.'[16]

Breaking the truce of God

Seven hundred clergy of the Northern Province then presented a petition to York Convocation criticizing the Bishop of Liverpool for breaking 'the truce of God', which the aging Archbishop of Canterbury had called for in the Church while awaiting a report from the Royal Commission on Ecclesiastical Courts.[17] The outspoken Dean Church expressed the feelings of many High Churchmen when he commented: 'The Bishop of Liverpool is surely as obnoxious to all High Churchmen as the Bishop of Lincoln can be to any Low, either for ritual defects or his extravagant pronouncements about the Eucharist.'[18]

Bell-Cox was cited to appear before the Chancery Court of York on 31 July 1885, but he ignored the injunction and refused even to engage counsel to advise him. His reason was the usual one given by ritualists facing such an order, that he did not recognise the jurisdiction of the Lay Court. In his absence Lord Penzance heard the case, and found him guilty of illegal practices in his church and ordered him to stop forthwith. If he failed to obey the injunction he was warned that the next step would be suspension and finally imprisonment. Bell-Cox persistently ignored the order of the court and was again instructed to appear. Once more he refused to appear and on 11 December he was suspended from office for a period of six months. In an interview with a local paper, Bell-Cox told a reporter, 'If anyone thinks that by means of such prosecutions as the present, he is going to stamp out what is called "ritualism" or to force all men into one groove, he is vastly mistaken.'[19]

A leading article in the *Guardian*, a popular Broad Church paper, posed the question, Who Breaks the Peace of the Church? The editorial was a rejoinder to a letter Ryle had written to the *Record* explaining why he had refused to exercise the episcopal veto. The leader writer contended that the peace of the Church had been broken by the determination of the Bishop of Liverpool not to use the discretion with which he had been invested by law. Ryle considered the article a misrepresentation of the facts and felt it his duty to publicly defend himself and his actions. His reply to the *Guardian* was published on 31 December 1885:

> This is a heavy charge and I am not disposed to submit to it in silence. Would it not have been more accurate, and much more fair, if you had made the following statement? The peace of the Church has been disturbed by an incumbent in the Diocese of Liverpool, who refused to obey the friendly admonitions of his Bishop, and abstain from practices in the administration of the Lord's Supper which have been declared illegal by the Queen's court. To the law suit against the incumbent which has been instituted, the Bishop is no party, though he has not prohibited it. I fail to see the justice of your language about the Bishop who upholds the law and declines to prohibit its enforcement, while you cannot find a single word of disapproval for the incumbent who has habitually disobeyed the law, and has twice within five years refused to listen to the Bishop's friendly admonitions about things which are not essential to the Lord's Supper. Which of the two has broken the peace of the Church? The Bishop or the Incumbent? It is vain to cry 'Peace, Peace', where there is no peace. We are practically in a state of anarchy about ecclesiastical discipline.

The Rev J. Bell-Cox jailed

After Bell-Cox had twice been suspended from office, and twice disobeyed the ruling of the Court, Lord Penzance had no alternative but to sentence him to a period of imprisonment for 'manifest contumacy' and 'contempt of court'.[20] Bell-Cox now engaged Digby-Thurman, a Liverpool barrister and a devout Anglo-Catholic, to appeal on his behalf to the higher court of the Queen's Bench for a review of the judgment against him. His counsel obtained a rule nisi, but only until March when three judges of the Court of Appeal gave a final judgment that Lord Penzance had been correct in his decision. On 5 May 1887 Bell-Cox was arrested by the sheriff's enforcement officer as he was about to enter St Margaret's to say Mass. He was taken in a carriage to Walton Jail and as he left the church he told reporters that he hoped Mr Hakes would sleep that night with an easy conscience as he would himself. The Bishop was away at the time. When he returned to Liverpool he was clearly upset by the turn of events and immediately instructed Archdeacon Bardsley to do everything possible to secure the release of the imprisoned clergyman. In a letter to the local press he said he had the greatest respect for Bell-Cox, whom he believed was a sincere and hard-working clergyman and he was pained that he had been sent to prison. He would have preferred him to be deprived of his benefice rather than be sent to prison and was concerned that no one had brought forward a short bill to substitute suspension for incarceration.

The *Church Times* immediately campaigned for the release of the imprisoned priest by publishing a large notice surrounded by a wide black edge, saying, 'Arrested, May 5th 1887. The Prayers of the Church are desired for Bell-Cox, priest. In Prison, For Obedience to the Church's Law.'[21] On 16 May his legal counsel obtained a writ of habeas corpus in the hope of obtaining his release from custody. Digby-Thurman had discovered a technical peculiarity in the Court's proceedings. The legal order under which Bell-Cox had been found 'contumacious' had apparently expired before the date of the issue of the writ, and secondly, the Surrogate who had delivered the judgment, had no legal authority to pronounce him guilty of contempt. These flaws in the legal procedures were most fortunate for Bell-Cox, since anyone guilty of contempt could only be released if he purged his contempt and promised to obey the ruling of the court; he had gone to jail determined to stick by his principles whatever the consequences. After legal argument the rule nisi was made absolute and the court ordered the immediate discharge of the prisoner. On 20 May he was welcomed back to St Margaret's in triumph. He had been in jail for fifteen days.

Once released from prison Bell-Cox admitted that he deserved all he got and was happy that he had been imprisoned for 'contempt' and not for 'ritualism'. He publicly expressed his gratitude to the Bishop and the Archdeacon of Liverpool for their efforts to secure his release. S. Baring Gould, a notable High Churchman, saw in the Bishop's gesture an attempt to quieten an uneasy conscience, however. 'Probably because he was heartily ashamed of what he had done to the Vicar of St Margaret's, he went out of his way to be gracious to Mr Bell-Cox. As the priest said in a letter to me, "His kindness and confidence was most touching."'[22]

Bell-Cox was a free man, but the suit was not ended. Hakes took his case to a higher court and the Court of Appeal reversed the judgment and declared that Bell-Cox had been wrongly released from prison. Bell-Cox was forced to go to the House of Lords, the final Court of Appeal. After a long deliberation the court on 8 May 1888 found in favour of him by a majority, and ordered Hakes to pay the full costs. The next day *The Times* commented that 'Hakes has meddled with an affair with which he has no concern in the world, and he has burnt his fingers in consequence.' The editor said of the priest, 'He has suffered martyrdom for his cause, but he has gained his crown.'[23] Back at St Margaret's, Bell-Cox gave thanks for 'the wonderful answer to prayer and the Eucharists which have been offered for us in all parts of the world', and continued the ritual as before.[24]

Protestant disturbances

The militant Protestants in Liverpool had questioned the Bishop's Protestant loyalty when after arriving in the diocese he failed to close down the two or three Anglo-Catholic churches in the city. Sometimes they took the law into their own hands and set out to cause disturbances in ritualist churches. There were disgraceful scenes inside St Jude's Church, Hardwick Street, in August 1882. Angry members of the congregation protested against the innovations in worship introduced by the vicar, and the police had to be called to restore order. The parishioners twice appealed to the Bishop to put a stop to the ceremonialism, but he felt powerless to take action. Protest meetings were held at street corners in the parish, and eventually the Chief Constable had to give a warning that any persons found loitering near the church on Sundays intent on disturbing the service would be arrested. One Saturday night the protesters adopted a new tactic. They pasted orange coloured placards on lamp posts and walls throughout the neighbourhood, with the bold headings, 'God Save Protestantism'. Underneath was a list of their complaints:

> The parishioners oppose the profanation of the services because of:- monkish cassocks, a surplice choir, church processions, preaching in a surplice, intoning the prayers, weekly morning (fasting) celebration of the Lord's Supper, naming the Lord's Table the Altar and bowing to it, a cross and flower vases on the Lord's table, teaching the Real Presence and baptismal regeneration, turning to the east and bowing is anti-scriptural and Papalistic, and therefore likely to promote tumult. Protestants help in opposing these pranks until they are withdrawn.[25]

The next day at the Sunday morning service there was brawling, and again the vicar was assaulted and the police were called in. The magistrates fined each of the offenders £5 and reminded them that if they had any complaints, the proper procedure was to appeal to the Bishop and not take the law into their own hands. Eventually the Bishop did act and the incumbent was suspended from office for three years.

Another problem for the Bishop centred on St Agnes' Church, Sefton Park, a new church built by Douglas Horsfield, a wealthy businessman and passionate High Church patron. To celebrate the consecration of the new church on 21 January 1885 and the induction of the new incumbent, a series of special preachers were invited. They included Father Black, who was a Cowley brother, Canon Knox-Little, and the Rev A. S. Machonochie, all revered ritualists. Hundreds of Orangemen in the city protested against the proposed services and the appointment of the Rev C. C. Elcum as vicar. Twenty-four Evangelicals in the diocese signed a memorial to the Bishop asking him not to consecrate the new church and not to institute Elcum into the living. Elcum was known to be a member of the English Church Union, a society formed in 1859 to defend High Church principles and practices in the Church of England. Ryle replied that Elcum had assured him that he would not act contrary to the law of the Church and went on:

> I am unable to see how I could refuse to consecrate St Agnes' Church on the ground of your suspicion that something may possibly be done there at some future time which the law has forbidden.... Every one of the preachers holds an episcopal licence and not one of them is under inhibition...my business is not to make the law but administer it.[26]

As a final fling the Protestant opposition staged a noisy demonstration outside the church on the day of the consecration and distributed pamphlets. The Bishop was left in no doubt that many churchmen disapproved of his leadership in this affair. A black-edge paragraph appeared a few days later in *The Protestant Standard*, announcing 'The mournful death of Bishop Ryle's Evangelical and Protestant principles'...and lamented that 'the heaviest blow that Protestants have received since the dawn of the Reformation has been inflicted on it by the Bishop of Liverpool.'[27]

Throughout his episcopate Ryle was verbally attacked by extremists in all parties. Some of his severest critics were a hard core of militant Protestants, not all of whom belonged to the Church of England, who made the wildest accusations against the Bishop in the local press. Yet he never allowed himself to be detracted from what he believed to be the right course. 'Abusive language', he would say, 'is a favoured weapon of many people when they run short of arguments.'[28] Ryle was sympathetic to the Protestant cause, but he did not approve of adopting violent methods. He would have taken a more positive action against ritualism in the diocese, but he felt his hands were tied and he could only act within the law.

Sometimes the harsh criticisms directed at him and other bishops roused him to anger and drove him to defend their actions. He told the Diocesan Conference in 1888:

> If they sit still and do nothing and look on with folded arms, they are blamed. If they allow any steps to be taken illegally, they are blamed

again. 'Blamed', did I say? The phrase is 'euphemism' indeed! That word is too weak to convey the idea of the fierce, violent language, which is poured on the devoted heads of the bishops, by the extreme writers on both sides. Whatever they do, they are wrong.

Protests failed to change anything and at the beginning of the new century Protestants came to accept that litigation had failed to stem the tide of ritualism within the Anglican Church. It was a fact that a younger generation of priests had reintroduced a ritualism and symbolism which went 'far beyond what the older generation thought natural and sufficient.'[29] There was no turning back. On the last occasion Ryle stood before the Convocation of York on 8 June 1898, he declared, 'Nothing would induce me now to institute a prosecution.' The trials strengthened the cause and made martyrs of the recalcitrants. Litigation and even the imprisonment of ritualists had done nothing to halt the progress of the Catholic movement and by the end of the century the Protestant societies realised that the way forward was to focus attention on 'education' rather than 'litigation'. The National Protestant Church Union in 1893 declared its future policy. It would continue to hold public rallies and arrange lectures, but it would abandon litigation and instead, 'we shall use our endeavours to refute error and proclaim the truth, but this we shall do by influencing public opinion, and it will be our endeavour to speak the Truth in love, and ever to keep a spiritual aim in view.'[30]

Chapter Fourteen

We must unite

Ryle believed division among Christians to be a scandal. His deep feelings over unity are clearly expressed in his exposition on Jesus' 'fervent prayer of intercession to the Father' that his people might be 'one' (John 17:21). He pointed out that this is the only recorded prayer of Jesus in the Gospels and that Christian unity was important in the mind of Jesus. He continued:

> How painfully true it is that in every age divisions have been the scandal of religion, and the weakness of the Church of Christ. How often Christians have wasted their strength in contending against their brethren, instead of contending against sin and the devil. How repeatedly they have given occasion to the world to say, 'When you have settled your own internal differences we will believe.'[1]

He believed that divisions and secessions in the Church damaged the cause of Christ, hindered the work of the gospel and delayed the answer to Christ's prayer. If Christians showed they were united in Christ, and the things which divided them were less important, then the world would be more disposed to believe.

Unity within the Church of England
However, Ryle did not equate unity with uniformity. He had no sympathy with those extreme churchmen who believed that the Church of England should be a narrow communion with a strict code of doctrine and practice. Down the centuries the National Church had been able to tolerate divines who differed 'about the Church, the ministry and the sacraments, about the meaning of some words and phrases in the Prayer-book and about the relative place and proportion they assigned to some doctrines and verities of the faith.'[2] Ryle rejoiced in the comprehensiveness of the Church of England. The National Church, he maintained, is like our National Army which is made up of different regiments, each

173

convinced of its own importance – the Guards, the Cavalry, the Artillery. So the Church of England includes High, Broad, Evangelical and No-Party men. Though they hold to their own distinctive beliefs and practices, they are united on the essential doctrines of faith, love the same Bible, subscribe to the same Articles, believe the same Creeds, use the same Prayer-book.[3]

Ryle longed for greater unity, however. He saw that the want of unity and scriptural charity was undermining the mission of the Church and making it a laughing-stock in the world. He had a generous and tolerant spirit and early in his ministry he adopted the principle of Robert Meldenius, which he often quoted, In necessariis unitas, – in non necessariis libertas, – in omnibus caritas. 'Unity in essentials, liberty in non-essentials, charity in all things.'[4] When he was consecrated Bishop of Liverpool he was determined to work amicably with men of High, Low and Broad traditions, who were faithful members of the Church and loyal to her formularies. He was devoted to the cause of reconciliation; reconciliation in the world between sinners and God and in the Church between Christians of different traditions. From time to time he felt he had to speak out about 'the unhappy divisions in the Church' and voice his concerns that 'the gulf between clergymen and clergymen becomes wider and wider and ministers of the same Church keep aloof and separate from one another, as if they did not belong to the same communion.'[5] He was troubled that churchmen could remain suspicious of each other and act as though they belonged to another Church. He confidently believed that a greater degree of unity could be achieved among the different traditions, if we would only see that a man's heart may be right with God even if we think him wrong in doctrine; if we could learn to be more charitable and courteous with those who differ from us; if we tried to understand what churchmen who differ from us believe; if we made the effort to meet men of other schools of thought and get to know them better, and if we co-operated with other churchmen wherever we can.[6]

For those clergy and laity of other schools who through ignorance considered Ryle more a dissenter than a churchman, he had a ready response:

In the matter of true and real attachment to the Church of England I will not give place by subjection to those who are called High Churchmen, for one moment. Have they signed the Thirty-nine Articles ex animo and bone fide? So have I. Have they declared their full assent to the Liturgy and all things contained in it? So have I. Have they promised obedience to the Bishops? So have I. Do they think Episcopacy is the best form of Church government? So do I. Do they honour the Sacraments? So do I. Do they think them generally necessary to salvation? So do I. Do they labour for the prosperity of the Church? So do I. Do they urge on their congregations the privileges of the Church of England? So do I.[7]

With all its faults and need of radical reforms, he was proud of the Church of England in which he had been baptized and confirmed, converted to Christ, ordained to the ministry and consecrated a bishop. He was not ashamed to be known as an Evangelical Churchman.

He frequently encouraged churchmen of all parties to be more tolerant and forbearing. He would say:

Let High Churchmen believe that most Low Churchmen are not necessarily anxious to become Dissenters and love the Church and the Prayer-book as much as they do. Let Low Churchmen try to believe that High Churchmen are not necessarily half papists and have no desire to go over to Rome. Let Broad Churchmen try to believe that other schools of thought may be just as friendly to free enquiry, science and exercise of reason.[8]

One of the benefits he gained from attending the Church Congress was the opportunity of meeting and talking with men of different churchmanship from his own and thus helping to lessen prejudices. He hoped that men of other traditions might gain similarly by meeting and talking with Evangelicals. At the Islington Conference in 1872, in an effort to promote a greater degree of unity between those of different traditions, he offered a serious proposition:

Let a few churchmen of mark, from each school be got together...Let them be put down at the Borrowdale Hotel, keep them away from letters, newspapers, *The Times, Guardian, Church Times, Record,*

give them nothing but their Bible, their prayer-book, pens, ink and
paper, and ask them to talk matters over quietly among themselves
to find out wherein they differed and wherein they agreed, and to
put it down in black and white.[9]

The suggestion never materialized, but he firmly believed that
such a gathering would prove churchmen of different schools could
agree on many more things than they disagreed on.

Ryle was proud to be an Evangelical, but sad that Evangelicals
had the reputation of being 'Independents and not Churchmen'.[10]
They were adept at organizing their own meetings but were not
keen to attend diocesan meetings; refused to go to the Church
Congress but would regularly attend evangelical conferences. A
useful purpose was served by the evangelical gatherings, but
Evangelicals had a valuable contribution to make outside their
own fraternities. He was sure that Evangelicals would have a
stronger voice in the Church and a more effective witness in the
world if they were more united and ceased to stand aloof from the
corporate activities of the diocese. In an attempt to bring
Evangelicals closer together, Ryle wrote numerous letters to the
Church press. At the Islington Conference in 1868 he delivered a
paper entitled 'We must Unite' in which he mercilessly scolded
his friends, saying: 'Every evangelical churchman does what is
right in his own eyes and every district goes to work in its own
way. We have no organized union at all. We have God's truth on
our side. We have numbers, strength, good will and the desire to
do what is right, but from lack of organization we are weak as
water.' It was a strong and persuasive address forcefully delivered,
but it fell on deaf ears and failed to move the audience to action.
Almost in despair he described Evangelicals as men who 'preached
the same doctrines and held the same opinions... yet clung
tenaciously to their old Protestant right of private judgment'; it
was beyond the power of any central committee to organize them
into a coherent whole.

The boundaries of the Church's comprehensiveness, Ryle
insisted, are clearly defined in the Scriptures and the Thirty-Nine
Articles. Nothing should be tolerated which contradicts the Bible,
the Articles and the Prayer-book.[11] However, he acknowledged

that some things are of secondary importance and that Churchmen may hold different opinions about beliefs which are not necessary to salvation. Each is to be persuaded in his own mind about matters on which Scripture is either silent or gives no clear directive. So he had no quarrel with the clergyman who preferred to conduct services in a cassock and surplice rather than a black gown or tried to improve the standard of worship by training a choir and introducing choral works.[12] However, there must be boundaries to the Church's comprehensiveness, and he warned against 'the growing disposition to sacrifice dogma on the altar of so-called unity.'[13] Peace is precious, and he loved it, but he loved truth more. Lowering scriptural standards and departing from the historic confessions of faith was too great a price to pay for unity. He was adamant on this point: 'Unity purchased at the expense of creeds and doctrines is a miserable, cold, worthless unity. I, for one, want none of it.'[14]

Co-operating together in Christian service was possible. Probably Evangelicals might not wish to open their pulpits to a High Churchmen, or invite a Broad Churchman to share with them in the work of evangelism, and in turn, they might not wish to reciprocate. But there were ample opportunities in temperance work, moral and social work for loyal churchmen to unite in doing good.

Relations between Anglicans and Nonconformists

Ryle had a passionate loyalty to the Church of England and undoubtedly preferred Episcopacy to Presbyterianism, the liturgy to extempore prayer and the parochial system to congregationalism. Above all, he liked the clearly defined doctrines of the Church set forth in the Articles and Prayer-book. Outside the Anglican tradition, however, he had a deep respect for Nonconformity and longed to see improved relations between Church and Chapel. His reading of English Church history showed that Dissent was created by the narrow, intolerant belief of the Church leaders in Stuart times. The breach had been further widened in the eighteenth century by the apathy of the Church, the extravagance of the bishops, and the absenteeism of her clergy, and again in the nineteenth century by the resurgence of ritualism in the Church. For forty years Ryle worked to bring closer unity between Churchmen and Nonconformists, but there was one big stumbling block. A small but vocal group of Nonconformists aimed to disestablish and disendow the Church, 'and if Dissenters will not let the Church alone, and will not rest until they have destroyed the Establishment, I give up all hopes of unity.'[15]

He never forgot his family connections with Nonconformity, and often spoke in affectionate terms of the evangelistic work of John and Charles Wesley. He admired the Methodist preachers' boldness in proclaiming the gospel, denouncing sin, uplifting the Saviour and pleading with sinners to repent. Shortly after his arrival in Liverpool, Methodists in the city expressed their good wishes and presented him with a copy of the Bible and The Methodist Book of Praise. This delighted him, and was the beginning of a long and friendly association with Nonconformists in the diocese. Soon among the Free Churches he became known as 'The Nonconformist Bishop of Liverpool'.[16] He could claim, 'I have often cooperated with Dissenters on behalf of the London City Mission and the Bible Societies. I have spoken side by side with their ministers on many platforms. I have entertained the leading members of the Wesleyan Conference at my own home in Liverpool.'[17]

The Bishop saw love for Christ as the common meeting place for Christians of different denominations. All Christians were united in the bonds of love by the cross of Christ. He would say:

> I leave it to others to excommunicate and unchurch all who do not belong to their own pale, and do not worship after their own particular fashion. I have no sympathy with such narrow-mindedness. Show me a man who repents and believes in Christ crucified, who lives a holy life, and delights in his Bible and prayer, and I desire to regard him as a brother. I see him as a member of the Holy Catholic Church, out of which there is no salvation.[18]

However, though he advocated the closest co-operation between Protestant denominations he saw no possibility of an organic union between Anglicans and Nonconformity.

We must not waste time and energy on the pleasant but quixotic idea that we can bring about a wholesale reunion of Church and Dissent. I am sorry to throw cold water on the charitable plans of some of my brethren. I freely admit that nothing is impossible. But of all improbable and unlikely things, I see none more improbable and unlikely than a fusion and amalgamation of Methodists, Independents and Baptists with the Church of England. Whatever may happen in isolated cases, it is not reason to suppose that trained and educated Dissenting ministers, as a rule, will ignore their own orders, and seek to be re-ordained. Nor is it reason to suppose that their congregations would follow them.[19]

Though Ryle did not expect to see all divisions abolished, he did hope to see the walls dividing the churches brought so low that churchmen and dissenters could see each other and talk together. 'Surely', he insisted, 'it is not right to say we expect to spend eternity with men in heaven, and yet cannot work with them in the world.'[20] He therefore delighted in the growing understanding and desire for closer cooperation between members of the episcopal and non-episcopal churches. Support for the British and Foreign Bible Society, the Sankey and Moody missions and the Keswick Convention brought together evangelical Christians from both Church and Chapel, and often they found the means of working together at a local level. For the sake of more unity among Churchmen and Christians of other denominations he believed in cooperation wherever possible.

The Church in Scotland
The Bishop was very fond of Scotland and he and his family sometimes spent their summer holiday at Pitlochry. Before taking his vacation in 1883, he wrote to the incumbent of the Episcopal church in Pitlochry, Holy Trinity Church, informing him that he intended to stay six weeks in the town but would not attend his church. He hoped he would not regard his absence from church on Sundays as a mark of personal disrespect.[21] The Episcopal Church in Scotland in its Articles of Faith accepted the doctrine of baptismal regeneration, which Ryle rejected. Consequently he felt he could not with a clear conscience worship in the Episcopal

Church, and did the courteous thing by letting the incumbent know his reason. The incumbent, the Rev. St John Howard, replied, 'I deeply regret your Lordship's decision, because if you attend any other place of worship it will cause grave scandal and shock the feelings of numerous members of our communion here during the season.'[22]

A few days later Howard wrote an irate letter to the national press stating that he had just seen a public notice in the village announcing that the 'Lord Bishop of Liverpool' would be preaching in the Kirk the following Sunday. Dr Ryle had preached there the year before, and while his fellow clergy considered the Bishop had committed a breach of ecclesiastical order, he believed the responsibility for action lay with the Church in England.[23] His presence at a Sunday service in a Presbyterian church attracted widespread publicity and produced a spate of critical letters in the press. Ryle had theological reasons for not attending the Episcopal Church in Scotland, and as for officiating in the Scottish Kirk when invited to do so, he asked:

> What law of the Church or State do I break? I know of none. The Kirk is a sound Protestant Church of Christ; her Confession of Faith is Scriptural; the Canons of 1804 enjoin churchmen to pray for her, the Queen always attends when she visits her people over the border. The Queen is the earthly head of the Church of England. Her Majesty is also the earthly head of the Church of Scotland. Each Church has a creed to which he could subscribe. If the Church of Scotland is good enough for the head of the Church of England, a loyal servant could, without his conscience reproaching him, preach in a church belonging to the Scotch Establishment.[24]

One notable Scottish minister paid a glowing tribute to Bishop Ryle's ministry in Scotland:

> I had heard him preach ere I left my country parish in Edinburgh, in a barn hard by, and had been profoundly impressed by his eloquence and ability. Coming forth from hearing divers of our preachers, one might say, 'that was very eloquent and striking,' or like words of similar appreciation. But after listening to Ryle, some felt that criticism would have been profanation. Get away by yourself, and solemnly think how it is indeed with you.[25]

Roman Catholicism

Though Ryle had a deep respect for Nonconformity and counted many Nonconformists among his friends he had a different attitude toward Roman Catholicism. In the course of his pastoral ministry he had met many Roman Catholics with a sincere and devout faith in Christ, and he was sure that many of them were disenchanted with their Church and were seekers after truth. But he saw Romanism to be a growing threat to the Reformed and Protestant faith of England. In his Visitation Charge of 1890 the Bishop warned that

> The edge of the old British feeling about Protestantism seems blunted and dull. Some profess to be tired of all religious controversy, and are ready to sacrifice God's truth for the sake of peace. Some look on Romanism as simply one among many English forms of religion, and neither worse nor better than others. Some try to persuade us that Romanism is changed, and not so bad as it used to be.

He saw the growing dominance of Romanism as a menacing threat intent on destroying the benefits of the English Reformation and gave this warning:

> Let us resolve to have no peace with Rome, till Rome abjures her errors, and is at peace with Christ. Till Rome does that, the vaunted reunion of the Western Churches, which some talk of and press upon our notice, is an insult to the Church of England.[26]

Religious feelings sometimes ran high in Liverpool and the hostility between Roman Catholics and Protestants was symptomatic of the deep religious factions embedded in the very culture of the city's lower classes. Early in his episcopate the Bishop and Mrs Ryle had been attacked by a mob of Irish Catholics as they left St Michael's in the Hamlet, where he had been preaching to a large congregation of working-class men and women. Stones were thrown at his carriage but no one was hurt and the Bishop paid little attention to the incident. Such hostile incidents were not unusual, particularly on St Patrick's Day, when Roman Catholics marched in processions, and on 12 July when the Protestants commemorated the Battle of the Boyne. Street fights ensued, and many were arrested before the end of the day.

Protestants and Roman Catholics lived separately in their own districts of the city. Mixed marriages were exceptional. Catholic children attended Catholic schools and Protestant children went either to the Church or National school. Catholics and Protestants patronized their own shops and drank in their own pubs, and generally Protestants who had the vote supported the Tories and Catholics favoured the Liberals. Politically, economically, culturally and religiously, Liverpool was at this time a divided city.

Chapter Fifteen

Desire to die in harness

The demands of the diocese put a tremendous strain on Ryle as he grew older. In 1889 the seventy-three-year-old bishop reported to the Diocesan Conference that in the first five months he had preached thirty-five sermons, conducted forty confirmation services, attended the registrar's office for interviews, spent two weeks in the House of Lords reading the daily prayers, one week in attendance at York Convocation and another week examining candidates for ordination. A report of the work accomplished in the diocese in his first ten years is a stimulating account of difficulties overcome and progress made by faithful ministry and God's blessing. It is a narrative of healthy growth in the number of clergy serving in the diocese, a rise in the number of new churches and mission halls; an increase in the number of church schools and pupils attending; more Scripture readers commissioned, and numerous societies working to relieve the misery of 'the abject poor' in Liverpool and other towns on Merseyside.[1]

Surveying the first decade of his administration, the Bishop could point to encouraging progress in both spiritual and social work. 'The work done for young men and women, for the sick and for orphans, for fallen women, for waifs and strays, for sailors, for carters, for railwaymen, the good work is endless.'[2] When he considered the great variety of religious and philanthropic agencies supported by the Church in the diocese, he confidently claimed, 'These were enough to show that they did not deserve the bitter remark that they were a "Dead See".'[3]

Henrietta's death
The death of Mrs Ryle in 1889 was a hard blow for the Bishop to bear. Henrietta was sixty-four years of age and they had been married for twenty-seven years. Devoted to her husband and his

work, she was always by his side, gracious, kind and thoughtful, a woman of simple Christian faith. Every Sunday afternoon she and her daughter, Isabelle, held a small Bible class in the Palace drawing-room for the benefit of the household servants and quietly taught them in the things of God. She frequently addressed women's meetings in the diocese and gave her practical support to several missionary societies. She was warmly welcomed by the clergy wives who appreciated her sympathetic understanding of their needs and problems.

It was while she was attending the great Liverpool Exhibition in 1886 on the occasion of the Queen's visit to the city, that Henrietta caught a chill from which she never fully recovered. Over the next two or three years she consulted numerous doctors, but her health continued to deteriorate. Eventually the family arranged for her to go to Harrogate for treatment, but the journey proved a great strain and her conditioned worsened. Miss Ryle telegraphed home requesting the Bishop to return immediately to Harrogate, and the message was passed on to him at Christ Church, Bootle, where he was conducting a Confirmation service. Henrietta had a further relapse and quietly passed away on 6 April 1889. Her body was brought back to Liverpool for burial in Childwall churchyard.

On the day of the funeral between five and six thousand people stood in Abercromby Square with heads bared to witness the cortege leave the Bishop's Palace, and pay their respects to a greatly loved Christian lady who had devoted much of her life to the spiritual and moral welfare of ordinary people. Among the wreaths placed near the grave was one from Liverpool railwaymen, a body of men whom Mrs Ryle had sought to help through the distribution of tracts and homely comforts. The dominant note throughout the funeral service was one of praise to God, and the congregation united in giving thanks for a life so wholly dedicated to the Lord and his service. Standing by the graveside at the close of the burial service, the Bishop was moved to speak quietly to the mourners standing nearby:

I feel so much in my heart that indeed I must say a few words to you.... You do not know the extent of the loss you and others in the diocese have sustained in the removal of her by whose grave you now stand. She always rejoiced in your successes; she was always concerned in your every difficulty; and she bore you, and everyone who was working for the Master, from the richest to the poorest, unstintingly on her heart to the King of Kings. I would like here to testify that her faith was simple, and in that faith she lived and died. May the prayers she has often presented to the Throne of Grace be followed by showers of blessing over the whole diocese.

Then in a subdued voice and with deep emotion he said as he turned away from the grave, 'Till the Lord Jesus comes, we part.'[4] A year later he still felt the loss most keenly and in one of his letters to Herbert, his eldest son, he confessed, 'Life has never been the same thing, or the world the same place since my wife died.'[5]

From this time on the Bishop came to rely more and more on the help of his daughter, Isabelle. She was devoted to her father and acted as his housekeeper, secretary and general factotum. Every Tuesday they went together to Childwall to lay flowers on the grave until eventually his failing eyesight made it impossible. As his secretary she wrote between twenty and thirty letters a day on matters relating to the diocese, and always accompanied the Bishop on his preaching engagements. A committed Christian, she was hospitable, kind and completely dedicated to caring for her father throughout the rest of his life. It was a great consolation to the Bishop that his three sons had succeeded in their chosen careers. Reginald was now practising medicine in Brighton. He specialized in the study of mental disorders and at one time was President of the Medico-Sociological section of the Medical Association. Arthur, the youngest son, was a successful artist and a member of the Royal Society of British Artists. Herbert was the President of Queen's College, Cambridge and a distinguished career lay ahead of him. He wrote in his autobiography of the close bond which always existed between father and son: 'Much as father differed from me in many points he never suffered a shadow of difference to come between us in the intimacy of affection. And since the time I went to school at the age of nine and a half I have never received from him a harsh word. And the sense of companionship grew between us until the rarity of meeting one another caused that growth to grow, and simply left us supremely happy to meet and be together.'[6]

In 1891 the Bishop suffered a slight stroke. He made a speedy and remarkable recovery, but it was obvious that if he was to avoid a complete breakdown he needed to share his responsibilities. Bishop Peter Sorenson Royston had recently returned to England after serving for thirty-five years in the colonies with the Church Missionary Society, nineteen of them as Bishop of Mauritius. For many years Ryle had been pressing radical reforms on the Church including more bishops with smaller dioceses. He had been against the proposal to revive the office of suffragan bishops thinking that they would be no better than 'episcopal curates'. Now however at the age of seventy-five, he was delighted to appoint Royston as his assistant bishop. Since there was no available endowment for an assistant bishop, Ryle contributed towards the bishop's stipend out of his own pocket until five years later a vacancy occurred at All Saint's, Childwall, and Royston was then able to combine parochial ministry with his episcopal duties. Ryle described Royston as 'a dear and saintly man'. He in turn had the greatest respect for his Diocesan. He frequently recalled in later life how he went each week to the Bishop's Palace for a staff meeting which always ended with the two bishops kneeling together in prayer and commending themselves, their ministry and the diocese to the Lord.

Continued controversies in the Church

Since Ryle moved to Liverpool, episcopal responsibilities had given gave him less time for writing. Nevertheless, he did publish some collections of sermons and addresses. In 1884 he published *Principles for Churchmen*, a sequel to *Knots Untied*, containing papers relating to imminent dangers facing the Established Church. In a long Introduction he describes in some detail the problems besetting the Church from two causes. One was 'the continual existence of a body of Churchmen, who seem if words and actions mean anything, determined to unprotestantize the Church of England'.[7] The second he believed to be 'a spirit of indifference to all doctrines and opinions in religion', so that any extreme opinion was accepted. [8] The chapter titles include 'The Church's Distinctive Principles', 'The Importance of Dogma', 'Thoughts on the Supper of the Lord' and 'Disestablishment' while three of them, 'The Church,' 'Worship,' and 'Baptism,' are reprints from his earlier book. Admirers of Ryle welcomed the volume, but one critic described its aim as an attempt to 'undo the work of the Catholic Revival'.[9]

Four years later he published *The Upper Room*, a collection of some of the sermons he had preached during his forty-five-year ministry. In the Preface he wrote, 'I have reached the age when I cannot reasonably expect to write much more.' It would have been a great loss not to have his sermons on 'Luke, The Beloved Physician', 'Simplicity in Preaching', 'Foundation Truths,' and 'Athens' since they are so full of definite and distinctive evangelical truths. In 1891 he added two more chapters to *Bishops and Clergy of Other Days* and republished it under the new title, *Light From Old Times*. It contains fascinating chapters on the Christian witness of several Reformation martyrs and Puritan divines, including Rowland Taylor, Rector of Hadleigh and William Gurnall, Rector of Lavenham in Suffolk, Ryle continued to use his influence to counsel against secession. In 1890 a case was brought by the Church Association against Edward King, the Bishop of Lincoln, for taking the eastward position at the Communion Table, mixing water and wine in the Chalice and using the sign of the Cross. Archbishop Benson gave a ruling that the eastward position adopted by the minister at the Holy Communion was legal, provided that the manual acts could be seen by the congregation. He also said that no doctrinal significance was attached to the position of the officiating priest at the Holy Table. This judgment caused consternation among Evangelicals, and some felt driven to secede from the Anglican Church in protest. Many more would have followed but for the reasoned counsel of Bishop Ryle. He wrote to the *Record* appealing to waverers to stand firm by the Church of England:

I charge my brethren not to listen for a moment to those who counsel secession. I have no sympathy with the rash and impatient men who recommend such a step. So long as the Articles and the Prayer-book are not altered, we occupy an impregnable position. We have an open Bible, and our pulpits are free.[10]

He saw no valid reason why loyal churchmen should abandon the ship because of a small leak, and warned those who contemplated leaving the Established Church that they would find that 'the chimney smokes in chapel as well as church.[11] The time to leave the Church would be:

When the Thirty-Nine Articles are altered, when the Prayer-book is revised on Romish principles and filled with Popery, when the Bible is withdrawn from the reading desk, when the pulpit is shut against the Gospel, when the Mass is formally restored in every parish church by Act of Parliament... then it will be time to leave the Church of England. Then we may arise and say with one voice, 'Let us depart, for God is not here.'[12]

Evangelistic efforts

Throughout his ministry Ryle was deeply concerned about the thousands of people living in England who were ignorant of the gospel. 'Ask them,' he said, 'what they know about Jesus Christ and you will be astonished at the gross darkness which covers their minds.'[13] In the 1850s in an effort to reach those without Christ, Ryle, along with Hugh McNeile, an eloquent Irishman known for his remarkable ministry in Liverpool and J. C. Miller, the Evangelical vicar of St Martin's in the Bullring, Birmingham, had conducted what was probably the first parochial mission in a parish church. It was a simple preaching service at which the reserved pew system was suspended and the poor of the parish were invited to fill the church. This untried venture proved successful and similar missions were led by the same team in Ipswich and Islington.[14] Ryle was happy with the occasional parish-based mission but was not enthusiastic about mass-evangelism of the revival type, for he felt they were often hot, sensational and emotional gatherings. However, he did give his wholehearted support to the visit of the Sankey and Moody mission to Britain which culminated in the great Mission to London in 1875. In 1883 he welcomed the evangelist and gospel singer to Liverpool for a city mission, and sat on the platform of a huge wooden structure erected in Henglis Circus when the American evangelist preached to five thousand people with further large numbers in overflow meetings. One critic, who disapproved of the Bishop's active support of the mission, wrote to the press, 'The Bishop of Liverpool in seeking the assistance of Mr Moody is in the position of a qualified physician calling on the aid of an unauthorised practitioner who, in medical phraseology, would be termed a quack.'[15] In spite of such criticisms, at York Convocation Ryle happily paid tribute to the evangelist's ministry. He did confess however that neither revivalist nor parochial missions really succeeded in reaching the lower classes. Long experience in the ministry had taught him that while an occasional evangelistic mission may speak to those who are not regular church attenders and even to those who are, real and lasting work for God was more often achieved in the parishes by regular pastoral work: 'Ask any clergyman who works his parish and visits his people and knows their character, what is the chief difficulty with which he has to contend and I am certain he will tell you it is neither Romanism, nor extreme Ritualism, nor Broad Churchmen, nor any other "ism", but the half dead, torpid indifference about any sort of religion.'[16] He firmly believed that evangelism is most effective where the minister knows and loves his people, and faithfully in church and home, school and street, speaks to them of their need of Christ.

At the beginning of 1894 as part of the diocesan effort to stem the working class flow out of the churches, the Bishop sponsored the Liverpool General Christian Mission. It was led by two of his evangelical friends, Prebendary W. E. Askwith of Taunton and the Rev W. Hay Aitkin of Bedford. The publicity for the Mission included a pastoral letter from the Bishop urging Christians to pray for its success, to attend as often as possible, and to invite as many as possible to hear the gospel message:

The object of the Mission is not so much to tell people new things as to induce them to feel old things more deeply. The benefits of the Mission do not consist in temporary excitement and running after strange preachers, but in the new sense of the value of souls, leading to repentance, faith and practical holiness. It is only when the Bible is read, the Lord's Table better attended, that a mission does any good.[17]

Almost every parish in the diocese supported the Mission, and afterwards the clergy reported that prayers had been answered and blessings received.

Other engagements

The once robust Bishop attended less engagements outside the diocese in his later years, though he continued to attend a select number of evangelical conferences and annual meetings of the missionary societies as often as he could. He was duty bound to attend the occasional meetings of bishops at Lambeth Palace, but thought the discussions 'weak, evasive and impotent'.[18]

He wrote to Herbert after one visit, 'I came away vexed and annoyed and am not at all disposed to go up again to London for a night for such a waste of time.'[19] He continued to attend the Church Congress and spoke at Derby on 'Evangelism at Home', at Wakefield on 'The Church in Rural Areas', and attended his last Congress in 1890 at Hull when he gave a paper on 'Foreign Missions'. He was also a regular attender at the Upper House of York Convocation and took part in several debates on controversial issues. As senior bishop Ryle became a member of the House of Lords in 1884, though he never used the opportunity to speak on political or social problems and attended only when he was on the rota to say Prayers. At the Third Lambeth conference of Anglican Bishops he contributed papers on 'Sunday Observance' and 'The Care of Emigrants'. It was this Conference which issued the Encyclical containing the Lambeth Quadrilateral, a statement of four articles considered a fundamental basis for any reunion between the Eastern and Western Churches. Ryle went on holiday to Scotland before the Conference ended and only read details of the agreed Encyclical in *The Times*. He immediately wrote a sharp riposte dissociating himself from the statement in the plainest terms. Archbishop Benson was quick to reply. He pointed out that only eight bishops of the Anglican Communion were absent when the Quadrilateral was drafted and 'we did not unfortunately have the advantage of his presence for cooperation and criticism on that day.... If he preferred to be on holiday in Scotland rather than at Lambeth that was his fault.'[20] A local paper in Liverpool picked up the report of the altercation under the heading, 'Our Bishop Ryled.'[21]

Ryle was often at his best when addressing working class laymen. A special feature of the Church Congress was the evening meeting for working men. In 1882 he was one of the main speakers at the Working Men's meeting in Derby, during which he paid a fine tribute to the work going on in one of the working-class parishes of his diocese:

I know at this moment a parish of five thousand people in Liverpool with not a rich man in it but only small shopkeepers, artisans and poor. There are only thirty families in it which keep a servant, and not one family which keeps two. There are 195 houses with more than one family in each. There are 133 families living in cellars. Many of these cellars are within a few yards from the church, and under its shadow. In short, that this is a thoroughly poor, working-class parish, I think no one can deny. In a plain brick church, holding one thousand, built thirteen years ago, there is a simple hearty service, and an average attendance of 700 on Sunday morning, 300 in the afternoon, and 950 in the evening. About half the sittings are rented and half free. In three mission rooms there is an average attendance of about 350 in the morning and 450 in the evening. The communicants are almost all of the working classes and nearly half men. I myself once helped to administer the consecrated elements to 395 persons, and I saw the hands which received them and I knew that many of them were dock labourers and foundry men. The worthy minister of this parish began his work alone about fourteen years ago, with four people in a cellar. After this church was built, he had only eight communicants at his first administration of the Lord's Supper. He has now eight hundred communicants and is aided by two paid Curates, one paid Scripture reader, one paid Bible woman, and one paid organist. But he has besides 82 voluntary Sunday School teachers, 120 church workers, 18 Bible Classes with 600 adults on the register, and 1,700 Sunday scholars. There are six services in church every week, and four services in mission-rooms throughout the year, besides two prayer-meetings every month. The practical and moral results of the church's work in this parish are patient and unmistakable. Of course some of the people remain to this day irreligious, careless, unchanged, and like the 'wayside hearers' in the parable of the sower, the wheat and the tares will grow together till the harvest. No minister can give grace, however faithfully he may preach it. But there are plain proofs in this case that labour is not in vain. It bears 'fruit that remains'. The congregation raises eight hundred pounds a year for the cause of God. There are 1,100 pledged abstainers in the district. There is not a single house of ill fame or a single known infidel in the parish.[22]

The Bishop's account of Canon Hobson's ministry at St Nathaniel's Church, Upper Parliament Street, aroused much interest and two statements so astonished members of Congress that their accuracy was later questioned. At the Bishop's request the churchwardens checked the registers and assured him that there were actually 802 bona fide communicants, most of whom lived within the parish boundaries, and the police confirmed that to their knowledge there was not a disreputable house in St Nathaniel's parish.

Eightieth birthday celebrations
In May 1896 the bishop celebrated his eightieth birthday. He rejoiced in the love and good wishes of his family and friends and only wished that his wife had been spared to share that special time with him. Representatives of the clergy and laity presented him with an Illuminated Address as a token of their respect and loyalty. Among their number was James Bell-Cox, who shook the Bishop's hand most warmly, and received a kind and appreciative response. The Bishop was overcome by the affectionate terms of the Address and a few days later wrote to the Archdeacon of Liverpool:

I came to the diocese knowing well that every English bishop to this day must make up his mind to be severely criticized and that in all his actions, and words, and opportunities he will displease somebody. I came among you as a man of very decided opinions, and I think it likely that many of you would have preferred a bishop of a different school of thought; with rare exceptions I have found no difficulty in working with you all.[23]

Still no Cathedral, but a Church House

Ryle still considered the lack of a cathedral to be one of the wants of the diocese, and was disappointed that the diocese had failed to start work on building a new Cathedral. 'In this respect,' he said in his Visitation Charge of 1896, 'we are far worse off than the new dioceses of Wakefield and Newcastle, each of which has a fine church to begin with.'[24] However, this failure eventually turned out to the advantage of the diocese, as Sir Frederick Radcliffe, chairman of the Cathedral committee, admitted, 'It left us free to secure a glorious building on a splendid site.'[25]

The proposal at the end of the century to build a Church House in Liverpool was not in any sense a second choice to a Cathedral, but had been conceived by Ryle in the early days of the episcopate. Without a Church House important documents and papers relating to the new diocese had to be stored in Chester. The Bishop concluded in his Charge, 'We want a Church House, a plain building in a central position, containing one or two large committee rooms, a diocesan registry, a room for Bishop's interviews, offices for some of our chief societies, and a reading-room where churchmen could meet one another. Cost fifty-thousand pounds, but where from?'[26] After preliminary meetings to discuss the project, an excellent corner site was secured in the commercial district of the city. The architect's plan was for a three-story building, with the ground floor to be let as shops and offices. Ryle himself subscribed an initial donation of £1,000 to the building fund. He was still the bishop when the Countess of Derby laid the foundation stone of the new building on 1 August 1899, but did not live to see the official opening on 18 May 1901 by the Archbishop of York.

Ryle had bequeathed to the trustees of Church House his library of 5,000 books on Reformed Theology and three cases of paintings, most of them attributed to his son, Arthur. The library was a rare collection and included some valuable editions of Reformation and Puritan literature. The works of Cranmer, Latimer, Owen, Goodwin and Baxter had been his constant sources of study and enjoyment. Such a huge set of theological and devotional works left no one in any doubt where the Bishop stood doctrinally and spiritually. Some in the diocese disliked the particular brand of theology embodied in Ryle's library, and some years later it was alleged that without diocesan authority or public discussion many of the more pronounced Protestant and Evangelical tomes had been removed and replaced by more liberal works.[27]

Persuaded to retire
Bishop Ryle preached his last sermon in May 1899 on behalf of the Church Missionary Society in St Silas Church, Toxteth. In the course of his address he told the congregation that he had just received a postal order for twenty-three shillings from a nurse who wished the money to go to missionary work.[28] When at the close of the service the offertory was taken up it was found that someone had placed a gold chain in one of the collecting boxes in response to the Bishop's challenging appeal. The total collection at the service amounted to £120, a record missionary collection for the church.

Another serious illness now left the Bishop weak and infirm and it was decided that he should go to Lowestoft, his favourite resort, to rest and recuperate. In September Herbert went over from Cambridge to the east coast to see his father. He was shocked to find how enfeebled he had become in hearing and walking, and that his memory was also affected. He felt compelled to advise him to resign the See and retire with Isabelle to East Anglia. The Bishop saw the wisdom of his son's counsel, and in Herbert's words, 'Evidently pleased that the suggestion should come from another, almost welcomed it – and in twenty-four hours had practically determined upon it.'[29] It was a hard decision to make since he had wished 'to die in harness'. Nevertheless, on his return to Liverpool in October he immediately notified the Archbishop of York that it was his intention to reign from the bishopric at the end of February 1900.

Bishop Royston was now responsible for carrying out almost all the episcopal duties. The aged Bishop conducted his last ordination in October, privately in Oxford, when he ordained Professor P. S. Margoliouth, a converted Jew and Professor of Arabic at the University. A charming account of the Bishop's last visit to St Nathaniel's Church used to hang over the fireplace in the Vicar's vestry until the church was pulled down some years ago. The simple inscription read:

> For some months in 1899 he had been in poor health, but he rallied towards the end of the year. As the clergy were about to begin the eleven am service on Christmas Day, a tap was heard on the vestry door, and when it was opened, there was the Bishop quite bent, with his family, including his son, Herbert, afterwards Bishop of Exeter and Dean of Westminster, hoping to make a quiet entrance into the church. They all took their place in the vicar's pew, as was his custom, in the corner where Mrs Ryle who predeceased had been wont to sit. Many of the congregation were deeply affected by the sight of their venerable Bishop, always so straight and commanding, now bowed down by infirmity. At Holy Communion he came to the rail followed by his children, who knelt on either side of him. For a moment the good vicar was overcome with emotion. The Bishop looked at him, and said softly, 'Go on.' When the service was over they all waited behind and on the vicar's approach, he reached out a trembling hand, drew him close to himself, and said as the big tears rolled down his deep furrowed cheeks, 'This is the last time. God bless you. We shall meet in heaven.'

Before the Bishop left the diocese, he gave one of his study Bibles to his friend, Canon Richard Hobson, vicar of St Nathaniel's. These black, leather bound volumes were carefully marked and underlined on each page where the Word of God had spoken to his servant. As he handed Richard Hobson the well-used copy of the Scriptures, he said to him, 'I have been thinking what memento you might like to have of me. I have thought you might like to have one of my Bibles which I have been using on my study table for over fifty years.' Taking up his pen, he wrote on the flyleaf: 'Given to R. Hobson by J. C. Ryle first Bishop of Liverpool, With very much Christian love, 22nd January 1900.' Canon Hobson recorded: 'Handing the book to me, he said, "Now let us have a parting prayer." I knelt by his chair, and oh, what a prayer he offered for me! I shall never forget it.'[30]

The Bishop felt very deeply the necessity of laying down the work which for so long had engaged his time and energy. For close on twenty years he had been bishop of a new and important diocese, leading and encouraging his clergy and laity and the many diocesan evangelistic and moral agencies. Though his administration had not pleased everyone, he was respected, if not loved, by clergy and laity in the diocese as a true man of God, a born leader, and a man of integrity, generosity and wise counsel. His Farewell Letter to the Diocese reveals the heart of the man and his deep love and concern for the spiritual wellbeing of its people:

> I am about to resign a post which years and failing health at the age of 83 told me I was no longer able to fulfil...I shall never forget you. I had ventured to hope that I might be allowed to end my days near the Mersey, and to die in harness, but God's thoughts are not our thoughts, and He has gradually taught me that failing health and the huge population of the diocese require a younger and stronger Bishop. Before I leave you I ask you to accept a few parting words from an old minister.... Let me then charge all the clergy... never to neglect their preaching... a lively, Christ-exalting minister will always have a Church-going people.... Last but not least, be at peace among yourselves.... In a little while we shall all meet again, I hope, on the King's right hand and few on the left...
>
> > I remain your affectionate Bishop and lasting friend,
> >
> > J. C. Liverpool.[31]

When it became known that the Bishop intended to retire, his many friends urged him to publish a last book of sermons 'as a memorial of his sixty years in the ministry'. He was delighted to do so and invited Archdeacon Madden to make a selection from his manuscripts. The resulting collection of sermons, entitled *The Christian Race*, was published in 1900. It reveals Ryle's customary forceful, expressive and epigrammatic style with an appeal to the heart. The sermons also clearly illustrate where the emphasis lay in his preaching, for they deal with the doctrines of Sin,

Redemption, Regeneration, Sanctification and practical Holiness.

The farewell gift from the diocese was presented by the Archdeacon of Liverpool. It was a piece of silver plate and an illuminated address signed by 391 clergy, all of whom he had ordained. It gave him great satisfaction to know before he left Liverpool that the Queen had appointed his friend, Francis James Chavasse, Principal of Wycliffe Hall, Oxford, as the next Bishop of Liverpool. He was confident that the Evangelical and Protestant character of the diocese would be maintained.

Having bowed to the inevitable with good grace he decided to retire with his daughter to Lowestoft. The seaside resort was not far from Cambridge and he looked forward to seeing Herbert and his family more often. He planned to leave Liverpool on 6 March but was taken ill the day before, and the journey to Suffolk was postponed until the middle of the month. So it was on 22 March 1900 that the Bishop and his daughter Isabelle left the Palace for the last time. He was taken in an invalid carriage to the station and seen off by a group of his closest friends. Their new home, Helmingham House in Lowestoft, was pleasantly situated with delightful views over the North Sea. However, he quickly became weaker and less mobile, and less than two months after leaving Liverpool he died. It was Trinity Sunday. The next day would have been the twentieth anniversary of his consecration. He passed on, trusting in his Lord and Saviour whom he had faithfully served for sixty-three years, confident in the resurrection hope and of seeing his Lord face to face.

Herbert felt the bereavement more acutely, perhaps, than any other member of the family. From Queen's Lodge, Cambridge, he wrote to his friend, Arthur Benson, son of the late Archbishop of Canterbury, to tell him the circumstances of his father's death:

> The summons came unexpectedly and I left this house on Sunday morning at twenty minutes notice; but all was over – an hour previously before I reached the house at Lowestoft. The sudden blow – however long expected – comes suddenly, and is a blow to which nothing can be compared. You have been through the experience and know what it all means. And I, to whom it was an intense stimulus to think of pleasing my father as a boy and a young man, feel how

greatly he has filled up the picture of my life. In the country life of Suffolk he was everything to us, taught us games, natural history, astronomy, and insisted on our never being idle, and carefully fostered our love of books, to us boys he was extraordinarily indulgent and he was tolerant to a degree little known or recognized.... It was a merciful end, for the powers were used up, and there was little pleasure left in existence.[32]

The body in a simple oak coffin was taken by train to Liverpool to be received at the station by Bishop Royston, and rested overnight in Childwall parish church. A quiet and sustained joy characterized the funeral service in the crowded church and outside in the churchyard. Hundreds travelled by special trains and by vans and carts to attend the funeral and to pay their last respects to their old and venerable Bishop. Among those who stood at the graveside was a policeman who had often been on duty at the Landing Stage in Liverpool when the Bishop took his customary walk at lunch time, and whose life had been changed by the kindly words of the Bishop. All were deeply moved when the huge congregation sang two of the Bishop's favourite hymns, 'Rock of Ages' and 'Come, let us join our friends above'.

So the first Bishop of Liverpool was laid to rest by the side of his wife. The little black Bible which he had used throughout his preaching ministry was placed next to his heart and buried with him. The brass plate on the coffin bore the inscription, The Rt. Rev. John Charles Ryle, DD, Born 10th May 1816, Died 10th June 1900. First Bishop of Liverpool, Consecrated St Barnabas Day, 11th June 1880, Resigned 1st March 1900.

The carefully chosen words of Bishop Chavasse in his funeral address summed up the feeling of many in the diocese at the time:

The noble Bishop is no more, Liverpool is the poorer for his passing. This work is done, and done handsomely and to the full. The remark 'We shall not look on his like again,' may be trite, but it is peculiarly applicable to the splendid personality of Bishop Ryle.[33]

When the memorial stone was placed at the head of the grave to mark his resting place it was inscribed with two of the Bishop's favourite texts. They were 2 Timothy 4:7: 'I have fought a good fight, I have finished my course, I have kept the faith'; and Ephesians 2:8, 'By grace are ye saved though faith,' the verse which had made such an impression when he heard it read in an Oxford church, and which had led him to faith in Christ.[34]

Chapter Sixteen

A Victorian Bishop

Shortly after it was announced that J.C. Ryle had been appointed the first Bishop of Liverpool, a seventy-one-year-old labourer wrote to the Bishop of Manchester, saying:

> I read this morning of a great ceremony which is to take place at the consecration of Canon Ryle as Bishop of Liverpool. He is a man whom I admire very much. I hope he will not lose any of that plainness of manner, which is so characteristic of him after his elevation. He has been speaking very plainly to the bishops formerly, by saying if they were to doff their lawn and preach in earnest, and go more among the people, then six or seven of them would do more good than the whole Bench, or something to that purpose. Now we shall see whether he will put these precepts into practice or not?[1]

That his elevation to the episcopate did not change the man is confirmed by the story of an old lady who went out of her way to hear Bishop Ryle preach. After the service she told a friend that she had been very disappointed, 'I never heard a Bishop,' she said, 'I thought I'd hear something great. He's nowt. He's no Bishop. I could understand every word.'[2] When the Bishop heard the story he said it was the greatest compliment he had ever had paid to his preaching.

Bishop Ryle was far from being an undistinguished figure in an age of great men. Those who knew him recognised a commanding personality endowed with remarkable gifts of leadership and possessing an unusual strength of character. Not only had the Bishop the appearance of a prophetic figure with his flowing white beard, but in his preaching he proclaimed the Word of God with prophetic boldness, denouncing sin, and upholding God's standard of righteousness.

There were times when 'My Lord Bishop', as he always liked

to be addressed, appeared arrogant, authoritarian and puritanical, acting the prelate with an undue sense of the dignity of his office. Bishops were held in awe in his day and it is said that he never forgot, nor allowed others to forget, that he was 'the first Bishop of Liverpool'.[3] He was a proud man, proud of his academic achievements, proud of his outstanding prowess in sport and proud of his preferments in the Church. A man of weighty stature, with a 'strong personality and a magnificent presence', he towered over many of his contemporaries.[4]

Ryle's achievements as bishop

More than a century after the founding of the new diocese on the banks of the Mersey, it is appropriate to consider how Ryle measured up to the office of Bishop. Did his episcopate enhance the hierarchy? What were his achievements? How successful was he as a diocesan administrator? What were his failures? Did his administration have any lasting effects? What place should we assign to him in the life of the Church and nation?

It is clear that his nomination to the newly created diocese caused apprehension in many minds. He was hardly known in the north of England. 'Not one Liverpudlian in fifty,' it was said, 'knew before the bishop arrived that there was such a place as Stradbroke, and such a man as Ryle.'[5] He was getting on in years, at a time in life when most men of his age were thinking of giving up work, not taking on great tasks. Furthermore, he was a country parson who had spent most of his ministry in country parishes, and Liverpool was a bustling diocese closely allied to commerce and industry. He was also a leading spokesman for the Evangelicals in the Church of England, and an uncompromising Protestant. He was thought too narrow and dogmatic in his views to be a bishop in a Church which accommodated men of fundamentally different opinions and practices.

A hundred years later, we can see that there were few more influential Evangelicals in the Victorian era than Bishop Ryle, though it is a matter of opinion whether he did his best and most lasting work as pastor in Suffolk or as bishop in Liverpool. If the crowning period of his life was the episcopate it was due in part to his strong and robust physique at sixty-four years old, his enormous reserves of energy and his capacity for starting and completing difficult tasks. His capacity for work was astonishing, his use of time was intense, and he was far more active than many younger clergy.

Ryle and politics

A few months after Ryle's consecration, a contemporary wrote of him:

> It is impossible to think of him... without picturing him as an important figure in the House of Commons. If a particular turn had not overtaken him and placed him on the road that has led him at last to Liverpool, we should have seen him long ago in Downing Street, giving away bishoprics, instead of accepting one; we should have seen him now at the right hand and now at the left of the Speaker's chair at Westminster, we should have watched the stalwart figure playing a part among diplomats and statesmen. His particular qualities would more easily have made him a cabinet minister than they made him a bishop.[6]

Remembering his youthful ambition to enter politics after leaving Oxford, we might have expected him to exercise some influence in and through Parliament when he became one of the spiritual Lords. But over the years he appears to have lost all interest in politics and devoted himself entirely to spiritual work. He was called to the Upper Chamber in 1884 and eventually became the oldest serving bishop on the Bench, yet there is no record that he ever addressed the Lords. Any political opinions were confined to extolling the virtues of Disraeli and vehemently criticising the politics of Gladstone. He was an 'Establishment' figure, yet maintained that the less the Church had to do with Parliament the better. There was one notable exception, when together with a group of Evangelical clergy he publicly opposed Gladstone's Liberal party in the 1868 General Election and wrote a pamphlet *Strike, but Hear!*, a defence of those clergy who opposed Mr Gladstone at the last Parliamentary Election. The opposition centred on Gladstone's intention to disestablish and disendow the

Irish Church. It was thought Ryle opposed because he was a Tory, but the tract recorded an interesting disclaimer, 'Tory politics were not my reason. I am not a Tory and never was; if I have any politics, I am a Liberal.'[7]

His aims as a bishop

It was Ryle's resolve to fulfil as a bishop all the solemn promises he had made at his consecration. According to the Prayer Book service of the Consecration of a Bishop, these were 'to instruct the people' in the Holy Scriptures, and 'exhort with wholesome doctrines'; to 'drive away all erroneous and strange doctrines'; to 'live soberly, righteously and godly'; to 'maintain and set forward... quietness, peace and love among all men; to be faithful in ordaining,' and 'be merciful for Christ's sake to poor and needy people'. It was his honest intention to oversee the diocese fairly and well, and to 'be to the flock of Christ, a shepherd.' He was not deterred by age but regarded his appointment to the bishopric as a fresh starting point in an already full and varied career.

Administration

The Diocesan Year Books for the last two decades of the nineteenth century confirm that he set up all the necessary agencies for carrying out the work of the Church. Liverpool was the first diocese to have a Sustentation Fund to raise the stipends of the clergy, and the first to inaugurate the Incumbents' Pension Fund. Some dioceses had created Diocesan Synods, but Ryle was opposed to these because 'no Bishop will like to preside over a Church assembly in which a large and important section of his clergy have no place at all'.[8] Instead, in 1881 he established a Diocesan Conference with a broad constitution. He favoured a liberal and not an exclusively elected constitution, allowing all the clergy and two elected lay representatives from each of the deaneries to attend.[9] The annual Conference, held in St George's Hall, was a lively affair and often engendered frank and heated exchanges. Occasionally the Conference went against the Bishop's known wishes, but he took defeats in his stride.

The bishop was required to hold a Triennial Visitation in one of the main towns of the diocese at which he gave his Charge to the clergy. This gave him the opportunity to express his mind on parochial and diocesan affairs and the clergy were left in no doubt about his views. Ryle was not without wit and good humour and once told his audience, 'When a bishop has passed the stage of three score and ten he is bound to remember that each Triennial Visitation may be his last – so leaves nothing unsaid'.[10]

During his episcopate the diocese built 44 new churches. The number of curates serving in the diocese rose from 120 to 230, and the total number of clergy to around four hundred. He encouraged evangelical ordinands from the Universities to come to Liverpool, and many took titles in the diocese because it was known to be resolutely Evangelical. Unlike some bishops, he refused to include a Diocesan Board of Patronage in his plans, believing that, 'for the sake of peace men of decided opinions would be passed over in favour of moderate men, until the diocese was filled with colourless, tame, no-party men, theological jelly-fish, who would do no good.'[11] Instead he gradually increased his own influence in patronage and encouraged evangelical trustees in their appointments. He advocated the adoption of more reverent and orderly services. The number of churches open on weekdays grew, confirmation numbers and frequency of Holy Communion services increased.

Criticisms and controversies

Ryle had his champions but also his critics. It was alleged that he did not wish to see a new Cathedral built and he was severely criticized for this. There was not a grain of truth in the allegation. However, he did consider a new cathedral not such a priority as the other places of worship which were needed to evangelize the thousands of 'unchurched' in Liverpool and other towns in the diocese. His priorities were to meet the spiritual needs of the people in the populous districts before turning to the enormous task of building a new Cathedral. Surprisingly, *The Church Quarterly Review* agreed with him: 'Had Ryle succeeded in guiding the Cathedral scheme to an issue and left these other necessities of his Diocese untouched, his episcopate might have left its evident

monument; but it would have been open to serious criticism and
the charge of many things left undone. Late in his episcopate Ryle
always said he regarded other needs more pressing. It was a
question of priorities or energies and resources'.[12]

Events proved that it was the right policy. Sir Frederick
Radcliffe, chairman of the reconstituted Cathedral committee, said
of Ryle:

> He left in 1900 to Bishop Chavasse, his successor, an effective
> diocese, so organised that it was possible, in the very first year of the
> episcopate, to hope for active support for a Cathedral on a good site,
> not only from the city of Liverpool, but from the considerable centres
> of population in other parts of the Diocese.[13]

Another criticism related to the decline in church attendances
which was highlighted in the local press during the 1880s-90s.
Gladstone described the figures as 'a dismal spectacle' showing
that myriads of Liverpool people attended no place of worship.
There were many reasons to account for this. The Sabbath was no
longer observed with the same reverence as earlier in the century
and there was no longer the same deference paid to the Church.
Other Sunday attractions such as cheap train excursions to the
seaside took thousands off to Wales, Southport, and Blackpool
for the day. In addition, there were band concerts in the parks and
museums and art galleries were open. Wages were increasing and
working families felt better off. Many workers now had Sunday
off and found other activities more interesting than church
services.[14] Even the recent invention of the bicycle took people
away from Church and the children from Sunday School. The
changes affected all denominations, not only the Church of
England.

It is unfortunate that Ryle's episcopacy was marred by bitter
controversy which was none of his making. He was at heart a man
of peace and hated controversy. He was genuinely troubled by
'the unhappy divisions' in the Church and throughout his
episcopacy he prayed and worked to bring about closer relations
between the clergy. Though unashamedly an Evangelical, he was
more a Church-man than a Party-man and was always ready to

acknowledge that the National Church is a comprehensive Church, accommodating High, Broad and Evangelical Churchmen who are loyal to her formularies. He had a profound respect for men who held decided opinions, even though they might differ from his own. He was not the bishop of any one particular party and tried to be fair and just in his dealings with all his clergy. His constant advice to the clergy was 'Always cultivate the habit of treating Christians of other schools of thought than your own with kindness, courtesy and respect'.[15] This attitude brought him respect in return.

It is reported that one day, shortly after the Bishop's death, James Bell-Cox, his former antagonist, was walking through Abercromby Square. As he looked across the gardens to the Bishop's Palace he suddenly raised his hat. His companion asked, 'Out of respect for Bishop Chavasse?' 'No,' Bell-Cox replied, 'Out of respect for Bishop Ryle.'[16] At a Memorial Service to the late Bishop the same priest paid a remarkable tribute, referring to 'Dr Ryle's largeheartedness to those who differed from him in theological matters. In this respect to know him was to esteem him, and... to love him also. Under his rugged exterior beat one of the warmest hearts he had ever met.' Bell-Cox never forgot how the Bishop had shown him great kindness and nobility without rancour in the ritualist controversy, and confessed: 'It seemed to me he could never do enough for me nor ask me to do enough for him. He was straight and fair all through, I miss him tremendously.'[17] Another Liverpool priest is reported to have said of Ryle: 'He came here as Saul the persecutor, and became to us Paul the Apostle.'[18]

Ryle was sometimes criticised for not doing enough to relieve the poor and needy. The 'submerged tenth' of the population lived in dreadful conditions, especially in times of unemployment and trade depression. It seemed to some that the Church was not aware of the great social changes taking place before their eyes. But in fact there were many religious and philanthropic agencies working in the diocese to ease distress and improve the lot of the poor, and Ryle was proud of this. Knowing firsthand something of their achievements, he confidently claimed Liverpool was not 'a Dead See'. 'I believe the "black spot on the Mersey" as some are pleased to call us, is one of the most liberal and Samaritan cities in the world.'[19]

Though known in the diocese as 'the working man's bishop', he made no pretence to be a champion of the poor. He was not an F. D. Maurice or Charles Kingsley, the revered leaders of the Christian Socialist Movement, who saw as their primary task to improve the welfare of the poor by opening cooperative workshops. Sometimes Ryle touched on social problems in his addresses, but it was not 'Muscular Christianity' he had to offer. He believed 'the poor would always be with us' and felt the best advice was to exhort the rich to do more for the poor and the poor to do a good day's work for a fair day's pay. The power of the gospel, he believed, could achieve more in hearts and lives than all the Acts of Parliament, for saving a man's soul was the best way of lifting him out of the gutter and setting him on the road to a better life. In company with the majority of Victorian bishops, he felt it was not the business of the Church to attempt to deal with political and social problems.

Ryle the man

Ryle was reserved by nature and few outside the small circle of ministerial friends really knew him. But those who worked closely with him saw 'the kindest, most humble, unselfish and generous of men'. As age, illness and infirmity combined to soften and melt his stern, blunt and stubborn character, he became warm-hearted and amazingly tolerant. Behind the apparent overbearing manner, the dignified exterior which mellowed with age, they saw a man of deep personal faith; a man who loved Christ with all his heart; a man versed in the Scriptures, who took God at his word; a man who believed in the power of prayer; a man of strong individuality and with the courage of his convictions, who never budged from his principles; a man with a loving concern for his clergy and people; a man called to preach with prophetic ardour, denouncing sin, and lifting up the Cross, pleading with sinners to repent and believe in Jesus, and exhorting believers to live sanctified and holy lives. He was a man totally committed to the service of God.

His friend Richard Hobson, preaching at a commemoration service in the pro-Cathedral at the close of his episcopate, said, 'I am bold to say that perhaps few men in the nineteenth century did so much for God, for righteousness, among the English-speaking race and in the world as our Bishop.'

Ryle's legacy

J.C.Ryle is probably best remembered for his writings, particularly *Knots Untied* and *Holiness*, which have been published in many editions and are still widely read. He could also be justly proud, however, of what he had accomplished during the twenty years of his episcopate. He met the challenge of administrating a new diocese with vigour and energy, and left an indelible mark which remains to this day. His successor, Bishop Chavasse, on arrival in the diocese applauded Ryle's leadership and all that had been achieved during his episcopate, saying:

> His twenty years Episcopate was a turning point in the history of the Church on the Mersey. Gifted with a strong personality, a significant presence, a well-spring of pure English, a fearless courage and an indomitable will, even those who least agreed with his principles could not but be attracted to the man. Beneath a somewhat brusque and peremptory manner there lay hidden a depth of tenderness, a devotion to duty, a wide interest in the affairs of men and a love for all created things, which threw a spell over those who knew him well. His affection for Liverpool and his Diocese amounted to a passion. He began his work as a Bishop at an age when most men are beginning to think of rest, and he laboured on 'without hasting and without resting' so long as his brain could think, and his hand could write. An earnest conception of the size of the mountain and its position in a range, is rarely to be formed by those who stand at its feet. In another half century our children will be able to appreciate more justly than we can the work of Bishop Ryle, and his place in the history of the Church of England.[20]

Bishop David, the third Bishop of Liverpool, confirmed fifty years after Ryle's death, 'The main tradition of the diocese is evangelical. Its fruits in work are manifest in the invaluable services of such agencies as the Scripture Readers Association, the Ladies Parochial and Bible Mission, local branches of the Church Pastoral-Aid Society and other societies. and in the steady increase of its contributions to Overseas Missions.'[21] A correspondent in the *Record* in 1941 wrote of Bishop Ryle: 'It is no exaggeration to say that his virile personality dominated two generations of Evangelicals and set its ineradicable mark upon a third.'[22]

Ryle's administration attracted evangelical clergy to the diocese and some of Ryle's men were raised to prominent positions in the Church. These included J.W. Bardsley, Bishop of Carlisle, William Lefroy, Dean of Norwich, J. Denton Thompson, Bishop of Sodor and Man, J. W. Diggle, Bishop of Carlisle, and H. Gresford Jones, the first Bishop of Warrington.

Not everything he did was wise or has stood the test of time. With the benefits of hindsight, for instance, it is evident that too many churches, and far too large, were built at a time when statistics showed that church attendances were declining year by year. It was probably not wise of the Bishop to hold on to the episcopate so long. An appropriate time to resign might have been following Henrietta's death in 1889 or a couple of years later when he suffered a stroke, but he had a strong wish 'to die in harness'.

However, the thriving nature of the modern diocese of Liverpool may fairly be attributed in part to Ryle's wise leadership and sound administration. Some of the radical reforms he had advocated earlier in his ministry are now well established, including shorter services, higher stipends and greater use of the laity. The diocese continues to attract evangelical clergy to work in its varied and challenging parishes and often after gaining experience as curates to remain in the diocese as incumbents. The High Church and the Anglo-Catholic traditions are well represented, yet the Evangelical influence remains strong and the majority of congregations continue to be drawn to those churches with an evangelical message.

The Bishop was considered 'an antiquarian' by some because he never changed his theological stance to adopt more liberal views in line with modern thinking. Today some of the issues he regarded as important, such as Sabbath Observance, Worldiness, and

Election and Predestination are regarded as dated and irrelevant. But Ryle never abandoned the beliefs of his youth. Throughout the whole of his ministry he continued to hold the same views on Scripture, man's helpless condition without Christ, the all-sufficiency of the Atonement, justification by faith alone, sanctification by the Spirit, and the return of Christ for his own, which had strengthened and supported him throughout the whole of his Christian life and ministry. He had no reason to be ashamed of these fundamental beliefs and 'found nothing to retract, cancel or withdraw'.[23] His friend Richard Hobson, described him as 'Bold as a lion for the truth, the truth of God's Word and his Gospel.'[24]

NOTES

Chapter One

1. Richard Hobson, *What Hath God Wrought* (1903), pp. 327-328.

2. *Macclesfield Courier*, 10 May 1816; P.Toon, *J. C. Ryle, A Self-Portrait* (1975), p. 3. This fragment of autobiography written by Ryle in 1873 when he was vicar of Stradbroke, touches on family life from the time of his birth until the death of his second wife in 1860.

3. P. Toon, JCRSP, p. 10.

4. P. Toon, JCRSP, p.10 .

5. P. Toon, JCRSP, p.11.

6. P. Toon, JCRSP. p. 9.

7. P. Toon, JCRSP, p.11.

8. P. Toon, JCRSP, p.12

9. Regular advertisements appeared in the *Church Times* similar to the following: 'The Vicar of a country parish receives a limited number of Private Pupils between the ages of 9-13 to prepare for the Public School. The house is very large and well situated and the sanitary arrangements are perfect. Ten Guineas per term.'

10. P. Toon, JCRSP, p.15 .

11. Some earlier details of the Ryle family in Cheshire are to be found in John Ryle's Notes, 1649-1721, in the County Record Office, Chester, Ref. OOX 23, Acc.51.

12. P. Toon, JCRSP, p. 4;

13. Ryle had a genuine concern for his workers, but the Dispensary was a good investment since it was in Ryle's interest to get sick workers back to their looms as quickly as possible, C. Stella Davies, *A History of Macclesfield* (1961), p. 254.

14. P. Toon, JCRSP, p. 4.

15. P. Toon, JCRSP, p. 53.

16. P. Toon, JCRSP, p.22.

17. P. Toon, JCRSP, p.16.

18. P. Toon, JCRSP, p.17.

19. J. St John Thackery, *Memoirs of Edward Craven Hawtrey* (1896), p. 51; P. Toon and M. Smout, *John Charles Ryle, Evangelical Bishop* (1976), p.15.

20. P. Toon, JCRSP, pp. 23-24.

21. P. Toon, JCRSP, p.19.

22. P. Toon, JCRSP, p.37.

23. P. Toon, JCRSP, p. 38.

24. P. Toon, JCRSP, p. 20.

25. J. C. Ryle, *Knots Untied* (1874, my copy 1896), p.102.
26. P. Toon, JCRSP, p. 21.
27. P. Toon, JCRSP. p. 21.
28. P. Toon, JCRSP, p. 25.
29. P. Toon, JCRSP, p. 20.
30. P. Toon, JCRSP, pp.18-19.
31. P. Toon, JCRSP, p.17.
32. *Macclesfield Courier*, 12 December 1832.
33. C. Stella Davies, *A History of Macclesfield* (1961).

Chapter Two
1. P. Toon, JCRSP, p. 30.
2. P. Toon, JCRSP, p. 30.
3. P. Toon, JCRSP, p. 29.
4. H. C. Thomson, *A Memoir of H. G. Liddon* (1899), p. 28.
5. H. C. Thomson, *A Memoir of H. G.Liddon*, p. 28.
6. P. Toon, JCRSP, P. 30.
7. Lillywhite's *Scores and Biographies*; J. D. Bentham, *Oxford and Cambridge Cricket Scores and Biographies* (1905), pp.142-143; P. Toon and M. Smout, *John Charles Ryle, Evangelical Bishop* (1976), p. 21; M. Guthrie Clark, *J. C. Ryle* (1947), p. 6, states that Ryle rowed in the Oxford Boat against the Light Blues, but there is no record of this in C. M. Pitman, *The Record of the University Boat Race 1828-1909* (1909).
8. P. Toon and M. Smout, JCREB, p. 25.
9. J. S. Reynolds, *The Evangelicals at Oxford* (1953), p. 4; V. H. H. Green, *Religion at Oxford and Cambridge* (1964), p. 202. Oxford at this time was dominated by High Church teaching. Evangelicalism never flourished in the University as it did in Cambridge, even though it was the birthplace of Methodism.
10. P. Toon, JCRSP, p. 36.
11. Maurice H. Fitzgerald, *A Memoir of Herbert Edward Ryle* (1928), p. 4; P. Toon, JCRSP, p.36.
12. P. Toon, JCRSP, p. 39; P. Toon and M. Smout, JCREB, p. 26; *Record*, 15 June 1900.
13. P. Toon, JCRSP, p. 39; C. Stella Davies, *A History of Macclesfield*, p. 335.
14. P.Toon, JCRSP, p. 40.
15. Canon A. Christopher, 'Canon Christopher's Reminiscences', in the *Record*, 15 June 1900; P. Toon and M. Smout, JCREB, p.109, note 73.
16. P. Toon, JCRSP, p. 43; W. H. Griffith Thomas, *The Work of the Ministry* (1911), p.185.
17. J. W. Diggle, *Quiet Hours with the Ordinal* (1906), p. 72.
18. P. Toon, JCRSP, p. 40.

19. P. Toon, JCRSP, p. 34.

20. P. Toon, JCRSP, p. 31.

21. J. C. Ryle, *The Christian Leaders of the Last Century* (1868, my copy 1891), p. 221.

22. P. Toon, JCRSP, p. 40. Canon John Ryle Wood, tutor to Prince George and later Canon of Worcester, was 'horrified' when he heard of John Charles' conversion, JCRSP, p. 41. The renunciation of all worldly pleasures (the theatre, dancing, gambling, drinking, billiards) was a distinctive characteristic of Evangelical teaching, but Ryle did not include cricket, considering it a pleasant and wholesome activity, P. Toon, JCRSP, p. 47.

23. P. Toon, JCRSP, p. 41.

24. P. Toon, JCRSP, p. 45; M. W. F. Macray, *The Right Reverend John Charles Ryle* (1900), tells us 'Ryle loved Cheshire' and used to say 'no county breeds better and taller men', p. 13.

25. P. Toon, JCRSP, p. 46.

26. P. Toon, JCRSP, p. 46.

27. P. Toon, JCRSP, p. 47. J.C. Ryle, KU, p. 107. With the rise of ritualism in the Church of England several clergy resigned their livings and became Nonconformists, some taking their congregations with them. At the Triennial Visitation in 1893 Bishop Ryle commented: 'I am old enough to remember the secession of Baptist Noel.... I believe (he) lived to see that secession was a mistake'. See also Owen Chadwick, *The Victorian Church* (1966), I, pp. 250-271; G. R. Balleine, AHEPCE, pp. 222-228.

28. P. Toon, JCRSP. p. 47.

29. P.Toon, JCRSP, p. 46.

30. A local historian says he possessed several five pound notes issued by the Macclesfield and Cheshire Bank, and one dated 14 January 1841, and signed 'J. C. Ryle'. J Earles, *Streets and Houses of Old Macclesfield* (1915), p.113.

31. F. Leary, *The Earl of Chester's Regiment of Yeomanry Cavalry, 1797-1897* (1898), p. 120.

32. G. W. Hart, *Bishop Ryle, Man of Granite* (1963), p. 4; P. Toon, JCRSP. p. 47.

33. P. Toon, JCRSP, pp. 48-49.

34. P. Toon, JCRSP, p. 47.

35. P. Toon, JCRSP, p. 49.

36. *Macclesfield Courier*, 4 September 1841. See also G. Leo Grindon, *Manchester Banks and Bankers* (no date), pp. 111-117.

37. P. Toon, JCRSP, p.52; M. H. Fitzgerald, AMHER, p. 2.

38. P. Toon, JCRSP, p. 53.

39. P. Toon, JCRSP, p. 54.

40. *Macclesfield Courier*, 2, 16 October and 4 December 1841 has a full account of the legal proceedings and the financial outcome.

41. P. Toon, JCRSP, p. 53.
42. P. Toon, JCRSP, pp. 55-56.
43. P. Toon, JCRSP, p. 57.
44. P. Toon, JCRSP, p. 54.
45. P. Toon, JCRSP, p. 58.
46. P. Toon, JCRSP, p. 56.
47. P. Toon, JCRSP, p. 5; P. Toon and M. Smout, JCREB, p. 31. C. Stella Davies, *A History of Macclesfield*, p. 239; *Macclesfield Courier*, 15 June 1900.
48. *Record*, 15 June 1900.
49. J. C. Ryle, *The Upper Room* (1888), p.88.

Chapter Three
1. P. Toon, JCRSP, p. 60.
2. P. Toon, JCRSP, p. 60.
3. P.Toon, JCRSP, p. 60.
4. P.Toon, JCRSP, p. 59. His brother Frederick was also ordained and two of his sisters married clergy friends who were his contemporaries at Oxford.
5. Algernon Coote, Harry Arkwright, William Courthorpe and Charles Daniel were some of his Christian friends who were ordained after taking their degrees.
6. G. H.Sumner, *Life of Charles Richard Sumner* (1876), p.143. G. R. Balleine, *A History of the Evangelical Party in the Church of England* (1911, my copy 1933), p.195.
7. L. E. O'Rorke, *The Life and Friendships of Catherine Marsh* (1917), p. 41, mistakenly gives the date of Ryle's ordination as 12 December. Actually he was ordained on 21 December, St Thomas ' Day, 1841.
8. P. Toon, JCRSP, p. 60.
9. P. Toon, JCRSP, p. 61.
10. P. Toon, JCRSP, p. 61.
11. P. Toon, JCRSP, p. 63.
12. P. Toon, JCRSP, p. 64.
13. P. Toon, JCRSP, p. 62; See also J. C. Ryle, TUR, pp. 31-33. A nineteenth century doctor published a pamphlet to assist clergy in this aspect of their ministry entitled, 'Instruction for the Relief of the Sick Poor in Some Diseases of Frequent Occurance, Addressed to the Parochial Clergyman Residing at a Distance from Professional Aid.'
14. P. Toon, JCRSP, p. 62.
15. J.C.Ryle, TUR, p. 31.
16. P. Toon, JCRSP, pp. 65-66. Dr Jepson was known far beyond Leamington for his treatments and Mrs Tollemache and John Ruskin were among his patients.

17. P. Toon, JCRSP, p. 66. See also Anne Thicke, *Notes on the History of the Former Church of St Thomas and St Clement, Winchester*.

18. P. Toon, JCRSP, p. 67. Ryle made an eloquent appeal on behalf of the infant School and raised £20, M. H. Fitzgerald, AMHER, pp.14-15.

19. P. Toon, JCRSP, p. 68.

20. P. Toon, JCRSP, p. 67.

21. P. Toon, JCRSP, p. 67.

22. P. Toon, JCRSP, p. 68.

23. P. Toon, JCRSP, p. 69.

24. P. Toon, JCRSP, p. 68.

25. P. Toon, JCRSP, p. 74.

26. P. Toon, JCRSP, p. 69.

27. P. Toon, JCRSP, pp. 74; P. Toon and M. Smout, JCREB, p. 97.

28. P. Toon, JCRSP, p. 75.

29. P. Toon, JCRSP, p. 43.

30. P. Toon, JCRSP, pp. 68-69.

31. P. Toon, JCRSP, p. 71.

32. P. Toon, JCRSP, p. 71. E. D. H.Tollemache, *The Tollemaches of Helmingham and Ham* (1949).When in London the Tollemaches resided in a fine house at St James or at Ham House in Richmond. John devoted nine years to creating Peckfordton Castle, a mock tudor castle almost under the shadow of the historic Beeston Castle in Cheshire, a genuine medieval ruin.

33. E. D. H. Tollemache, *The Tollemaches of Helmingham and Ham*, p.163.

34. E. D. H.Tollemache, *The Tollemaches of Helmingham and Ham*, p.170.

35. T. H. L. Gilmour in *The English Churchman*,11 February 1995, gives a full description of the paintings and a complete list of texts Ryle employed at Stradbroke after the church restoration.

36. P. Toon, JCRSP, p. 73.

37. J. C. Ryle, JCRSP, p. 63; J.C. Pollard, 'Evangelical Clergy 1820-1840', *Church Quarterly Review*, 1958.

38. J. C. Ryle, *Light from Old Times* (1890, my copy 1898), p. 391.

39. J. C. Ryle, LOT, p. 409.

40. J. C. Ryle, LOT, p. 345.

41. J. C. Ryle, LOT, p. 349.

42. J. C. Ryle, LOT, p. xvii; J. C. Ryle, *Holiness* (1877, my copy 1900), p. 14.

43. J. C. Ryle, LOT, pp. 247-251.

44. J. C. Ryle, PCh, p. 159.

45. J. C. Ryle LOT, pp. 328-329.

46. J. C. Ryle, LOT, p. 337.

47. J. C. Ryle, LOT, p. 409.

48. J. C. Ryle, LOT, pp. 400-401.

49. J. C. Ryle, LOT, p. 329.

50. J. C. Ryle, LOT, pp. xv, 337.

Chapter Four

1. J. Baldwin Brown, 'Is the Pulpit losing its power?' in *The Nineteenth Century,* May 1877, pp. 97-112.

2. G. Herbert Wright, 'The Suffolk Pulpit, 1857-1861', in *The Suffolk Chronicle,* 23 March 1858.

3. G. Herbert Wright, *The Suffolk Chronicle,* 23 March 1858.

4. J. C. Ryle, *Expository Thoughts on the Gospel of St Luke,* vol.I (1858), p. 356.

5. J. C. Ryle, TUR, pp. 45-46.

6. W. H. Griffith Thomas, *The Work of the Ministry* (1913) p. 214; P. Toon, JCRSP, p. 69.

7. J. C. Ryle, *Knots Untied* (1874), p.149-155

8. J. C. Ryle, KU, p. 51.

9. G. H. Wright, *The Suffolk Chronicle,* 23 March 1858.

10. J. C. Ryle, TUR, p. 53.

11. G. H. Wright,*The Suffolk Chronicle,* 23 March 1858; P. Toon and M.Smout, JCREB, p.45.

12. J. C. Ryle, *Principles for Churchmen* (1884, my copy 1900), p. 413.

13. J. C. Ryle, PCh, p.160.

14. J. C. Ryle, PCh, p. 413.

15. J. C. Ryle, PCh, p. 97.

16. J. C. Ryle, PCh, p.165.

17. J. C. Ryle, PCh, p.166.

18. J. C. Ryle, TUR, p. 54.

19. J. C. Ryle, PCh, p. 414.

20. J. C. Ryle, PCh, pp.154-155.

21. J. C. Ryle, PCh, p.163.

22. J. C. Ryle, ETG, St Luke, I, p. 292.

23. J. C. Ryle, York Convocation, 23 February 1892.

24. J. C. Ryle, York Convocation, 23 February 1892.

25. J. C. Ryle, PCh, pp.164-165.

26. J. C. Ryle, TUR, p.36.

27. J. C. Ryle, Address to Wakefield Church Congress, 1886. Typical of his challenge to the clergy 'never to neglect their preaching... your people will not be content with dull, tame sermons; they want life and light and fire and love in the pulpits as well as in the parish, never forget that a lively, Christ-exalting minister will always have a church-going people' is taken from his Farewell Letter to the Diocese in PCh, pp. v-vi.

28. J. C. Ryle, H, p. 388.

29. J. C. Ryle, H, p. 388-9.
30. M. Guthrie Clark, *J. C. Ryle,* pp. 14-15.
31. G. R. Balleine, AHEPCE, p. 272
32. M. Guthrie Clark, *J. C. Ryle*, p.15.
33. *The Times*, 11 June 1880.
34. The *Record*, 8 March 1880.
35. G. R. Balleine, *A History of the Evangelical Party in the Church of England*, p. 279 footnote. See also G. W. Hart, *Man of Granite* (1963), p. 6.
36. W. F. Macray, *The Right Reverend John Charles Ryle*, p. 44.
37. G. W. Hart, *Bishop J. C. Ryle, Man of Granite*, p. 6; Liverpool Courier, 1 March 1880. More than a million copies of Ryle's tracts were published in English and many European languages.
38. P. Toon, JCRSP, p. 72.
39. P. Toon, JCRSP, p. 72.
40. P. Toon, JCRSP, p. 80.
41. P. Toon, JCRSP, p. 80.
42. P. Toon . JCRSP, p. 80
43. *The Suffolk Chronicle*, 27 January 1858
44. G. R. Balleine, *A History of the Evangelical Party in the Church of England*, p. 246.
45. W. Knight, *A Memoir of Henry Venn* (1880), p. 312.
46. H. Gresford Jones, F. J. Chavasse (1947), p. 29

Chapter Five
1. See J. B. Burke, *History of the Landed Gentry of Great Britain and Ireland* (1937), pp. 1820-1821.
2. P. Toon, JCRSP, p. 73; Maurice H. Fitzgerald, *A Memoir of Herbert Edward Ryle*, p.10.
3. P.Toon, JCTSP, p. 73.
4. P.Toon, JCRSP, p.77.
5. P.Toon, JCRSP, p. 78. Apparently Ryle did not get on too well with his mother-in law, and after his wife's death, wrote, presumably for the benefit of his three sons in particular, 'It is my deliberate conviction when a young woman marries and leaves her home, that the more she and her husband are left alone and the less they are meddled with and interfered with by other persons, the happier and better it will be for them,' P.Toon, JCRSP, p.76.
6. J. C. Ryle, ETStL, I, p.285.
7. P. Toon, JCRSP, p. 78.
8. P. Toon, JCRSP, p. 75.
9. The sermon was later published under the title, 'Be not slothful, but followers', a Sermon from Hebrews vi, 2, on G. I. Tollemache. See also E.D.H. Tollemache, *The Tollemaches of Helmingham and Ham*, p.167.

10. P. Toon, JCRSP, p. 75. After the death of his wife Tollemache closed 'the dame school' and built a new school in the village, provided a cottage for the teacher and gave him a small salary. Ryle went each week to the school to take prayers and teach Scripture.

11. See J. B. Burke, *History of the Landed Gentry of Great Britain and Ireland* (1952) p.2613; Ryle mistakenly states that the marriage took place in 1849, P. Toon, JCRSP, p. 78, but it was 1850 according to the marriage register.

12. P. Toon, JCRSP, p. 81.

13. P. Toon, JCRSP, p. 79.

14. P. Toon, JCRSP, p. 80.

15. P.Toon, JCRSP, p. 80.

16. P. Toon, JCRSP, p.81. Ryle records that his wife 'was confined five times', but his first wife had one daughter Georgina Matilda, and his second wife had four children, Jessie Isabelle, Reginald John, Herbert Edward, and Arthur Johnson.

17. E. D. H. Tollemache, *The Tollemaches of Helmingham and Ham*, p. 170.

18. P. Toon, JCRSP, p.71.

19. P. Toon, JCRSP, p.80.

20. E. D. H. Tollemache, *The Tollemaches of Helmingham and Ham*, p. 171.

Chapter Six

1. Maurice H. Fitzgerald, *A Memoir of Herbert Edward Ryle* (1928), p. 11.

2. William Legh Clowes was the largest landed proprietor in the borough of Salford. He was the head of a well-known evangelical family who had distinguished himself in the Peninsular War. See also *The Victorian History of Lancashire*, Vol.IV (1911), p.218.

3. Maurice H. Fitzgerald, AMHER, p.17.

4. Maurice H. Fitzgerald, AMHER, p. 358.

5. Maurice H. Fitzgerald, AMHER, p. 358.

6. Maurice H. Fitzerbert, AMHER, p. 36.

7. Maurice H. Fitgerald, AMHER, p. 31.

8. Maurice H Fitzgerald, AMHER, p. 302.

9. Maurice H. Fitzgerald, AMHER, p. 303.

10. P. Toon, JCRSP, p. 78.

11. P. Toon, JCRSP, p. 3.

12. P. Toon, JCRSP, p. 43.

13. Article in *Public Men of Ipswich and East Suffolk*,1875.

14. Ryle believed idleness was of the devil and would reprimand any youths in the parish he saw at the street corners. Once he shouted at a group of lads, 'Don't stand there idle; it would be better if you went and got into

mischief!' Maurice H.Fitzgerald, AMHER, p.13.

15. J. C. Ryle, TUR, p. 312.

16. J. C. Ryle, TUR, p. 308.

17. J. C. Ryle, TUR, p.308.

18. Maurice H. Fitzgerald, AMHER, p. 11.

19. Liverpool Diocesan Board of Education and School Society Report, 1889.

20. J. C. Ryle, TUR, p. 29.

21. Maurice H. Fitzgerald, AMHER, p.14; P.Toon and M. Smout, JCREB, p. 51. Ryle was following the example of Grimshaw at Haworth and other early evangelicals who displayed texts in their churches. David Streeter in his little book on *The History of All Saint's Church, Stradbroke*, p. 8, states 'parishioners contributed £45.11s.6d towards the cost of the restoration, Miss Ryle gave £75 towards an organ and clock', and Ryle gave £150, 'in addition to paying for the chancel restoration' in memory of his father, p. 8.

22. P.Toon JCRSP, p.86.

23. J. C. Ryle, PR, p. 314.

24. J. C. Ryle, PCh, p. 409.

25. J. C. Ryle, Hull Church Congress, 1890.

26. J. C. Ryle, UR, p. 334.

27. Ryle was able to afford clerical assistance with a grant he received from the Church Pastoral-Aid Society. One of his seven curates, C. O. Mules, became a bishop in New Zealand.

28. J. C. Ryle, TCLLC p. iv. The chapters first appeared separately in the monthly journal *The Family Treasury* and when their success was assured they were published in book form.

29. J. C. Ryle, KU, p. v.

30. S. Baring Gould, *The Church Revival* (1914), p.195.

31. The *Record*, 30 April 1880; M Guthrie Clark, *John Charles Ryle*, pp.17-18.

32. J. C. Ryle, OP (1877, my copy, 1900), p. viii.

Chapter Seven

1. J. C. Ryle, KU, p.55.

2. F. Warre Cornish, *The English Church in the Nineteenth Century* (1880), II, p. 218; Desmond Bowen, *The Idea of the Victorian Church* (1968), pp.160-172.

3. P. Toon, *Evangelical Theology, 1833-1856* (1979), p.117.

4. J. C. Ryle, OP, p. 34.

5. J. C. Ryle OP, p.16; ETG, St John, I, 1865), pp. vii-viii.

6. J. C. Ryle, KU, p. 4.

7. J. C. Ryle, TCLLC, p. 26.

8. J. C. Ryle, ETG, St Luke, I, p. vii.
9. J. C. Ryle, KU, p. 4.
10. J. C. Ryle, KU, p. 4.
11. J. C. Ryle, ETG St Luke, I, pp. 371-372.
12. J. C. Ryle, KU p. 436.
13. J. C. Ryle, ETG, St Luke, I, p. 5; J. C. Ryle, KU, pp. 4-5.
14. J. C. Ryle, H, p. 413.
15. J. C. Ryle, Address to Annual Meeting of the British and Foreign Bible Society, 23 October 1880.
16. J. C. Ryle, KU. p. 411.
17. J. C. Ryle, H, p. 414.
18. J. C. Ryle, ETG, St Matthew (1856, my copy no date), p. 2. See also Arthur Pollard, *The Churchman*, lxxxiv, September 1960, pp. 166-167.
19. J. C. Ryle, ETG, St John, III, 1873, my copy 1880), p. 160.
20. J. C. Ryle, ETG, St John, III, p. 92.
21. J. C. Ryle, KU, p. 410. See also J. C. Ryle, Preface to C. H. Waller, *The Authority and Inspiration of Holy Scripture*; H. D. McDonald, *Theories of Revelation* (1959), pp. 219-287.
22. J. C. Ryle, OP, p.19.
23. J. C. Ryle, OP, p.17.
24. J. C. Ryle, OP, p.18.
25. J. C. Ryle, OP, pp. 17-18; J. C. Ryle, ETG, St Luke, I, p. 4. See also J. I. Packer, *Fundamentalism and the Word of God* (1953), pp. 78-79; A. Pollard and M. Hennell, eds, *Charles Simeon, 1759-1836* (1959), p. 46.
26. J. C. Ryle, ETG, St Luke, I , p. 4.
27. J. C. Ryle, OP, pp. 28-29;
28. J. C. Ryle, ETG, St Luke, I, pp. vi-vii.
29. J. C. Ryle, ETG, St Luke, I, p. vii.
30. J. C. Ryle, KU, p. 61.
31. J. C. Ryle, UR, p. 46.
32. J. C. Ryle, PR, p.103.
33. J. C. Ryle, PR, p.113.
34. J. C. Ryle, ETG, St John, I, p. v.
35. J. C. Ryle, ETG, St John, I, p. xii.
36. J. C. Ryle, ETG, St John, I, p.xii.
37. J. C. Ryle, ETG, St, John, I p.xii. John Ferus, a sixteenth century Franciscan monk, and Toletus were renowned Bible commentators and Ryle was happy to quote both occasionally in his Notes.
38. J. C. Ryle, ETG, St John, I, p. xiii
39. J. C. Ryle, ETG, St John, III, pp. x-xi.

Chapter Eight

1. J. C. Ryle, LOT, p. xix.
2. J. C. Ryle, LOT, p. xx.
3. J. C. Ryle, KU, p. 4.
4. J.C. Ryle, KU, p. 4
5. J. C. Ryle, KU, p. 5.
6. J. C. Ryle, KU, p. 6.
7. J. C. Ryle, KU, p. 6.
8. J. C. Ryle, OP, p.186. While some theologians treated the 'Substitutionary Theory' of the atonement with contempt as an affront to intelligence, Ryle was convinced that this interpretation was the one most in accord with the Scriptures.
9. J. C. Ryle, TUR, p. 20.
10. J. C. Ryle, ETG, St John, III, p. 394.
11. J. C. Ryle, OP, p. 387.
12. J. C. Ryle, OP, p. 221.
13. J. C. Ryle, H, p.147.
14. J. C. Ryle, H, p. 152.
15. J. C. Ryle, KU, p. 7.
16. J. C. Ryle, *Plain Speaking*, p. 37. *Plain Speaking* (1847) like *Home Truths* (1859) was a miscellaneous collection of tracts on various subjects.
17. J. C. Ryle, KU, p. 8.
18. J. C. Ryle, OP, p. 300; H, p. 27.
19. J. C .Ryle, KU, p. 8.
20. J. C. Ryle, OP, pp. 304-312.
21. J. C. Ryle, KU, p.12.
22. J. C. Ryle, KU, p. 257.
23. J. C. Ryle, KU, p.257.
24. J. C. Ryle, KU, p. 272.
25. J. C. Ryle, ETG, St Matthew, p. 197.
26. J. C. Ryle, KU, p. 271.
27. J. C. Ryle, PCh, pp. 119-120.
28. J. C. Ryle, KU, p.13.
29. J. C. Ryle, KU, p.14.
30. J. C. Ryle, H, p. 399.
31. J. C. Ryle, KU, p. 347.
32. J. C. Ryle, KU, p.13.
33. J. C. Ryle, KU, p.13.
34. J. C. Ryle, KU, p.107.
35. J. C. Ryle, KU p.107.
36. J. C. Ryle, KU, p.111.
37. J. C. Ryle, KU, p.113.
38. J. C. Ryle, KU, pp. 113-114.

39. J. C. Ryle, KU, p.116.
40. J. C. Ryle, KU, pp.121.
41. J. C. Ryle, KU, pp. 118-119.
42. J. C. Ryle, ETG, St Luke. I, p.102.
43. J. C. Ryle, KU, pp. 126 and 130.
44. J. C. Ryle, KU, p.166.
45. J. C. Ryle, KU, p.167.
46. J. C. Ryle, KU p.165.
47. J. C. Ryle, PCh, p. 257.
48. J. C. Ryle, PR, pp.153-154.
49. J. C. Ryle, KU, p. 201.
50. J. C. Ryle, KU, p. 247.
51. J. C. Ryle, KU, pp. 247-248.
52. J. C. Ryle, KU, p. 249.
53. J. C. Ryle, H, pp. 83 and 416f.
54. J. C. Ryle, H, p. 251.

Chapter Nine

1. David W. Bebbington, *Evangelicalism in Modern Britain* (1989), pp. 164-165; John Kent, *Holding the Fort, Studies in Victorian Revivalism* (1978), p. 31.
2. J. Kent, HTF, pp. 74-76.
3. J. Kent, HTF, pp. 89-90.
4. The Palmers encouraged believers 'to lay down their all on the altar that God might sanctify the whole'..
5. J. Kent, HTF, p.111; J.C.Ryle, H, pp. 428, 432; *Suffolk Chronicle*, 27 January 1858 and 4 September 1859.
6. J. Kent, HTF, pp.107-113; D. Bebbington, pp. 8, 162.
7. *The Suffolk Chronicle*,15 February and 10 June 1861; P. Toon and M. Smout, JCREB, p. 55.
8. D. Bebbington, pp.164-165. J. C. Pollock, *The Keswick Story* (1964), p. 13.
9. G. R. Balleine, AHEPCE, p. 301.
10. D. Bebbington, p.154; J.Kent, HTF, p. 354
11. G. R. Balleine, AHEPCE, p. 300-301; John Kent, HTF, p.345; J.I. Packer, *Keep in Step with the Spirit* (1984), pp.146-148.
12. D. Bebbington, p.160; John Kent, HTF, pp. 298, 316-317.
13. G. R. Balleine, AHEPCE, p. 301.
14. D. Bebbington, pp.304-305; M. L. Loane, *John Charles Ryle, 1816-1900*, p.72.
15. John Kent, HTF, pp. 298-299; P. Toon and M. Smout, JCREB p. 69; Owen Chadwick, *The Victorian Church*, II (1970), pp. 471-472, J. I. Packer, *Keep in Step with the Spirit*, pp.161-162. Handley Moule's deflection to the

Keswick Movement did not affect the relationship which he and Ryle had enjoyed over many years.

16. J. C. Ryle, H, p. vi.

17. John Kent calls Ryle 'the self-appointed conscience of Anglican Evangelicalism', HTF, p. 351.

18. John Kent, HTF, pp. 340-351.

19. John Kent, HTF, p. 353.

20. John Kent, HTF, p. 355.

21. John Kent, HTF, p. 355; The *Record*, December, 22, 1875.

22. J. C. Ryle, H, p. vi.

23. J. C. Ryle, H, pp. xv-xviii.

24. J. C. Ryle, H, p. xi.

25. J. C. Ryle, H, pp. xx-xxiii.

26. J. C. Ryle, H, pp. xxix-xxx.

27. Ryle published *Holiness* in 1877. It was reprinted in an enlarged format two years later and has gone into several editions and is still widely read. In the Preface to the new edition (1953), Martyn Lloyd-Jones says 'Ryle's books are a distillation of true Puritan theology presented in a highly readable and modern form.... Ryle like his great masters had no easy way to holiness to offer, and no "patient" method by which it can be attained.' John Kent, *Holding the Fort,* p. 352, is mistaken when he delineates the publication as 'Ryle's most famous book', that epithet surely belongs to *Knots Untied*, Ryle's magnum opus.

28. J. C. Ryle, H, p. 19.

29. J. C. Ryle, H, pp. ix-x, 425-428.

30. J. C. Ryle, H, p.1.

31. J. C. Ryle, H, p.18.

32. J. C. Ryle, H, pp. 23-24.

33. J. C. Ryle, H, p. 44.

34. J. C. Ryle, H, p. 44.

35. J. C. Ryle, H, p. 44.

36. J. C. Ryle, H, p. 44.

37. J. C. Ryle, H, pp. 128 and 448.

38. J. C. Ryle, H, p. 45.

39. J. C. Ryle, H, pp. xii-xiii.

40. J. C. Ryle, H, p. 54-55.

41. J. C. Ryle, H, p. 55.

42. J. C. Ryle, H, p. 51.

43. J. C. Ryle, H, p. 41.

44. J. C. Ryle, H, p.132.

45. J. C. Ryle, H, pp. 126-131.

46. J. C. Ryle, H, p.133.

47. J. C. Ryle, H, pp. xxvi-xxvii, 31-32.

48. J. C. Ryle, H, p. 82.

49. J. C. Ryle, H, p. 30.

50. J.C. Ryle, H, pp. 31-32,74-96; PR., p.12.

51. S. Barabas, *So Great Salvation* (1952), p.100.

52. J. C. Ryle, H, p. xxix

53. J. C. Ryle, H, p. viii.

54. J. C. Pollock, *The Keswick Story*, pp. 77-78; Marcus L. Loane, *Makers of our Heritage* (1968), p. 40. See also Elizabethan, 'J. C. Ryle, and the Keswick Movement,' in *The English Churchman*, June 1955.

Chapter Ten

1. Maurice H. Fitzgerald, AMHER, p.13.

2. *The Times*, 31 January 1879.

3. G. R. Balleine, AHEPCE, pp. 276-277.

4. P. Toon and M. Smout, JCREB, p. 67.

5. E. Stock, *A History ot the Church Missionary Society* (1899), II, p. 342.

6. E. Stock, p. 455.

7. J. C. Ryle, PCh, p. 62.

8. Owen Chadwick, *The Victorian Church*, II, p. 363.

9. G. R. Balleine, AHEPCE, p. 272.

10. J. C. Ryle ETG, St John, II, p.173.

11. Owen Chadwick, p. 363.

12. J. C. Ryle, PCh, p. 62.

13. C. H. Spurgeon, 'The Sword and the Trowel' (1879) in I. H. Murray, *The Forgotten Spurgeon*, p.137.

14. G. R. Balleine, AHEPCE, p. 272.

15. Eugene Stock, *The English Church in the Nineteenth Century* (1910), p. 61. Ryle earned the art of cut and thrust in debating when he became a prominent member of the 'Eton Society', an exclusive group of twenty-five boys which met regularly outside the college for heated debates.

16. Eugene Stock, *My Recollections* (1909), p. 96.

17. J. C. Ryle, PCh, pp. 78-79.

18. J. C. Ryle, PCh, p. 78.

19. The *Church Times*, 23 April 1880.

20. J .C. MacDonnell, *The Life and Correspondence of William Connell Magee, Archbishop of York*, I (1896), p.195.

21. J. C. Ryle, PCh, p. 398.

22. The *Record*,15 June 1900.

23. The sermon is found in Ryle's book, *The Upper Room*, pp. 56-71.

24. A. R. M. Finlayson, *The Life of Canon Fleming* (1909), p. 178 footnote.

25. The *Macclesfield Courier*,1 May 1880.

26. *The Times*, 6 March 1880.

27. The *Church Times*, 12 March 1880.

28. W. Meynall, *Benjamin Disraeli* (1903), pp.117-118, M. L Loane, *John Charles Ryle*, p. 83.

29. The *Macclesfield Courier*, 1 May 1880; 'The Bishop's Consecration and Master Brown', in *The Porcupine*,1 May, 1880.

30. G. E. Buckle, ed, *Letters of Queen Victoria*, Second Series, Vol 111, p. 78.

Chapter Eleven

1. R. Muir, *History of Liverpool* (1907), p. 81, described the Port of Liverpool as 'like a whirlpool which sucked all trade towards itself.' See also G. Chandler, *Liverpool* (1957).

2. S. G. Checkland, *The Rise of Industrial Society in England* (1964), pp. 228-229.

3. J. B. Lancelot and T. W. Tyrer, 'The First Fifty Years of the Diocese, 1880-1900,' in *Liverpool Review*, vol. V, July 1930, p. 240. Beresford Hope, a Tory back-bencher and vice-president of the English Church Union was a strong protagonist for the establishment of an episcopal see on Merseyside.

4. Frederick Radcliffe, *The Liverpool Review*, July 1930, p. 291; See also Abraham Hume, *A Detailed Account, of How Liverpool Became a Diocese* (1881), pp.10-16.

5. The Tait Papers, 47/48, Cross to Tait, 13 March 1876.

6. Hansard Parliamentary Debates, Third Series, CCXXXVIII, 18 March 1878.

7. *Macclesfield Courier*, 1 May 1880; Marcus L. Loane, *John Charles Ryle, 1816-1900*, p.84. The Bishop was delighted with the Palace in all respects but one, he wished to have a larger library. 'A bishop,' he told members of the Bishopric Committee, 'should have a large library. Mine is a very large and important library of Protestant theology, and whether it will be necessary to convert the stables, for which I shall have no use, into a library, I don't know,' *Liverpool Courier*, 13 February 1900.

8. R. Hobson, *What Hath God Wrought* (1903), p.139.

9. The *Record*, 7 May and 15 June 1880.

10. The *Guardian*, 12 April 1880.

11. Marcus L. Loane, *John Charles Ryle*, p. 84.

12. L. G. Lockhart, *Charles Lindley, Viscount Halifax* (1935), Vol.I, p.249.

13. *The Times*, 12 April 1880.

14. The *Church Times*, 13 February 1900; The *Guardian*, 12 April 1880.

15. The *Guardian*, 21 April 1880.

16. *The Rock*, 23 April 1880; *The Porcupine*, 3 September and 30 June 1886.

17. The *Church Times*, 23 April 1880.

18. Q. Hughes, *Architecture and Townscape in Liverpool* (1964), pp. 108-109.

19. *Macclesfield Courier*, 1 May 1880.

20. *Macclesfield Courier*, 1 May 1880. William F. Forwood, a member of the Bishopric Committee who worked closely with the Bishop, said: 'Dr Ryle, our first Bishop, was a recognised leader of the Evangelical party, and a prolific writer of tracts. He was also an able preacher, a good platform speaker after the old fashioned pattern, and had a very inspiring and episcopal presence', *Recollections of a Busy Life* (1910), p.190.

21. Edward Garbett and John Ryle were contemporaries at Oxford and founder members of the Church Association and Wycliffe Hall, Oxford. Garbett became editor of the *Record* from 1854 to 1867. An eye-witness at the ceremony said Bishop Ryle was 'most reverent' and made the responses 'with considerable feeling'.

22. M. Guthrie Clark, *J. C. Ryle*, p. 22.

23. *Liverpool Courier*, 15 February 1900; Owen Chadwick, *The Victorian Church* II, pp. 310-311.

24. *The Times*, 28 June 1880.

25. M. Guthrie Clark, *J. C. Ryle*, p. 21; Liverpool *Daily Post*, 2 Jule 1880; The *Record*, 1 July 1941.

26. *Liverpool Courier*, 20 March 1900.

27. The *Church Times*, 23 April 1880.

28. E. Stock, *My Recollections* (1909), p. 61.

29. J. C. Ryle, Triennial Visitation Charge, 1893.

30. M. F. Macray, *The Right Reverend John Charles Ryle*, p.13.

31. *Liverpool Courier*, 10 March 1900.

32. R. Hobson, *What Hath God Wrought*, p.145.

Chapter Twelve

1. The *Record*, 21 June 1880. Ryle did not appoint a Dean to the pro-Cathedral. He believed the office of Dean should be suppressed, and the Bishop act as Dean of his Cathedral. He gave the administration and arrangement of services to the incumbent Canon A. Stewart, and arranged to preach regularly on the first Sunday afternoon of the month.

2. Marcus L. Loane, *John Charles Ryle, 1816-1900*, p. 89.

3. J. C. Ryle, PCh, p. 396.

4. J. C. Ryle, PCh, p. 402.

5. J. C Ryle, PCh, p. 415.

6. V. Cotton, *The Book of the Cathedral* (1964), p.1.

7. Report of the Bishop of Liverpool's Commission, 1901-1902.

8. Q. Hughes, *Seaport Architecture and Townscape in Liverpool* (1964), p. 113.

9. J. C. Ryle, Liverpool Diocesan Conference, 1888.

10. W. B. Forwood, *Recollections of a Busy Life*, p.195; Ryle is reported to have stated quite bluntly, 'that if this thing is to be done at all, it will be done well,' The *Guardian*, 2 May 1883. Eventually at a meeting in the Town Hall on 17 June 1901 a resolution was passed, though not unanimously, that a new cathedral should be built on St James' Mount. The foundation stone was laid amid great rejoicing by King Edward VII on 19 July 1904.

11. *Liverpool Mercury*, 10, 14, November 1888.

12. J. C. Ryle, KU, p.15.

13. The Church of England Year Book,1885, p. xviii.

14. F. Warre Cornish, *The English Church in the Nineteenth Century* (1880), II, p. 214.

15. *Liverpool Courier*, 11 June 1900;

16. *Liverpool Albion*, 2 March 1882.

17. Hume concluded the Survey proved that the majority of city dwellers in Liverpool were Anglicans, but profession was not backed up by attendance. The Bishop saw two reasons for this: dull and ineffective preaching in some parishes and a want of constant and friendly contact between clergy and people.

18. *Liverpool Daily Post*, 3 November 1891. In F. R. Barry's words, 'The Church in Victorian Times was rich in manpower beyond the dreams of avarice', *Vocation and Ministry* (1958), p. 71.

19. The *Record*, 3 May 1881.

20. Later he appointed W. H. Barlow, Principal of the Church Missionary Society College, Islington, and his own son, Herbert, who was principal of St David's College, Lampeter.

21. M. H. Fitzgerald, AMHER, p. 132; See also H. Kirk-Smith, *William Thomson, Archbishop of York, 1819-1890* (1958), p. 55.

22. O. R. Clark, 'The First Bishop of Liverpool', *The Churchman* (LXIX, 1955), pp. 225-226

23. R. Hobson, *What Hath God Wrought*, pp. 192-193.

24. R. Hobson, p. 279.

25. J. C. Ryle, Hull Church Congress 1890.

26. The Bishop used to say. 'The first step in reaching the unchurched should be to send living agents from street to street... until not one say "The Church of England does not care for my soul," ' J. C. Ryle, PCh. p. 401.

Chapter Thirteen

1. Horton Davies, *Worship and Theology in England*, iv (1962), pp.114-131; Alec R. Vidler, *The Church in an Age of Revolution* (1961), p. 157.

2. The Tait Papers, The Queen to Tait, vol 197, 12 June 1874, pp.119-122; P.T. Marsh, *The Victorian Church in Decline* (1969), p.160.

3. Correspondence between the Bishop and the Rev. J. Bell-Cox.

Newspaper cuttings of the dispute are in the Institute of Education Library, Abercromby Square, formerly 'The Bishop's Palace'. The Rev. Bell-Cox was formerly curate to the Rev.Charles Parnell at St Margaret's against whom the Church Association complained to Bishop Jacobson of illegal practices in the services. Eventually Parnell was forced to resign and Bell-Cox was appointed in his stead. During the dispute Bell-Cox broke a confidence and published the letters in St Margaret's Monthly Paper of Church Information.

4. J. Bell-Cox, Correspondence.

5. J. Bell-Cox, Correspondence. Ryle insisted that 'Parishioners so aggrieved have a right to bring the matter before the Bishop. The Bishop has a right to call the clergyman to account, and ought so to call him,' J. C. Ryle, PCh, p. 54.

6. J. Bell-Cox, Correspondence.

7. J. Bell Cox, Correspondence.

8. *The Protestant Standard*, 25 March 1882.

9. Archbishop Magee, nicknamed the Church Association, 'The Prosecution Company Ltd'. The Association brought seventeen legal actions against Ritualists between 1845-1849.

10. J. Bell-Cox, Correspondence.

11. J. Bell-Cox , Correspondence.

12. A. C. Benson, *The Life of Edward White Benson*, II, p.243; W. B. Forwood, *Recollections of a Busy Life*, p.190.

13. J.C.Ryle, Liverpool Diocesan Conference, 1883. Bishop Fraser of Manchester refused to use the veto in a ritualist case in his diocese and S. F. Green went to prison, but several other bishops in similar disputes thought it right to use it.

14. J. Bell-Cox, Correspondence.

15. The *Record*, 18 December 1885.

16. J. Bell-Cox, Correspondence. On the advice of his Chancellor and the Archbishop of York, Ryle had to allow the prosecution.

17. The *Guardian*, 22 January 1886. P. T. Marsh, *The Victorian Church in Decline* (1969), pp. 264-289.

18. M. C. Church (ed), *Life and Letters of Dean Church* (1897), p. 405.

19. J. Bell-Cox Correspondence; Michael Smout, *Bishop Ryle – Protestantism and Reaction in Protestant Britain* (1974), p.11.

20. S. Baring Gould, *The Church Revival* (1914), p.196. Gould is mistaken when he states Bell-Cox was imprisoned for 'ritualism'. Ryle regarded 'the imprisonment of a clergyman for contumacy as a relic of barbarism', Triennial Visitation Charge, 1887. The Bell-Cox case was the last prosecution in the Victorian era, Owen Chadwick, *The Victorian Church*, II, p. 349.

21. The *Church Times*, 6 May 1887. *The Times*, 6 May, contended the

law needed changing, but the priest was guilty of 'a deliberate act for which he must throughout have been prepared to take the consequences'.

22. S. B. Gould, *The Church Revival*, p.195.

23. *The Times*, 21 May 1887.

24. St Margaret's Monthly Paper, June 1888. The English Church Union appealed for £1,000 from its members to pay the priest's legal fees.

25. *The Times*, 29 August and 19 September 1882.

26. *Liverpool Daily Post*,17 January 1885; *Liverpool Courier*, 20 January 1885; P. Toon and M. Smout, JCREB, p. 87.

27. *The Protestant Standard*, 24 January 1885; See also J. C. Ryle, PCh, pp.x-xiv.

28. J. C. Ryle, What is Written about the Lord's Suppper? See also Charles Smythe, *Cyril Foster Garbett* (1959), pp. 415-416.

29. M. C. Church, *Life and Letters of Dean Church* (1897), p. 405.

30. G. R. Balleine, AHEPCE, p. 294

Chapter Fourteen

1. J. C. Ryle, ETG, St John, III, p. 221.

2. J. C. Ryle, PCh, pp. 34-35.

3. G. R. Balleine, AHEPCE, p. 295.

4. J. C. Ryle, PCh, p.110. Nothing is known about Meldenius and the name may be a pseudonym. The saying was quoted by Baxter and the Puritans.

5. J. C. Ryle, Triennial Visitation Charge, 1887.

6. J. C. Ryle, PCh, pp. 68-80.

7. J. C. Ryle, Triennial Visitation Charge, 1884; KU, p. 190.

8. J. C. Ryle, Triennial Visitation Charge, 1884.

9. Eugene Stock, The History of the Church Missionary Society III, pp. 8-9.

10. J. C. Ryle, Triennial Visitation Charge, 1887.

11. J. C. Ryle, PCh, p. 36.

12. J. C. Ryle, PCh, p. 58; The *Guardian*, 21 August 1880.

13. J. C. Ryle, PCh, p.108.

14. J. C. Ryle, PCh, p. 66.

15. J. C. Ryle, PCh p. 334

16. The *Record*, 9 July 1880.

17. J. C. Ryle, PCh, p. 320.

18. J. C. Ryle, O P, pp. 285-286.

19. J. C. Ryle, PCh, pp. 308-309. The abolition of the Church Rate in 1868, the removal of the Religious Tests opening the older Universities to Nonconformists in 1871, and the change of the law permitting Nonconformist ministers to bury in church graveyards, helped to remove some of the long-standing grievances.

20. J. C. Ryle, Southampton Church Congress, 1870.

21. *The Scottish Guardian*, 31 August 1883.

22. *The Scottish Guardian*, 31 August 1883.

23. *The Scottish Guardian*, 31 August 1883.

24. *The Liverpool Courier*, 10 March 1900.

25. A. K. H. Boyd, *Twenty-Five Years at St Andrews* (1892), II, p.261.

26. J. C. Ryle, Triennial Visitation Charge, 1893; also H, pp. 423.

Chapter Fifteen

1. *The Liverpool Daily Post* had a series of articles entitled 'Squalid Liverpool' from 3 October to 17 November 1883 and 8 to19 March1886.

2. J. C. Ryle, Liverpool Diocesan Conference, 1890.

3. J. C. Ryle, Triennial Visitation Charge 1893.

4. *The Liverpool Daily Post*, 13 April 1889.

5. M. H. Fitzgerald, AMHER, p.10.

6. M. H. Fitzgerald, AMHER, p.135.

7. J. C. Ryle, PCh, p. viii.

8. J. C. Ryle, PCh, p. xix.

9. *The Church Quarterly Review* (1885), p. 257.

10. The *Record*, 12 August 1882.

11. J. C. Ryle, PCh, p. 312.

12. J. C. Ryle, KU, p. 226.

13. J. C. Ryle, H, p. 359.

14. J. C. Ryle, Triennial Visitation Charge 1887; M. L. Loane, *John Charles Ryle, 1816-1900*, p.70

15. *The Liverpool Review*, 14 April 1883; The Bishop welcomed Moody to Liverpool to hold a mission but refused the Rev J.L.Lyne, 'Father Ignatius', permission to hold a mission in a church, so he went off and hired a public hall and conducted his services. The refusal was because 'Father Ignatius' was a member of the Confraternity and was reputed to have introduced ritualism in the diocese of Norwich.

16. J. C. Ryle, Triennial Visitation Charge 1887. According to the Diocesan Year Book of that year there were ten clergy in the diocese commissioned to take parish missions.

17. J.C.Ryle, Pastoral Letter 1894.

18. M. H. Fitzgerald, AMHER, p.133.

19. M. H. Fitzgerald, AMHER, p.133.

20. *The Times*, 17 August 1888.

21. *The Porcupine*, 18 August 1888.

22. R.Hobson, *What Hath God Wrought*, p. 317. The same account is also recorded in J.C. Ryle, PCh, p. 418-420.

23. *Liverpool Courier*, 20 February 1900.

24. J. C. Ryle, Triennial Visitation Charge, 1896.

25. *The Liverpool Review*, Vol. V, July 1930, p. 297.

26. J. C. Ryle, Triennial Visitation Charge 1896. On another occasion Ryle said a Church House would 'Promote unity, bring clergy together, and facilitate every kind of diocesan business,' Diocesan Conference 1897. Ryle saw the foundation stone laid but did not live to see Church House opened on 18 May 1901 by the Archbishop of York. The Bishop gave £1,200 towards the cost and bequeathed his library of over five thousand theological works and three boxes of paintings, many by Arthur Ryle. Church House served the diocese well until 1941 when it was destroyed in the May blitz on the city.

27. *The Liverpool Courier*, 13 Feb 1900; The *Record*, 25 July 1940 and 11 July 1941. G. Harford compiled a catalogue of Church House Library.

28. Eugene Stock, *A History of the Church Missionary Society*, VI, p. 428.

29. Maurice H. Fitzgerald, AMHER, pp.133-134.

30. R. Hobson, *What Hath God Wrought*, p. 289.

31. J. C. Ryle, PCh, pp. v-vi.

32. Maurice H. Fitzgerald, AMHER, p.134.

33. F. J. Chavase, *The Liverpool Review*, June 1900.

34. After the consecration of the new Cathedral a recumbant memorial figure in honour of Bishop Ryle was placed on the west side of the nave.

Chapter Sixteen

1. J.W. Diggle, *Bishop Fraser's Lancashire Life* (1889), p. 336.

2. *The Liverpool Courier*, 1 March 1900.

3. The *Church Times*, 23 April 1900.

4. F.J.Chavasse, Liverpool Diocesan Conference, 23 October 1900.

5. *The Liverpool Courier*, 13 February 1900.

6. The *Record*, 29 December 1880.

7. J. C. Ryle, General Election pamphlet 1868 quoted by P. Toon and M. Smout, JCREB, p. 63. At the Diocesan Conference in 1885, Ryle described Gladstone as an 'impulsive statesman', since he had drafted a bill to disestablish the Irish Church in 1871 and handed over Protestant endowments to Papists.

8. Dublin Church Congress, 1865.

9. The *Church Times*, 23 April 1881.

10. J.C. Ryle, Diocesan Conference 1887.

11. *The Liverpool Courier*, 15 February 1900.

12. *The Church Quarterly Review*, iii (1920), pp. 46-47.

13. Frederick Radcliffe, 'Some Notes on the First Scheme for a Liverpool Cathedral', in *Liverpool Review*, Vol. V, 1930, p.121

14. J. C. Ryle, *Triennial Visitation Charge*, 1893.

15. J. C. Ryle, *Triennial Visitation Charge*, 1893.

16. *The Liverpool Courier*, 18 June 1900.

17. S. Baring Gould, *The Church Revival*, p.145.

18. S. Baring Gould, *The Church Revival*, p.145.

19. J. C. Ryle, Liverpool Diocesan Conference,1890

20. F. J. Chavasse, Liverpool Diocesan Conference, 1900.

21. Dr. A. A. David, the Bishop of Liverpool, 'The Diocese in 1930', in *The Liverpool Review*, Vol. V, 1930, p. 234.

22. Albert Mitchell in the *Record*, 11 July 1941.

23. J.C.Ryle, in Preface to new edition of *Knots Untied*, 1886.

24. R. Hobson, *What Hath God Wrought*, p. 294.

Persons Index

Places Index

Subject Index